A PRACTICAL GUIDE TO
KINGDOM LIVING

Seeing, Entering, & Manifesting

THE KINGDOM

DISCIPLING NATION SERIES #4

ABRAHAM JOHN

SEEING, ENTERING, AND MANIFESTING THE KINGDOM OF GOD

A Practical Guide to Kingdom Living
Discipling Nations Series #4

Copyright © 2020 by Abraham John

Published by Abraham John

www.TheKingdomNetwork.org
email: info@thekingdomnetwork.org
1-800-558-5020

ISBN: 978-1-948330-18-3

Printed in the United States of America

Unless otherwise indicated, all Scriptures are from the New King James Version®. Copyright © 1982 by Thomas Nelson. Used by permission. Scripture quotations marked (KJV) are from the King James Version and are in the public domain.

Scripture quotations marked (NIV) are taken from the Holy Bible, New International Version®, NIV® Copyright © 1973, 1978, 1984, 2011 by Biblica, Inc.® Used by permission. All rights reserved worldwide.

All *emphases* or additions in parentheses within scriptural quotations are the author's own.

All rights reserved. No part of this book may be reproduced or transmitted in any form or by any means, electronic or mechanical, including photocopying, recording, or by any information storage and retrieval system, without permission in writing from the author. Please direct your inquiries to info@thekingdomnetwork.org.

"It is the glory of God to conceal a matter, but the glory of kings is to search out a matter."

PROVERBS 25:2

TABLE OF
CONTENTS

PREFACE	7
INTRODUCTION	9

PART I: SEEING THE KINGDOM

Chapter 1: The Great Exodus	17
Chapter 2: Why We Received Jesus, But Rejected His Message	33
Chapter 3: Why Seek God's Kingdom First	51
Chapter 4: Why Must We Be Born Again?	67
Chapter 5: Seeing the Kingdom of God	93
Chapter 6: Let Your Eye Be Single	109

PART II: ENTERING THE KINGDOM

Chapter 7: Seek God's Righteousness	125
Chapter 8: Entering the Kingdom	143
Chapter 9: The Process of Entering the Kingdom	159
Chapter 10: The Unlearning Process	177
Chapter 11: Seven Entrances to the Kingdom of God	197
Chapter 12: The Seventh Entrance to the Kingdom	221

PART III: MANIFESTING THE KINGDOM

Chapter 13: Manifesting the Kingdom	243
Chapter 14: Why the Kingdom of God Is Not Manifesting	261
Chapter 15: Transitioning into the Kingdom	279

LIST OF OTHER BOOKS AND RESOURCES	293

PREFACE

Jesus said that if we seek first His kingdom and righteousness, then *all* we need (money, food, clothing, and shelter) will be added to us. How does this work in our everyday lives? Is this promise applicable to us today, or was it only for the first century believers, or some Jewish people? Will this work in our country now in the twenty-first century?

Since I have started to preach the gospel of the kingdom message, many people have asked me serious questions about it. Some are skeptical because they are hearing things for the first time and wondering why their church or leaders have not taught them about this before. Either that, or they are hearing things that are different from what they have heard for many decades.

When the COVID-19 pandemic emerged and churches were forced to close their doors, Christians were drawn away with the world and felt helpless. They didn't know what to do. They didn't have any answers or solutions to offer the world; instead, they looked to the world for answers.

As I've been saying, right now there is no difference between the church and world, except that we meet together in a building on a Sunday morning. Whatever happens to the world will happen to the church as well. That should never be the case.

The church has only two solutions to every problem and challenge that has risen in the world over the last five hundred years. The first solution they give is that the rapture is going to take place any minute, and the second one they will offer is that we are on the brink of *another* revival.

By implying those two thoughtless answers, they deny the reality and refuse to admit the inadequacy and the incompetency of their faith to come up with any real and practical solutions to what the world is facing. Some are already talking about a COVID-19 revival.

Many people believe that their church has already taught them everything they need to know about God, Christian life, and the kingdom, and everything is fulfilled, so the next event they are waiting for is the rapture. When that happens, they will be released from this world, and on that they place their hope. However, some prophets and seers from around the world are beginning to speak of glimpses of a kingdom age and kingdom move. This is really encouraging.

Every generation since Christ has believed the rapture would take place in their lifetime. They all died, and the church is still here. What if there are hundreds of years to come before the rapture? What if the church had a plan and vision for the nations and cities in which they exist instead of focusing on leaving the planet? Where would we and our children be today if our grandparents and the twentieth-century church leaders had a vision for our nation?

To do this, we need an entirely different system and structure of operation and a renewed vision from the Lord. I believe this book will provide the body of Christ with that new operating system and vision for the future. This book is a practical guide for every believer for how to fulfill their kingdom assignment on earth.

INTRODUCTION

Many want to know how and from where I received the message of the kingdom of God which I am preaching and writing about. Then they want to know if the message is working for me. They want to know I am able to live what I preach. To be blunt, they want to know if what I preach is putting food on my table and bringing in money to pay the bills and take care of my family.

First of all, I want to tell you that I don't do anything with the intention of making money. I don't live to make money. I live to fulfill the purpose and calling God has for my life. Money comes to me as a reward for doing that. I have been living like this since I was eighteen years old. Now I am forty-seven, and I can tell you I have never had to go hungry even once and never have gone without a place to sleep. God has been faithful. The One who called me has never let me down.

I am happy to share the secrets I have learned from the Lord about His kingdom with you. *All the questions I mentioned above and more will be answered in this book.* This is the most practical book God has given me on the subject of the kingdom of God. It is the foundation—a manual for anyone who is serious about living a kingdom life here on earth.

Before we can apply any other revelation of the kingdom of God, a person has to receive and apply the revelation contained in this book *first.* If what is written in this volume doesn't work for a person, then nothing else about the kingdom will work. It will be just another "pie in the sky" utopian ideology.

Throughout this book, I am going to explain the "nitty gritty" details of how to live out the kingdom message. How is each person supposed to live in the kingdom and benefit from it in this day and age? How will seeking God's kingdom first bring food to your table? Is the kingdom message applicable to us now? If so, how can each of us apply it practically? What does the kingdom look like when it manifests in the physical? The answers are in this book.

We can disciple nations *only after we learn and apply this.* To disciple a nation, the people in that nation should be released to fulfill their destiny. Then they can corporately release the destiny of their nation. That is what Jesus taught His disciples for almost three years. He taught them about how the kingdom works and how each individual fits in His kingdom mandate. Then when He sent them out to do the assignment He had given them, specifically telling them not to take any money or extra clothes with them (Luke 9:1–3).

Jesus wanted them to experience kingdom living. He wanted them to totally depend on Him and His kingdom to provide for the assignments He had for them. That's why He told them not to take any money or other material things with them. When they came back from their kingdom "outreach" or "practicum," He asked if they lacked anything, and they said no (Luke 22:35).

If you apply the principles revealed in this book, you will be able to experience this same kingdom living in your life. You should be able to say, "I don't lack anything." It may not happen right away. It didn't happen for the disciples in one day or one week; they were trained in the kingdom for three *years*. If you stick with it and don't give up, I can guarantee that this will work anywhere. I'm not saying it will be easy, but it will be worth it!

INTRODUCTION

How do we seek the kingdom of God and His righteousness first, so that all the things we need in our lives will be added to us as Jesus instructed in Matthew 6:33? A person should be able to apply and live it first before he or she can teach it to others. Since I have been living this for more than twenty-five years, I believe I have some credibility to teach about it.

When we live in the kingdom, we do not need to use any gimmicks or manipulate others to meet our needs. Jesus said that our heavenly Father already knows what we need before we ask (Matthew 6:8, 32). He also said this:

> Therefore do not worry, saying, "What shall we eat?" or "What shall we drink?" or "What shall we wear?"
> *(Matthew 6:31)*

How do we live that kind of life practically in this day and age?

That is the purpose of this book. This is not a secret I invented; this has been a theme throughout the Bible from Genesis to Revelation. This is how the people in the Bible lived. We have not been taught correctly about the kingdom of God among other things, so we missed out on this.

The message of the kingdom will work for anyone, in any country, on any continent, at any time or season. A person's financial or educational background, or the economic situation of the nation in which he or she lives, does not matter.

There is a reason Jesus did not call the most educated or the rich people to be His disciples. Instead, He went to the seashore to call a bunch of fishermen. To understand and apply the message of the kingdom, we do not need to be rocket scientists or possess a degree from a university. The message of the kingdom will work for anyone, regardless of their social, educational, or financial status.

By divine providence, God started to teach me about His kingdom and how it works from the time I was sixteen years old. I didn't recognize that it was the kingdom at that time because I didn't hear anyone talking about the kingdom in my church. I was a regular churchgoer and did everything others did—but I never fit into the normal church paradigm. I always felt like an outsider because many of the religious church practices did not make any sense to my heart.

I went into the ministry and tried to copy what others were doing in order to build a big ministry, but that didn't work for me either. I thought that maybe God didn't call me, and that I had made a mistake. But it wasn't a mistake; I just didn't recognize His specific calling for my life.

After reading the *Discipling Nations* series, many people ask me the same question: Why was this revelation not revealed before? Why haven't other people come up with this several hundred years ago? Why didn't they see this in the Scriptures after reading it hundreds of times?

The best answer to those questions is that the time was not right yet. However, now the time has come for the saints to receive the kingdom of God and fully understand the eternal plans and purposes of God for the earth and mankind. Now is the time to manifest the kingdom here.

Now that we know what we know, we will be held accountable for what we know. After reading these books, if we go back and keep doing what we have always done, we will face a greater judgment than the nations in the Bible that God judged.

To be honest, there are millions of people living and manifesting the kingdom of God on the earth today without even realizing what it is. Some of them may not even be church members or call themselves Christians!

INTRODUCTION

Ironically, at the same time, there are millions of believers around the world who are part of the church but are *not* benefitting from the kingdom of God. Though God made everything He owns available to us, they don't know why God put them on this planet. They are enslaved and stuck in the world system for their survival. This book is written to those precious believers to liberate them from this tyranny of life and fate.

We are supposed to be the light of this world and the salt of the earth. Instead, we have been functioning as parasites on this world system. We have been feeding on it, but have been in denial about that. We see this in the fact that we are singing songs that state that we don't belong in this world, and that this world is not our home. However, the reality is that we depend on this world for every little thing we need.

Since we lost our flavor (the salt), this world has been trampling on the church. If the world falls apart, the church will fall apart, too. We are dependent on the world. That shouldn't be the case. That is backward from the way it's supposed to be—and it will only change when we understand and function as kingdom people.

When the world falls apart, people should be running to the church. We received a kingdom that cannot be shaken (Hebrews 12:28). We have been living without the kingdom for too long. *It is time to rediscover our country of origin.*

It took me twenty-five years to receive these revelations and understand these truths. I am excited to share them with you. Your life will never be the same again! May the Lord use this revelation to help the next generation fully manifest the kingdom of God here on earth.

I would like to hear your comments and questions after you read this book. If this helped you in any way, I would like to hear that as well. You are welcome to correspond with me. My e-mail is info@thekingdomnetwork.org.

> It is the glory of God to conceal a matter, but the glory of kings is to search out a matter.
> *(Proverbs 25:2)*

Together we are going to search out some mysteries of the kingdom of God that have been concealed until now. Welcome to the journey!

PART I:
SEEING THE KINGDOM

CHAPTER 1

THE GREAT EXODUS

Thus says the Lord: "Let My people go, that they may serve Me." (Exodus 8:1b)

The body of Christ has been held captive by the enemy kingdom for a very long time. What do I mean by captivity? Aren't we saved and going to heaven? Is it possible for God's children to be in captivity? Yes, we see that in the Bible multiple times (Genesis 15:13; Romans 8:15; 2 Timothy 2:25–26).

This captivity is happening under the guise of religion and through the economic slavery of the Babylonian system. Very few are free to fulfill their God-given destiny. The majority are slaving away their precious life in survival mode. There needs to be a great deliverance, just like there was for the people of Israel when they left Egypt in the Old Testament.

In the Bible, Egypt not only means a historic country, but also a religious, political, and economic demonic system similar to Babylon, that keeps God's chosen people bound so that they are not free to fulfill their God given destiny (Isaiah 45:14; Galatians 4:24–25; Revelation 11:8).

WHY SLAVERY?

God told Abraham that his children would be slaves in a foreign land for four hundred years (Genesis 15:13). Many theologians have offered various theories for why God allowed His people to be slaves for that long. One of the primary reasons God mentioned was that once the time was ripe, He was going to judge the nation that was keeping them as slaves (Genesis 15:14). Our God is a just God and His justice system is perfect, as are all His ways.

God needs a legitimate reason to either bless or judge a person or a nation. By permitting the Egyptians to enslave His people, He was building up a case against them to judge them in the end. He allowed His people to be enslaved for a time to build a case to bless them later as well.

By being in slavery, God's people gave free labor to build Egypt. They built palaces, walls, gardens, roads, farms, storehouses, and the pyramids for Pharaoh. They built the economy of Egypt, and Egypt became the most prosperous nation of that time. They were not free to serve God.

In return, the Egyptians gave the Israelites just enough food to survive. Similarly, the majority of Christians today are financially broke and live in a mere survival mode. They are waiting for the rapture because they are tired of the oppression of the taskmasters in their lives. They find their lives completely meaningless.

They have been enslaved by various schemes of the enemy and don't know how to shake free from them—their destiny and calling have been held captive by the enemy. They do not know what to do to be free from this tyranny of the system. The message of the kingdom is the solution to every human dilemma out there.

The body of Christ has been serving this world system for their sustenance for too many years—and most of the time for a minimum wage. They have been serving the Babylonian system with their sweat and blood, and their nations have grown and become great.

TWO ALTERNATIVE SYSTEMS

There are two "nations" mentioned from Genesis to Revelation that are very significant to understand. They are not just two historic nations but demonic systems that the devil uses to enslave God's people in every generation, so they won't discover God's kingdom or fulfill their purpose.

These two nations are Egypt and Babylon. There is a specific reason they are mentioned from Genesis to Revelation. Egypt represents a religious system. It was the birth place of various religions, magic, sorcery, witchcraft and mind control. The purpose of religion is mind control. To enslave humans so that they became addicted to rituals and belief systems contrary to the kingdom of God.

On the contrary Babylon is a political and economic system. It includes all sorts of fun, human achievements, and entertainments. It is built on humanism. When Egypt represents the religious spirit, Babylon represents the spirit of this world. One *enslaves* God's people when the other take them *captive*. These are two branches or wings of the kingdom of darkness. If the devil cannot enslave an individual with the religious system he will use the Babylonian system to deceive them.

Babylon is the birthing place of all type of humanistic thinking and achievements. In Egypt people worshipped different gods and idols. In Babylon man becomes the center of everything and were worshipped as gods. It is the birth place of all sports, entertainment and industries.

If we look at the world today these spirits are prevalent from east to the west. When we study the systems of rulership of these two nations, we understand more how they operated. In Egypt the rulers were called Pharaohs, it was a title, like Pope in the Catholic church. In Babylon the rulers did not have a particular title, each had individual names.

The intention of both systems is to enslave God's people and keep them as captives making them depended on it, instead of God's kingdom and blind them from seeing it.

Egypt and Babylon were physical nations, but they also represent two demonic systems or entities that have been operating since the time of Genesis. We read about them in Revelation as well. In the book of Revelation Jerusalem, the city where Jesus died is depicted as Egypt (Revelation 11:15).

SERVING BABYLON

The Babylonian system is the alternative system that the devil established on the earth in place of God's kingdom. It represents the kingdom of darkness, and it tricks people into working for it and depending on it instead of depending on God and fulfilling their destiny. We thought this was normal, the way it should be, because we were blinded by the god of this world, the devil.

What are the signs of slavery?

- Slavery is when you are not free to do what you were born to do. God sent each one of us with a specific kingdom assignment. But the enemy doesn't want us to fulfill that. He wants to kill us before we get a chance to do it.
- Slavery is when you are doing something against your will and conscience. Many who are doing a job don't like what they are doing. But they are pressured and forced because of necessity.

- Slaves are not free to choose or make decisions for themselves. The sign of true freedom is when you are free to make decisions for yourself.
- Slaves are not permitted to own anything. We live in a false sense of ownership, when our houses and almost everything we own belong to banks and credit companies.
- Slaves are not free to fulfill their destiny. We do not have freedom because our time, skills, and strength are spent to build the world's kingdom and not God's.
- Slaves are not free to serve God or fulfill their calling. They are afraid and stuck in the world system for their survival. They do not know what to do or how to get out of it.
- Slaves are not free to build God's kingdom. They are busy serving money and living to make it. (Money was the other master Jesus mentioned in the Bible.)
- Slaves are not free to maximize their potential. They live in survival mode, focused on making a living.

We thought we were living for God and serving Him with our lives, but if we look at our daily lives from Monday through Saturday, that is not the case. Most of us have been serving the dark Babylonian empire instead. It has used God's people—our resources, our strength, and our skills—to build its palaces, global businesses, governments, and resorts.

> The woman was arrayed in purple an scarlet, and adorned with gold and precious stones and pearls, having in her hand a golden cup full of abominations and the filthiness of her fornication.......I saw the woman, drunk with the blood of the saints and with the blood of the martyrs of Jesus. And when

> I saw her, I marveled with great amazement.
> (Revelation 17:4, 6)

Many of God's people have been tangled in the grip of Babylon's tentacles—and it has destroyed their lives. By the time we are done living to make money, we don't have any more strength or time left to do what God created us to do.

We have lost generations of lives that were held captive by this Babylonian empire. They did not get to fulfill the destiny God sent them to this earth to fulfill. I do not want you to end up in that list, nor your children or grandchildren.

ENSLAVED BY THE ENEMY

We have been robbed and enslaved by the enemy. Too many have given their best years to serve this Babylonian system. Then they retire and waste the rest of their lives watching TV and enjoying other leisure activities that their flesh enjoys, all the while claiming that they were living for God all their lives. Lord, have mercy!

Even on Sunday mornings, we only give a maximum of two hours to God, and for the rest of the day, we enjoy the glitters of Babylon. We thought we were doing God a favor by giving ten percent (like a tip) to the church while we give the other ninety percent to prosper the demonic kingdom by paying our bills to companies and buying products and services owned by ungodly people.

The time has come for our deliverance. God has heard the cry and groaning of many of His children. They are tired of the torture and oppression by their taskmasters. The time for the judgment of the Babylonian system has come.

> Then one of the seven angels who had the seven
> bowls came and talked with me, saying to me,

> "Come, I will show you the judgment of the great harlot who sits on many waters." *(Revelation 17:1)*

> For in one hour your judgment has come. *(Revelation 18:10b)*

> For true and righteous are His judgments, because He has judged the great harlot who corrupted the earth with her fornication; and He has avenged on her the blood of His servants shed by her. *(Revelation 19:2)*

The world is getting darker and darker, and life is becoming more difficult because God is forcing His children to think differently and come out of the Babylonian system. They are beginning to think about building kingdom communities that are not dependent on this world's system (2 Corinthians 6:17). Kingdom citizens from all over the world are conceiving the blueprints of these communities and new cities as well, but they haven't given birth to them yet. It is coming.

The enemy has been using God's people and their resources to build his kingdom here. His taskmasters own most of the houses, buildings, companies, banks, and businesses God's people use and work for. They have sucked out every ounce of our energy, skill, and gifting, and built empires for their *gods*. When they are done with us, and we have lost all our vitality, they will send us home and say, "It's time for you to retire!" Which is to tell us that it's time for us to go home now—and wait to die.

THE EXODUS IS COMING

The time has come for the great exodus of God's people. The blindfolds that have covered our eyes for so long are falling off. We thought we were doing God a favor by going to church on a Sunday morning and serving the world system Monday through Friday to gain a living.

When the devil and his kingdom receive the best of us (our best years, strength, and finances) and God gets what is left over, we are in trouble. Is this what it means to love God with all our heart, soul, and strength? Surely not.

How do we justify our math in any way or form? We give God a couple of hours a week, and the majority of our time is used to serve the kingdom of darkness and further its diabolical agenda.

The reason God sent us to this earth was to build His kingdom. Our entire time on earth (and every gift and skill He gave us) should be used to build His kingdom. Most of us didn't know that. We were taught that our lives here were temporary, and that the most important thing we had to do was make it to heaven, where we would build God's kingdom or sing to Him for all eternity.

The religious spirit made us believe that God is waiting in heaven to hear us sing to Him so He could get a good night's sleep! Or our music will inspire Him to be in a good mood, so that He might show up and do something for us! That is a huge deception. He doesn't need to hear our singing to be happy. That's not the reason He created us. He doesn't need to hear you sing for Him to come down and bless you, either. He has already blessed you with everything He has. We just don't know how to tap into it yet.

Some of us were taught that we are made "free" so that we can do whatever we want to do with our lives. Oh, really? Did you do whatever you wanted when the COVID-19 virus made us shut down everything and forced us to stay home? If a tiny virus can dictate how you live your life, do you think you are really free? Think about that for a minute.

BUILDING THE DEVIL'S KINGDOM

I have heard that only twenty percent of believers in a church give a ten percent tithe. However, we give the other ninety back to the world and its companies from whom we receive various services and products. Unfortunately, that means eighty percent of believers give a hundred percent of their life and money to the world system and the devil to enjoy a few perks.

Have you checked to see how many of the bills you pay every month or the stores where you buy food and other products you use are owned by Christians? I can guarantee you that the majority of them are not owned by Christians.

If they are not owned by Christians, who are they serving, and for whom do their owners live for? Whose agents are they? Whose kingdom are they building using our money? The devil's, right? This should have never happened.

All that money is going back into the kingdom of darkness to spread its agenda. In truth, who does the devil use to build and keep his kingdom intact on the earth? Just like in the beginning when he used Adam and the Israelites, he still uses God's children to accomplish his will. This must stop *now*!

WHOSE KINGDOM ARE YOU BUILDING?

In the early church, none of the wealth or money owned by God's children went into the hands of the ungodly. It only went out to be invested to make more money for the kingdom. They established a kingdom banking system (a kingdom economy) to manage the wealth and meet the needs of everyone in the church. As a result, there was no one with an unmet need, even in a five-thousand-member church! That is kingdom living.

We were slaves to sin before salvation. We were sold under sin and Satan was our illegal owner. Jesus came to die for our sins, and with His blood bought us back from the devil. Once someone buys us, we belong to that person. Now we belong to the Lord because He bought us with His blood (see Romans 6:16–17, 20, 7:14; 1 Corinthians 6:20, 7:23).

Lord means "owner." Once we accept Jesus as our Lord, from that minute on, we belong to Him for all eternity. Not just for a couple of hours on a Sunday morning. *From the moment we are saved, we are supposed to be serving Him with our lives and everything we have.*

When we are saved, we are supposed to pick up our original assignment and continue the task God sent us here to do. That is what salvation is supposed to do for us, but we have not been taught correctly about what happened to us when we were saved.

That is what God told Moses. God wanted to deliver His people from slavery so they could serve Him (Exodus 7:16, 8:1). When they were slaves, they couldn't serve Him. Why? Because their life was sold out to serve their masters and Egypt. From the moment they woke up until they went to bed (if they got a chance to go to bed), they were forced to serve the kingdom of Egypt.

Their time, energy, and strength was spent building Egypt. If we check the life of most believers, the situation won't be much different. They work or serve the kingdom of darkness Monday through Saturday and rush to church on Sunday morning. Even then, many show up late.

Every time you buy something, you are making God's kingdom or the kingdom of darkness richer and furthering one of the two agendas. It depends on who owns the business and who made the product you bought. Just look around you right now where you are sitting and reading this book. How many products have you bought that made the kingdom of darkness richer?

What is the solution to this problem? Once a believer sees and discovers the kingdom of God and their purpose in it, they will wake up every morning to fulfill their eternal calling. If you are saved, you have a calling. Do you know what you are called to do? Are you free to fulfill your calling emotionally, physically, and with your time? If your answer was no, this book is meant for you. Keep reading.

Those Israelites who were slaves in Egypt went to heaven once they died, but their destiny, purpose, potential, calling and blessings were stolen from them and were being used to build the enemy's kingdom. How sad! What is the benefit of going to heaven when your life on earth was spent building the kingdom of darkness?

Who is benefiting the most from your life—God or the devil? God's kingdom or the kingdom of darkness? The time you spend here on earth is the most important segment of your life. The next life will be a reward for what you did while you were here. If you didn't do much for God's kingdom in this life, then there won't be a great reward in the next.

This must stop. God's people must wake up to their destinies and their true identity. We need to rise up, shake off the shackles and the yoke of the enemy from our shoulders, and take up the yoke of Jesus Christ, our King and Lord.

How do we do this in our day-to-day lives? Who will provide for us and our families if we leave our jobs to fulfill the calling of God? How will we feed our children? God gave me this book to teach you on this very thing: practically living out the kingdom.

HOW CAN WE FIND FULFILLMENT?

Jesus said His yoke is easy and His burden is light. Until now, we had very limited understanding about the salvation we received through Jesus. We limited it to an entry ticket to heaven. God told the people of Israel that He was delivering them so they could serve Him, not so He could take them to heaven.

So how did the Israelites serve God after they were freed from Egypt? They didn't go around conducting music concerts with smoke machines and colored lights. They possessed the land and established a nation (a kingdom) for God. In the wilderness, they were being prepared to function as God's nation or an *ekklesia* (Exodus 19:6; Acts 7:38).

How many of us are serving Him with our time, energy, skills, gifts, and breath? In other words, how many of us are free to obey the first and greatest commandment, which is to love God with all our heart, soul, and strength? But how can we love Him with all of our strength when the majority of that strength is being used to build another kingdom?

We need to serve God and His kingdom with our spirit, soul, and body. Every ounce of our energy, health, skills, and talents must be used to serve Him. How do we walk in that in a practical manner? Who will pay us to serve Him? Many would say there's no opportunity in our churches to serve Him with their particular skills or gifting. That is the problem with our churches. This must change.

This book is a manual for those who are interested in finding and fulfilling their calling on the earth. When we do that, everything we need in life will come to us as a reward. That is why Jesus said to seek His kingdom and righteousness first, and then all the things we needed would be added to us.

I did not say we need to serve the church. My entire focus here is the kingdom of God—and the kingdom of God is much bigger than church as we know it now. Each of us is supposed to be a kingdom builder, not a church builder. Jesus is the One who builds His church. Each of us are living stones, part of the same building and kingdom.

CREATIVELY BUILDING THE KINGDOM

As I mentioned in one of my earlier books, each believer must own at least one business if possible. When you discover your purpose and master a gift or a skill, you are qualified to start a business in that area. Once you mastered something, you need to learn everything you can about how to start a business that fits your unique talent and skill. Your business idea could be to start a cleaning business or a mobile coffee shop at the street corner. Our business prospects will be diverse as and unique as we are.

I believe that God will give each of us several opportunities, ideas, and inventions to start businesses during our lives, but most of us won't take them seriously. For example, I am writing this page while I am flying from Taiwan to India on China Airline. One thing I noticed in this particular airline is that they do not provide bottled water. When they serve meals, they give tap water from the airplane for passengers to drink. I was really shocked by this.

I don't even drink tap water at home, so I never would in an airplane. I read several times in the news about contamination in the tap water in airplanes. This is a perfect opportunity for someone to start a bottled water business and approach the airline and sell them those bottles. Provided the airline would go for it, that person could make millions in a year.

It is a good idea to keep a journal to write down ideas and opportunities that come to your mind. We all notice things as we go along our way. The time has come for the Great Exodus to begin for the body of Christ worldwide. We have been serving the Babylonian system too long. The enemy has been using us to build and serve his kingdom. The time has come for us to fully *and only* serve our Lord and King with everything we have. In this book, you will learn how to do this in your everyday life.

Since God created each one of us to rule and have dominion, we must end the slavery of the world system and start to reign instead. For this to happen, we need to discover our calling and follow the blueprint we got when we were born again. Each of us are supposed to manifest an aspect of the kingdom of God here on earth. That is why He put the kingdom within us. We need to start focusing on that. If we practice what is written in this book, I estimate that within three to five years, everyone in the body of Christ can be free from the slavery of the world system. We can turn this world upside down!

FINDING OUR PLACE

If God has called you to be in the Babylonian system to represent Him and His kingdom and to influence it, then go for it. Don't try to escape that calling. That was the case with Joseph, Esther, and Daniel. They served God in their capacity where God put them. There is nothing wrong with that, but everybody is not called to do that.

We are supposed to go into the world to find out where each one of us fits and which aspect of the world we are called to influence. Only the Holy Spirit can help us find that place. He is the only One who knows the will of God for our lives.

We need to make our calling and election sure. Therein lies the secret to our prosperity. Please make sure you read the book *Purpose, Calling, and Gifts,* which will equip you more on this subject.

Are you free to serve the Lord with everything you have? Or are you stuck in the world system for survival and you feel miserable in your heart and spirit, crying out to the Lord to set you free or take you to heaven as early as possible? Don't worry, He has a plan.

Getting saved to make it to heaven is not enough anymore. Once our spirits are saved, we need to work out our salvation in other areas of life. Our minds need to also be delivered and renewed so we are able to think and imagine with the mind of Christ. We must yield our bodies to the purposes of God as well.

We need to be healed from every emotional wound, abuse, fear, insecurity, memory of past trauma, and any other issue that taunts us and holds us back. Every thought and mindset that keeps us emotionally crippled, socially handicapped, and intellectually stupid must go. Each one's case will be a little different, but we all have our own baggage that we need to be healed and delivered from.

PAID BY GOD

The night before the Israelites left Egypt, God told Moses to tell His people to plunder the Egyptians (Exodus 3:22). This means that each person borrowed expensive clothing and jewelry of gold and silver from their neighbors and looted them left and right.

Through doing this, God was paying His people the salaries due to them for all the years of labor they did for Pharaoh. Every penny that was owed to them and more was restored to them in one night. This is what needs to happen to the body of Christ worldwide. All the wealth the Babylonian system created or built using our time and energy must be paid back at least a hundredfold. Are you ready to receive your inheritance?

Every resource and treasure God has put on the earth for His children must be restored to them to build His kingdom. This must happen before Jesus can come back. He is not coming back for a church that is poverty-stricken, begging Him to get them out of here. He is coming back for a church that is ready to rule the nations with Him.

Before God can judge the Babylonian system, this Great Exodus must take place. God's people need to see the kingdom and discover the assignment God has for them on earth. They need to know exactly what they are called to do and identify the gifts He deposited in them and begin to function in them. Otherwise, if God judges the system, we will go down with it.

To prevent that from happening, God gave me this book. Its aim is to equip the body of Christ so we can take back what was stolen from us, heal that which became crooked, and build that which has been demolished. May the Lord use this book to accomplish that goal in Jesus's mighty name. Amen.

CHAPTER 2

WHY WE RECEIVED JESUS, BUT REJECTED HIS MESSAGE

> *I have not spoken in secret, from somewhere in a land of darkness. (Isaiah 45:19a NIV)*

We believe Jesus died for our sins: He shed His blood as the price of our redemption, took away the sin and curse, made peace between us and God, and reconciled all things in heaven and on earth. If we believe that, then we might wonder why we do not see the manifestation of it. Why doesn't life on earth reflect anything in heaven? Why we are not able to reclaim anything the enemy has stolen from us?

Jesus bore our sickness and pain on the cross. He became poor for us. He defeated Satan and took the keys of death and hell. All authority in heaven and on earth has been given to Him; and in turn, He gave it to the church. Then why does the enemy seem so powerful, roaming freely and doing what He does?

Though the Bible says God shall supply all our needs according to His riches in glory in Christ Jesus, why are so many children of God absolutely broke? In Africa alone, ten thousand children die every day because of hunger or hunger-related causes.[1]

Though the Bible says Jesus has left His peace with us, many Christians are deprived of peace and live in anxiety and depression. Though the Bible says that the kingdom of God is righteousness, peace, and joy in the Holy Spirit, many people in church have no joy, and run to the world to have some fun after church.

Every one of these problems are the result of one thing: We received Jesus but rejected His message. We gave people a King without His kingdom. We were taught that He came with the message of taking us all to heaven. However, when we read the Word, we find that Jesus and the apostles never asked anyone if they wanted to go to heaven when they died. That shocked me.

THE PROBLEM WITH HEAVEN

God never asked anyone if they want to go to heaven. Heaven was *not* made for humans. If we die, it's true that we will go to a resting place in heaven to wait until we can come back to the earth, but there's not a single verse in the Bible that says the dead are praising Him now, or one that describes any humans doing anything in heaven.

Instead, the Bible clearly says the dead do not praise God. They are all sleeping or resting now.

> The dead do not praise the Lord, nor any who go down into silence. *(Psalm 115:17)*

---

[1] James Strong, "127. Adamah," Strong's Hebrew: 127. האדמה (adamah) -- ground, land (Biblehub), accessed May 12, 2020, https://biblehub.com/hebrew/127.htm)

Believers who are dead are not flying around in heaven singing. They are all resting and waiting for the day of resurrection. This is what God told Daniel in the Old Testament.

> But you, go your way till the end; for you shall rest, and will arise to your inheritance at the end of the days. *(Daniel 12:13)*

We have written many imaginary songs and stories about heaven and what we will be doing there, and we taught those songs in the church. They are the fruit which emerged from a miserable, purposeless life. This created an escapist mindset in us as result. We did not know the real reason why God put us on this planet.

God wanted the same quality of life that is in heaven to manifest on the earth. That is what Jesus meant when He prayed "on earth as it is in heaven." We have not captured that vision yet. *God is waiting on us.* Meanwhile, we are still waiting on Him. We should not be waiting for Him to do something anymore; we should be stepping up to the plate.

We received Jesus because we were told that we will end up in hell if we didn't. Out of that fear of going to hell (and to escape this earth), we received Him into our hearts. Going to heaven should not be the inspiration and motivation behind getting saved. Because of this mistake, we have been waiting to escape this planet and go to heaven ever since.

Nobody in the entire New Testament scared anyone with the message of hell and influenced them to receive Jesus to go to heaven. No one coerced anyone with heaven or prosperity to receive Him. Not even once!

We thought Jesus came preaching about how to be born again. But He never preached about being born again in public. He mentioned it only once in a private, night meeting with a Jewish rabbi. That doesn't mean that it wasn't important.

We thought Jesus came with a healing message. But Jesus never preached or taught on healing. He healed people everywhere He went, but that was not His message. He didn't come with a revival message either. He never asked us to pray for revival. His message wasn't even about starting churches or going to church.

In recent history, people received Jesus because they heard about the benefits He was offering: like healing, deliverance, grace, material blessings, salvation, and so on. They received those benefits, but rejected His message. Maybe the *true message* was never preached to them.

How can they hear and receive unless someone preaches? Today, people are excited about the message of grace. Jesus was full of grace and truth, but grace was not His message either. When will we, as a church, become excited about the subject Jesus is most excited about and preached the most?

THE GOSPEL OF THE KINGDOM

Before anything else, Jesus is a king. He was born a king. When the wise men came from the east, they came to see the King, not a healer, prophet, or deliverer.

Day and night, Jesus had only one message to convey to humanity. From the time He began His public ministry until the day of His ascension, He preached and taught about one subject: *the message of the kingdom of God* (Matthew 4:17; Acts 1:3).

We totally rejected it because it did not fit into our religious frame of mind. We did not know how it applied to our lives now. We thought *kingdom* meant something euphoric or applied to the far-away future. Or perhaps it referred to going to heaven when we die.

WHY WE RECEIVED JESUS, BUT REJECTED HIS MESSAGE

We thought that maybe when Jesus comes back, then we will be with Him in His kingdom. We were taught that church is the kingdom; and if we go to a church regularly, we are in the kingdom. No. Jesus never taught such a thing.

Some were taught that the kingdom will manifest only in the new earth and new heaven, so there is no point of doing anything good now in this life because everything will be burned up. That is a lie from the enemy. Whatever we do for God and His kingdom will remain forever on *this* earth (1 Corinthians 3:10–15). Everything else will be burned up. If this entire planet is going to be destroyed, why did God say He would punish those who destroyed the earth when He returned (Revelation 11:18b)?

The true gospel is the gospel of the kingdom. The word *gospel* means "good news," and it refers to the fact that the kingdom which mankind lost when they fell in the garden was being restored. Jesus came preaching the gospel of the kingdom because He was personally restoring it. This was the good news. However, the religious spirit distorted and twisted Jesus's message over time, and taught people that getting saved was a choice between going to heaven or going to hell.

Therefore, we do not make the proper choice from the very beginning of our Christian lives, and we are poised to continue to make poor choices from that point on. We need to have an accurate understanding of Jesus's kingdom and our place in it for us to accomplish what He has called us to do in our lifetimes. The gospel of the kingdom has always been the same: God is King, He has a kingdom, and He wants to see His kingdom established *on earth as it is in heaven*, just as Jesus prayed in the Lord's Prayer.

The kingdom of God can manifest anywhere at any time. He did not put any time limit on His kingdom; there is only a faith limit. I hope you have read the other books in the *Discipling Nations* series. I address these issues in those books in detail.

We told Jesus we did not want Him to reign over us or the earth now. We just wanted His benefits and blessings. We wanted Him to continue to do what we told Him to do: go there, come here, touch this person, and heal that person. We became the lord and He became an *errand boy* who does our bidding. This is Charismatic Christianity in a nutshell. This is not kingdom living. That is humanism at its best. Many treat their pets with much more respect and love than they do Jesus the King.

We need to realize that we are not the center of this universe; Jesus is. Earth was not created for us. We were created for the earth. We were expected to take care of it. The earth was here long before we arrived—even before Adam arrived—and it will be here after we are gone. It will be here forever (Psalm 78:69, 119:90).

We were taught incorrect doctrine which said that we were the crown of all creation. We are the crown of all *creatures* God made on the earth, but not all creation. If we mismanage the earth and don't do what He told us to do, He will wipe us out and give the earth to someone else who will do what He wants. He did that a few times in the Old Testament, and Jesus warned us that He will do the same when He comes back (Matthew 24:33–41; Luke 19:11–27).

We received the gifts of the Holy Spirit because they helped us overcome our insecurities and made us feel better about ourselves. However, we merchandized them and used them to build our own personal empires, and rejected the person of the Holy Spirit. Holy Spirit is much bigger than His gifts. Holy Spirit came with the kingdom to help us to administer it on earth. He is the Governor-General of the kingdom of heaven. We used His gifts and built ministries and empires with them; but in the end, they will all come crumbling down miserably.

The purpose of the Pentecostal movement was to reintroduce the Holy Spirit to the church. Many of the people who used God's gifts without knowing their purpose lived lives marked by misery and frustration. At the end of their ministry, they died feeling empty and broken because they had not discovered and accomplished their true purpose within the kingdom of God.

That is why Jesus said at the end that *many* (He didn't say a *few*, but *many*) would come and say, "Lord, Lord, have we not prophesied in Your name, cast out demons in Your name, and done many wonders in Your name?" Jesus will declare to them, "I never knew you; depart from Me, you who practice lawlessness" (Matthew 7:22–23). That will be the saddest and most shocking day ever for many.

We received the Father and want His love for us, but reject His dream. We have written many romantic songs and fictitious stories about His love. Do you know that our heavenly Father has a dream? His dream is not to see us all in heaven. If it were, He would have kept us all there. He has no use for us in heaven. His dream is to see His kingdom come *on earth* and for His will to be done *here* as it is in heaven. That has been His dream from the beginning of time. It has been delayed and deviated because of the disobedience of mankind.

THE RELIGIOUS GOSPEL

I grew up in church and went at least four times a week. It was a very traditional, legalistic Pentecostal church. Almost everyone in my church was physically sick and financially broke, but we made a lot of noise when we met. Compared to the church, the heathens outside were living a better life.

We were believing and preaching a "pie-in-the-sky" religious gospel. We believed that someday when we got to heaven, everything was going to be better, but right now this was all we had to live for.

We were supposed to pretend to be happy! My own mother became ill and died at a very young age.

I said to myself, "There's something wrong with this picture. If this is all God has for me in this life, I don't want to do anything with this kind of church or God." What they were experiencing was the result of the religious gospel they heard and received. It was not the true gospel. The religious gospel is heaven-focused. It preaches that we are to escape this planet as fast as we can and enter the next life. They called it "the eternal life." Eternal actually means no beginning and no end.

Poverty is part of the religious gospel; in fact, they glory in poverty. They say the poorer you are, the more spiritual and holy you become. If you look at any religion, their biggest hope is pinned on whatever their god promised them they would receive after they died. They make no promises for the here and now. There is nothing much in this life. The religious gospel glorifies poverty and makes it part of the means to attain holiness and spirituality.

I entered into ministry when I was eighteen years old. I didn't have a mentor, and my church wasn't part of any major denomination. I wished many times for a mentor and to be part of a large denomination. In that framework, it would have been easier to build a ministry. If you have a network of people and churches, you can roam around and minister and raise funds.

Now I thank God that I was not part of a denomination and did not have a mentor. If I had, I wouldn't be where I am today and know what I know. It was all part of His divine design.

I was taught that our life on earth was a mistake—a short and temporary existence—and that God never intended for us to live here. Earth and all its resources belonged to the devil and his children. I was taught that God wanted us all in heaven and He was waiting for us to die and reach heaven so we could enjoy life with Him. That is another deception the enemy has used to steal everything God has given us.

GOD'S PLAN FOR MANKIND

Adam was not created to die. Death came because of disobedience. God told Adam that the day he ate from the fruit of the Tree of the Knowledge of Good and Evil, he would die. That meant that as long as man did not eat the fruit of that tree, he wouldn't have died. That was God's original design. If Adam had not died, he and his children would still be here today. Though he's not here, his children are. We are his descendants.

Man is useless in heaven. He was not created to live there. The only place God gets any benefit from us is while we are here on earth. We can speculate that we would do other things for God in some other part of the universe after we die, but everyone who died believing in Jesus is now resting until the day of resurrection. At that time, they will receive a glorified body and come back to earth to rule and reign with Christ. The Scriptures are very clear about this.

YET ANOTHER GOSPEL!

When I reached the United States, I heard a different kind of gospel. It was the opposite of the religious gospel I heard in India. This gospel offered everything big: big cars, big houses, and the best life ever, filled with lots of fun and perks. It is called the *prosperity* or *humanistic gospel*. According to this gospel, the wealthier you are, the more spiritual and holy you are.

It is the gospel of big cars, big houses, and megachurches. It's as if Jesus had gone around preaching and offering people bigger donkeys and faster horses in exchange for believing in Him or for giving Him some money as an offering. It is all about accumulating material wealth. These preachers twisted Jesus and the gospel, and used it to make their bank accounts heftier. God forbid!

I became very excited about this gospel at first because it looked very attractive and appealing to my flesh and my selfish ambitions. When a person grows up in poverty and then hears that now they can be rich and famous, it sounds like a great idea. It sounded like winning the lottery. I received it with all my heart and I couldn't wait to go back to India and start doing ministry to help all those poor people who were stuck in poverty and religion.

I went back and started with evangelistic meetings, then church planting, then pastors and church networks. Then I started an orphanage, and a private Christian school, and I thought I was on my way to having the biggest ministry in my hometown. We had the fastest-growing church in town.

Our school had more than six hundred students and the orphanage was one of the best in all of India. We had five buses for the school, and I bought a new SUV with cash. We never had to buy a used car. Everybody who saw me thought I had arrived! I was not even forty years old.

I was invited to be on the "Praise the Lord" program on TBN twice. When all these events were happening, I felt like there was something missing inside me. Something was out of order. I thought the next ministry project, opportunity or position would fill that void and bring fulfillment. I did not feel fulfilled instead, I felt miserable, but pretended to be spiritual and happy because people were looking to me for leadership. Outwardly, I appeared to be successful.

I was on my way to building a big ministry and making a name for myself. I wanted to be like one of those famous TV evangelists of our time. We started conducting pastors' conferences and trained more than 8,000 pastors. We had more than one hundred churches in our network. I wanted to be famous. I wanted people to know my name.

Everything I did was all about me. Nothing was for the kingdom of God. That is what I learned from the people I admired: They all had a big, worldwide ministry with their own names attached. I thought I was supposed to have one too!

SEEING FOR THE FIRST TIME

Then one day, something happened. For the first time I heard the gospel of the kingdom—the real gospel Jesus and the apostles preached. I got born again—again. The first time I was born again by hearing the religious gospel to become a Pentecostal. I was taught that I would go to heaven when I died. But this time I heard the gospel of the kingdom, and I was truly born again.

The Lord opened my eyes, and for the first time I understood the real reason why God created mankind and put us here on earth. I saw the kingdom of God. According to Jesus, when a person is born again, he or she must *see* the kingdom of God (John 3:3).

According to Jesus the King, if you didn't *see* the kingdom of God when you were born again, you are not truly born again. You could be member of a church or even pastor a church. You could be filled with a religious spirit and speaking in gibberish, and still not *see* the kingdom of God—because you are not truly born again. It is very possible. I was once like that.

If the kingdom of God still remains a mystery to you, I strongly recommend that you become born again today for the right reason, and be delivered from the religious spirit and receive the Holy Spirit.

To me, discovering the kingdom was like finding a treasure hidden in a field. When I discovered that *treasure,* the choice came: either I could keep all the "dung" and "fame" I had accumulated by my own efforts and sweat, or leave everything I had and take the treasure. I couldn't have both. And so the battle began.

How could I give up all the things and positions I had spent years to build? What would I tell the people around me? What would happen to my reputation? If I gave up everything, how would I support myself and my family? Children and many families were dependent on the support we were giving them monthly. I had to battle all these fears and overcome them.

In His grace, God began to take away everything bit by bit. The church we started and churches that were part of our network were all gone. To be honest, they weren't true churches; not even one of them functioned as an *ekklesia*. They were religious centers where people gathered on a Sunday morning to practice religious rituals.

The school was closed down. I kept the orphanage running for another year, even though I had a clear order from the Holy Spirit to close it. Because of my delayed obedience, I paid a huge price by facing the worst opposition and challenges that I had ever encountered before. In the following year, I closed that down as well.

Holy Spirit began to give me downloads on the kingdom. I kept on writing one book after another. I didn't know why and for whom I was writing at that time. I didn't have a church or pastors I could share with. Sometimes I became frustrated and angry because I could not see the fruit of my labor. I could only see the immediate future. Since I had given up everything, I thought this might be the end of my life and ministry. People thought I was a failure and passed judgments on me without knowing the true story.

Remember the story of the disciples. They gave up their boats, businesses, and livelihood to follow Jesus. They couldn't have both. It was Jesus and His kingdom or this world. Jesus said the path that leads to life is narrow and straight (Matthew 7:14). Only a few find it.

Jesus didn't promise Peter a bigger boat and a better net for leaving his business and following Him. That's what we tell people today. Peter was released into his God-given destiny from that day forward. Sadly, the majority of the people in the church today don't get released to fulfill their destiny. They follow Him for a bigger *boat*, a better *net* and for more fish.

Many of the big prosperity preachers are coming forward now and apologizing to people for what they have been preaching. They realize now that it was not the whole truth. However, the deception and destruction that the prosperity gospel has caused worldwide is unfathomable!

I'm not sure how many years it will take to reverse the damage it caused in the body of Christ.

That treasure that I found was the kingdom of God. The field was this world (Matthew 13:44). I could not live without it. Even if I had to lose everything I earned and built, it was worth every bit. You may wonder why I had to close down churches and all the ministry programs we were doing.

The simple answer is that none of them had to do anything with the kingdom of God. They were not built on the right foundation or for the right reason. They were Abraham John's kingdom. They were all part of the religion called Christianity. I was tired and done with religion. I wanted the kingdom of God because I had been created for it. So are you.

We do not read about the apostles going into a town and starting an orphanage or a school. There's not even one example of that in the Bible. They established *ekklesias* that, in turn, discipled cities, nations, and regions. James said true religion was to *visit* orphans and widows in their trouble, not start orphanages or homes for widows (James 1:27). If you are called to do this, then it's not a problem, but don't do it just because others are doing it.

I thank God for the mercy He has shown me. Those ministries were burdens that I brought upon myself. They could have killed me and destroyed my family. They almost did, but God spared my life and my family because of His great mercy toward me. During all these times, God did not stop the supply of kingdom provision in my life. I thank Him for that.

Though I discovered the kingdom twenty years ago and the Holy Spirit helped me to write twelve books on the subject, I hid those books in my computer for almost fifteen years and did not publish them. I was nervous about who would listen to what I had to say. However, God kept pouring out more and more, and I kept writing books one after another. I have now completed almost twenty books on the kingdom of God.

OUR SEASON

Then in October 2016, the order came from the Father. He told me that it was now time to run with this message. Ever since that day, my heart beats and my lungs breathe for His kingdom to manifest on earth, and for others to discover His kingdom. If a person does not discover His kingdom, nothing else will satisfy them.

When the Lord saw that I was ready to run the race with no extra weight hanging around my neck, He said that now was the time to run with the message. The result has been amazing. Nations are opening up to the gospel of the kingdom. Africa is the continent that is ready to receive the kingdom, as one of their spiritual fathers, Sydney Elton, has said.

Noah had three sons: Shem, Ham, and Japheth. The entire human race on earth today came from those three sons. Each of these sons is the head of a complete race of people. Shem became the nation recognized by God as the nation of Israel. They were the custodians of the vision of God. God chose them to display His glory and carry His message of deliverance and restoration. We know that they failed.

Japheth has now taken up the challenge. God in the Old Testament—through the Babylonian Empire, through the Medes and the Persians, through the various Gentile empires—propagated the system of Japheth. And Japheth has proceeded to govern the Gentile world now…Japheth has had charge of the whole purposes of God, particularly in the last two hundred and three hundred years, in the European race in Europe, and later in America.

The Gentile world has failed to establish the kingdom of God on earth, so we are seeing the end of the Gentile rule, we are seeing the end of the Japhetic rule, and there remains only one son, one head of a new race—the sons of Ham. And we are seeing some of them come to operation in these last days to bring in, finally, the kingdom of heaven on earth."[2]

We are in the abovementioned season now. God is doing a new thing on the continent of Africa, especially in Western Africa. No amount of money, fame, anointing, or power will gratify a human soul. If you have them, they were all given for one sole purpose: to establish and expand God's kingdom here on earth. If you do not use them to do that, at the end of your life, you will be very sorry.

Though I closed down all the religious programs, we will now be starting kingdom *ekklesias*, Kingdom schools, universities, training centers, and businesses, as well as helping governments in every nation. This will be done for one reason: to establish and expand the

---

[2] Ayodeji Abodunde, Messenger: Sydney Elton and the Making of Pentecostalism in Nigeria (Lagos, Nigeria: Pierce Watershed, 2016), 377.

kingdom of God—not to promote a particular personality or person or the name of a ministry.

When we come into the kingdom, everything we were before that must die. Our identity based on a particular race, tribe, profession, or nationality must die. Our personal ambitions and dreams need to die. We do not live for ourselves anymore. We do not live in our own strength anymore either. We live for the King. We live to do His will. We surrender our lives to Him and live to see His dream come true. We are all citizens of the same kingdom and children of the same Father.

We should be able to say like Paul did:

> I have been crucified with Christ; it is no longer I (based on my nationality and race) who live, but Christ lives in me; and the life which I now live in the flesh I live by faith in the Son of God, who loved me and gave Himself for me. *(Galatians 2:20)*

> He died for all, that those who live should live no longer for themselves, but for Him who died for them and rose again. *(2 Corinthians 5:15)*

When I discovered the message Jesus preached, it changed my life forever. Then I knew what God had been doing in my life since I was sixteen years old. My eyes were opened and I saw the kingdom of God. What does the kingdom look like when you see it? I will answer that question in the following chapters.

Your very life depends on what you *see* in the kingdom. Before we discover that, I would like to urge you to receive the message Jesus preached, and not just His benefits. Make a commitment to preach and live for it until your last breath.

The kingdom of God does not refer to a Jewish kingdom or the kingdom of Israel exclusively. Many misunderstand this these days. In fact, even many believers run to Israel, thinking they will get in touch with the kingdom of God over there. Jesus never said such thing. God's kingdom is universal; it is in you, and God wants the entire earth to be under the domain of His kingdom.

When the disciples asked Jesus if He was going to restore the kingdom to Israel, He told them to go to the ends of the earth to witness for Him (Acts 1:6–8).

This is why when Jesus taught us to pray, He told us to pray for His kingdom to come and His will to be done on earth as it is in heaven. He did not say His will would be done just in Israel, *but in the entire earth*. Anyone from any country can tap into God's kingdom and His favor. You don't need to go to Israel to do that.

If you want to go and see the biblical historical sites for educational purposes, that's fine. If you wish to bless Israel, that's fine as well, but Jesus said that when we help one of the least of these from any country, we are helping or blessing *Him* (Matthew 25:40).

If you want to know what the gospel of the kingdom is and how it differs from other gospels people are preaching, please order the book *The Gospel of the Kingdom: Hope for the Church and the World*. I guarantee you will be blessed by it.

CHAPTER 3

WHY SEEK GOD'S KINGDOM FIRST

*Seek first the kingdom of God and His righteousness,
and all these things shall be added to you.
(Matthew 6:33)*

According to Jesus, the *first thing* we should do in life is to seek the kingdom of God and His righteousness. God wants us to seek His kingdom before we seek any relationship, vocation, or educational option. Seeking His kingdom should *precede* our pursuit of money. God knows that once we are trapped in the Babylonian system of working for money to buy food, clothing, and shelter, it is difficult to be free from it. It is a trap—a form of slavery.

Everything in this world is geared toward hindering or blinding us from discovering God's kingdom and fulfilling our kingdom destiny. Our culture, education, religion, and government condition us to believe that we need to seek to be successful first of all. We are taught that this can be achieved by getting an education, finding a good job that makes a lot of money, and a life partner. We have been conditioned to function that way naturally. Our natural instinct is to make choices based on trying to survive or make a living.

It is against the Word of God to work for food and try to make a living by trusting in our own strength. According to Jesus, all those things are a reward for those who seek and discover His kingdom. What are the "all these things" this verse says will be added to us when we seek His kingdom?

Jesus explained them earlier in Matthew 6:31 when He told us not to worry about food, water, and clothing. Those are the essential things that will be added to us when we seek and discover God's kingdom and His righteousness first. This makes sense, as those are the basic things we need to survive. Ninety-nine percent of people working any kind of job do it to provide themselves with food, shelter, water, and clothing.

Most people are trapped in the snare of the enemy and working to provide for themselves and their families. In truth, they are working against the Word of God and against the kingdom of God. What is the solution for this? How do we stop it before another generation goes into eternity without fulfilling their destiny? What if you have already lived most of your life? It is a worldwide problem.

You might say, "Doesn't the Bible tell us that if we don't work we should not eat?" (2 Thessalonians 3:10). That passage isn't talking about a job that you do to make a living. It is talking about fulfilling our kingdom assignment: the work God has prepared for you (Ephesians 2:10).

It is important to note that nobody in the Bible who God used did anything to make a living. They were living out their calling, and as a result, food, water, and clothing were added to them. They were busy fulfilling their calling, and the things they needed were supplied. It was only before they discovered their calling that they did something else for a living. David and Moses fed sheep until they were called.

There's nothing wrong with doing a job or anything else to survive until you discover your calling and are fully released into it. Jesus was a carpenter until He was released to fulfill His calling.

Unfortunately, most people get stuck with a job they don't like and never get released into their calling. Fear of death and the enslavement of the Babylonian spirit keep them in bondage their entire lives.

Your calling includes food, clothing, and every other provision you need. Peter, James, and John were fishermen until they discovered their calling. That's how they were supporting themselves. If kingdom provision is not coming to you, it means you haven't discovered your calling yet. The first step in discovering your calling is to see the kingdom of God.

We need to seek God's kingdom and His righteousness first. There are three kinds of righteousness. Righteousness according to the law (legalism), self-righteousness (humanism), and righteousness by faith (kingdom living). We will learn more about this later.

The four things that keep most people out of the kingdom of God is their pride, unbelief, self-reliance, and self-righteousness. (There are different kinds of pride too: religious, racial, family, personal, and so on.) It's hard for many people to trust God or depend on Him for anything. They are out there "to make it happen" by their own strength and ability. They will all fail miserably in the end.

If you ask people, they will tell you that they will go to heaven when they die. Why? Because they are good people and believe God will let them into heaven based on that. If that was true, then we did not need a Savior, and Jesus did not have to come to die for our sins. People say those kinds of things because of their pride and self-reliance, as well as their dependence on their own righteousness. They will not enter God's kingdom nor make it to heaven when they die.

GOD'S ORIGINAL INTENT

To understand why Jesus asked us to seek His kingdom first, we need to go back to the beginning. God is King and He has a kingdom. He wants to see that kingdom and His will established on the earth. That is the single reason for everything God does in relation to our planet and mankind.

God wants earth to be an extension of heaven. He wanted to colonize earth with heaven. He wanted the same quality of life, culture, economy, and everything else that is in heaven, to be manifested on the earth. He never imagined life on earth to be any different than life in heaven.

God wanted to rule the earth, but He had a problem. He is Spirit. Earth is a physical planet, and anyone living here must have a physical body. God doesn't have a physical body like ours. He could not live on this earth because of that. If He wanted to live and accomplish anything here, either He needed to create a body or He needed someone else who had a body who would permit Him use it.

So God came down to earth and made a body out of the earth, which would provide a house for His Spirit to dwell in the physical world. This body did not have any life in it until He breathed the breath of life into its nostrils.

When the breath of life from God went into it, this body became a living soul. It is God's breath (His Spirit) that gave us life. We carry the same essence of life as God's. Our bodies gave God and His Spirit a temple in which to dwell and the legal right to operate in the physical world. When His Spirit leaves, our bodies go back to where they came from—the earth.

God called this species "Adam" (or mankind). Adam's responsibility was to fulfill the assignment of His Father, who is in heaven. Because Adam has the same Spirit and DNA that God has, he is called the son of God (Luke 3:38). Adam's spirit came from God.

Adam was to the earth what God was in heaven. Adam's responsibility was to represent His Father and carry out the task He gave him, which is to rule the earth. God created us for His purpose and put us on the earth to do His will. His will is to see His kingdom established on earth, so that His will is done here as it is in heaven.

God also knew that man needed certain things to fulfill His purpose and live on the earth. He needed food, water, a place to stay, and clothing. He decided to provide those. God never intended for man to work for His food, clothing, and shelter. It was a provision (a benefit) added to him by God for doing His will on the earth.

God came down and planted a garden and took the man He created and put him in it. The garden came with his food, clothing, and habitation. Adam did not work for the garden for his food, clothing, or shelter; it was given to him by God. Food was ready before he arrived in the garden. They were part of the package; they came with the kingdom assignment God had for him. He did not have to worry about any of these needs as long as he fulfilled the task God had for him. It was not the plan of God for man to ever worry about provision. Man's task was to fully engage with the assignment God gave.

Why did God provide food and everything else Adam needed? God wanted Adam to be free to fully focus on the task. As long as man fulfilled the assignment God had for him and lived in His kingdom, he never lacked anything.

This was God's original intention and plan for mankind. Each person born after Adam would experience the same kind of life. They would continue the assignment God had for them, and in turn, He would continue to supply their needs, so that they could focus and fulfill their kingdom assignment.

It is sad that most people spend their precious lives trying to provide for themselves. They are unaware of the provision God has prepared for them in the kingdom. They are unaware of His kingdom and the assignment He has for them. Nobody taught them how to seek God's kingdom and discover their assignment in it.

When you discover your kingdom assignment and start to live it, everything you need in your life will be added to you. That is why Jesus said if we seek His kingdom and His righteousness *first*, all these things would be provided. God's plan and system did not change, and will never change. His kingdom is an everlasting kingdom and His dominion endures throughout all generations (Psalm 145:13).

CALLING AND PROVISION

I hope you find your individual kingdom assignment as a result of reading and studying this book. Every person has a kingdom assignment. Most do not fulfill it because they never hear anything about it. They live, work for their food, shelter, and clothing, and then they retire, age, and die. That is the normal life cycle for the majority of us.

That is why this earth is in its current shape. The people who were sent to fix and restore what is broken leave it in worse condition than before they came. This world is missing our contribution.

When a king sends you on an assignment, it is his responsibility to provide for you. A king will never ask you to come up with money to fulfill a task for him. He will not send you on his mission and not provide for your expenses. A king will always exceed the reward for anything we do for Him.

The people of Israel did not work for their food in the wilderness. Manna was provided for them from heaven for forty long years. Why? They were called out by God from Egypt to fulfill a mission for Him. He wanted them to be a kingdom of priests to Him (Exodus 19:6).

What did Moses, David, and Esther do to provide for their families when they were commissioned to perform their callings? Their provision was included in the calling. So is yours. If your provision is not coming, I doubt if you are fulfilling your calling.

When called, the disciples left their boats and businesses and followed Jesus immediately. Where did their next meal come from? How did they support their families? That was not their burden or responsibility. It was Jesus's responsibility to provide for them. He was the One who called them to do something for Him, and they were walking out His calling. When you obey God to fulfill His calling, it is His responsibility to provide for your needs.

Their needs were taken care of from the moment they committed their lives to Jesus. This is not something we initiate by our own choice. We need to respond to His calling. God is not a respecter of persons.

Our God is King. He has a plan for your life in His kingdom. There is not a single human being not included in His plan. It is our responsibility to seek His kingdom first and discover that plan. This book is designed to help you do that.

Jesus told us to seek His kingdom first before we tried to find a way to make a living that was dependent on the Babylonian system. He wants us to discover His kingdom and our assignment in it. Everything we will ever need comes with that assignment.

Once we get stuck in the Babylonian system, it is very difficult to be free from it. If we start with God's kingdom first, we will have to go through less pain to enter and inherit the kingdom and fulfill our calling.

> No one can serve two masters; for either he will hate the one and love the other, or else he will be loyal to the one and despise the other. You cannot serve God and mammon. *(Matthew 6:24)*

Either we serve the God and His kingdom, or serve the mammon. We cannot serve two masters at the same time.

Personally, by God's grace, I started with the kingdom from the very beginning in my life, but I did not know it was the kingdom because no one taught me about it. I never had to look for a job to support myself or my family. I started the journey of fulfilling my calling when I was eighteen, and God has been my provider ever since. It's been more than a quarter of a century now, and all I can say is that He has been faithful.

This should be the story of every individual alive today, not just a few or the people in the Bible. For some reason, God was gracious enough to me or I was crazy enough to follow what He showed me without looking to the left or right. Not everyone is called to do the same kind of ministry I do. *Whatever God called you to do is your ministry.* If you are called to be a farmer, that is your ministry. If you are called to be a doctor, that is your ministry. Our ministries are as varied as we are.

THE ELDER-BROTHER SYNDROME

One of my favorite verses in the Bible is Luke 15:31, found in the parable of the prodigal son. If you recall the story, the older son had been slaving away all his life for his livelihood. When he saw his father's response to the return of the younger profligate son, he complained to his father that he had never given him a goat to enjoy with his friends, showing that he thought his father was a stingy guy. What did his father say?

> And he said to him, "Son, you are always with me, and all that I have is yours." (Luke 15:31)

This is the same response our heavenly Father has for each of us. Everything the older brother's father owned had always been his, but he did not enjoy it because he misunderstood his father, his wealth, and what his father thought of him and wanted from him.

That son's life is a perfect example of someone who did not find his father's assignment, but was dependent on his own strength. He slaved away all his life to support himself instead. This son never took the time to ask his father about the purpose of his father's resources or his plan for him as his son.

Many children of God live like that today. They don't know God's plan for their lives. They do not know exactly what their heavenly Father thinks of them. They think He exists in the distant somewhere way up in heaven, and that they have been left to themselves down here, struggling to survive. They don't benefit from the wealth He created for them to fulfill His purpose.

KNOWING OUR FATHER

God says the thoughts He thinks toward us are for our peace, to give us a great future and hope (Jeremiah 29:11). We are coheirs with Jesus. Everything Jesus owns, we own with Him (Romans 8:17). It is all available for us to use to build His kingdom on earth right now.

Jesus told us to seek His kingdom first for the following reasons:

- Our assignment on earth is connected to His kingdom.
- Our provision is attached to His kingdom.
- Our purpose is connected to His kingdom.
- Our purpose is connected to this planet.
- The reason for our existence is His kingdom.
- We have been sent here to establish His kingdom and will.
- Our sacred duty is His kingdom.

- Without His kingdom, there is no meaning for life.
- His kingdom is our dwelling place.

Adam did not work for the garden he lived in. He only had to take care of it and protect it. It was part of the assignment God had for him. Similarly, when an ambassador goes to a foreign country to represent his nation, everything he needs will be provided by the government that is sending him ahead of his arrival. It is the same way in the kingdom of God.

Adam was sent by God to represent Him on the earth and to establish His kingdom and will on earth as it is in heaven. God provided everything Adam needed to fulfill that task.

We are citizens of heaven. God sent us to earth as His kingdom ambassadors. He promised to provide for us and cover all of our expenses, but when we were naturally born in different nations, we were spiritually dead and sold under sin. We were held captive by an enemy's kingdom.

God sent His Son to save us and give us another opportunity to be born into His kingdom. That is why He told us to seek His kingdom first, so that we would discover that original assignment He intended for each of us.

When God sends you to do something for His kingdom, He promises to provide for you and cover all your expenses. That sounds like a great deal to me. I don't think anybody will say no to such a great offer. Life couldn't get any better or easier than this!

THE IMPORTANCE OF UNDERSTANDING MATTHEW 6

> Therefore I say to you, do not worry about your life, what you will eat or what you will drink; nor about

your body, what you will put on. Is not life more than food and the body more than clothing? *(Matthew 6:25)*.

Jesus knows that most people spend the majority of their time dedicated to the never-ending pursuit of feeding themselves and their family. They are afraid for their lives and unsure how they will survive. Jesus tells us in this verse that we should not lead our lives in this way. There is a better way. There is something called "kingdom living."

There is enough provision in the kingdom to feed every living creature on earth. God has been doing that for centuries. The only species that struggles to find their provision is human beings, because most are not living in God's kingdom and fulfilling His kingdom assignment. They are doing their own thing or simply trying to survive.

Jesus said our lives are much more than the food we work for. This means our lives are more important than spending all our time and effort working to fill our bellies each day. It means we are supposed to be spending our lives doing something better than just earning wages so that we can buy some food that perishes (John 6:27). There has to be a greater reason for our lives. What could that be? It is the most important purpose that we could ever spend our lives on.

That purpose is spending our lives building God's kingdom here—to see His will be done on earth as it is in heaven. Jesus said our bodies are much more important than the clothing we wear. Our bodies were not made for the clothes we wear; that's not their purpose. People show off their bodies in advertisements and other places, promoting their shape as well as the name brands of their clothing. That display is not the reason God gave us our bodies.

Many try to find their significance in the kind of clothing they wear. Our significance comes through our purpose in the kingdom, not through our appearance and possessions.

The purpose of the body is to provide housing for our spirits and God's Spirit. It should function as a temple for God on the earth and give God legal access to operate here in the physical world.

After this, Jesus began to tell them about birds and the lilies of the field and how they lived. He said they did not work for their food and clothing, but that our heavenly Father fed and took care of them all. A bird doesn't work for its food; they go and pick it up daily. They collect what God has placed for them that day, just like the people Israel went out every morning and collected manna in the wilderness. The Israelites did not work for the manna; they only had to collect it each day. That is kingdom living.

Jesus was saying that if God exercised such care and precision over every creature and plant, He would provide what we needed with even greater care, because we are more precious than all the rest. It is important to note that Jesus said *"your* heavenly Father feeds them" and not *"their* heavenly Father" (Matthew 6:26). Those creatures don't have a Father like we do; they only have a Creator.

> Now if God so clothes the grass of the field, which today is, and tomorrow is thrown into the oven, will He not much more clothe you, O you of little faith? *(Matthew 6:30)*

Unfortunately, most of His children are not benefitting from their Father and His kingdom. They are slaving away for their entire existence trying to feed themselves. In the end, they are broken and dissatisfied. Why? They did not seek their Father's will in His kingdom.

From Adam on, every individual ever born should have been spending their life accomplishing God's kingdom assignment for them. That assignment is the reason for our existence. When we are born again, we get *to see* what that assignment is. God will show it to you as part of His kingdom. We will learn about this more later.

Jesus was telling the people how life was supposed to work on earth. God never intended for mankind to continually toil in an effort to survive. Jesus said only the Gentiles do that. Who are the Gentiles? Gentiles are those who do not believe in God. Those who have no part in His kingdom. Unfortunately, most believers live like the Gentiles. They spend the majority of their time working to feed themselves. It shouldn't be this way.

Jesus was saying that God's children are supposed to be seeking His kingdom assignment first, not what they would eat, wear, and drink first instead. They are supposed to discover why God sent them to this planet. When they discover that assignment and live it out, everything they need will be added to them as a bonus. He is saying *kingdom living should be the norm for every person.*

Why does our Father provide for us? He wants us to be free from wasting our time providing for ourselves. That makes us free to focus on His assignment instead. You're either fed by God as you fulfill His assignment, or you feed yourself by your own strength. Either you are fulfilling God's assignment, or the enemy is using you by keeping you as his slave to build his kingdom as you work for your own food. There is no neutral ground.

We have been taught that seeking God's kingdom means going to heaven when we die or joining a particular type of church or doing some kind of ministry. That is far from truth. Jesus never said anything like that! Because of this misinformation, our lives have been robbed and stolen by the enemy for too long.

KINGDOM PRINCIPLES

Communism and socialism are two counterfeits of the kingdom principle birthed out of man's search for the kingdom of God. When people like Karl Marx became tired of religion and discovered all the evil, abuse, and exploitation done in the name of religion, he went on a search to find a solution to replace and destroy religion. He wrote that religion is the "opium of the people" and harmful to people as it kept them from seeing what he considered to be the true reality around them: that they were oppressed and imprisoned.

The entire quote by Karl Marx was: "Religion is the sigh of the oppressed creature, the heart of a heartless world, and the soul of soulless conditions. It is the opium of the people." [3] He was right.

As the result of his search, Marx discovered a principle of the kingdom of God. Lenin implemented Marx's principle, which removed God (the King of the kingdom) from the picture. They replaced God and His kingdom with a man-made system of government formed by their ideology, and decided to provide for people's basic needs so that they did not have to work or worry about what they would eat or where they would live. Whether people worked or not, they received a portion from the government for their survival and a place to stay.

Instead of trusting God and His kingdom to provide for the people, the government played the role of God. People began to depend on their government for provision. Additionally, the government didn't give people the freedom to fulfill their purpose and calling. Instead, they oppressed and suppressed people and their creativity. As a result, people lived and died without knowing their purpose and identity. The vast majority did not have the opportunity to utilize their potential. They rejected God and His kingdom and made government their god.

If they had included God, acknowledged Him for who He is, and given people the freedom to fulfill their God-given destiny, their mission could have been a huge success. In time, democracy filled

---

[3] "Opium of the People," Wikipedia (Wikimedia Foundation, April 13, 2020), https://en.wikipedia.org/wiki/Opium_of_the_people)

that vacuum. This system offered freedom for people to become what they chose. However, a democracy allows people to believe in any god or anything they want—or not believe in Him at all.

As a result, people began to depend on their own strength and ability to provide for themselves, instead of the kingdom or the government. They began to build their own personal kingdoms instead of God's. One good thing about democracy is that it at least gives us the freedom to preach and practice the kingdom of God to those who want it. In the end, only a theocracy works, with God in His rightful place.

The bottom line between all these different kinds of governmental ideas is that they put man or a man-made system in the place of God. That is the foundation of humanism, which began in the garden of Eden with the lie of the serpent.

> Then the serpent said to the woman, "You will not surely die. For God knows that in the day you eat of it your eyes will be opened, and you will be like God, knowing good and evil." *(Genesis 3:4–5)*

The serpent was introducing a new way of living to mankind. Exclude God and His kingdom from the picture; you don't need Him. Separate yourself and be independent from Him. Make yourself god instead so you can decide for yourself what is good and what is evil. No one should tell you how to live or what to do.

You become the master and creator of your own destiny. You are the guardian of your soul. This is the root of all individualism and humanism. Religion is a branch of humanism, which depends on man's work or ability to please God or to become like god apart from God. Living this way is in direct opposition to the will of God for humanity.

Now that we know why we need to seek God's kingdom first, how do we find out what a person is called to do? How do we find our kingdom assignment? That is what we are going to look into next.

CHAPTER 4

WHY MUST WE BE BORN AGAIN?

Having been born again, not of corruptible seed but incorruptible, through the word of God which lives and abides forever. (1 Peter 1:23)

When God created Adam, the Bible says He took him and put him in the garden He had planted for him. As we have learned, the garden was the manifestation of the kingdom of God. When Adam opened his eyes, the first thing he saw in the natural was the garden. He saw the kingdom of God.

Later on when Adam and Eve sinned, they lost the ability to see the kingdom. Instead, they began to see what was wrong with them. A different set of eyes were opened, and they saw their weaknesses and defects instead (Genesis 3:7). They became sin-conscious instead of God-conscious.

God came up with a plan to re-open the eyes of our spirits. That plan is called being born again. When you are born again, you are supposed to *see* the kingdom of God just as Adam did in the garden. The only difference is that now you will see it in the spirit realm and not in the natural. Your assignment is to manifest what you have seen and continue to see in the spirit into the natural. We will learn how to do that later in this book.

Nicodemus was stuck in religion. He could quote Scriptures. He was very pious and looked spiritual outwardly. He may have even memorized the first five books of the Bible (the Torah). He was considered a "teacher" by the Jewish religious community; but in that state, he was useless to Jesus and the kingdom of God. He was not manifesting the kingdom of God. Why? Because he was not born again. He was too religious. That is why Jesus told him to be born again—so that he could see the kingdom of God (John 3:3).

We have many religious, pious people like Nicodemus around us. Some of them are leaders of churches and denominations. They can quote the Bible left and right, but they are not manifesting the kingdom. They are training people how to become more religious on a daily basis.

A person possessing only head knowledge of the Bible is of no benefit to God. Many can quote Bible verses. I did that for many years without knowing what it really meant. My life was not centered around building the kingdom because I was not truly born again.

HOW IS A PERSON BORN AGAIN?

In the beginning was the Word. God creates everything with His Word. We see that in Genesis chapter 1, the phrase "God said" is repeated ten times. That is why the Bible says, "By Faith we understand that the worlds were framed by the word of God, so that the things which are seen are not made of things which are visible" (Hebrews 11:3).

With the fall we also lost our sonship and citizenship in the kingdom of God. To regain those, God wants us to be born again and He uses the specific word that He used to create each one of us, to make us born again and see His kingdom. When we hear that word, our spirit-man comes alive.

WHY MUST WE BE BORN AGAIN?

Jesus told Nicodemus that he *needed* to be born again, but He did not tell him *how* to do it. He did not lead him in a prayer of confession or tell Nicodemus to receive Him into his heart. That's what we've been taught and have been doing for a long time. That's where we went wrong.

There is not a single reference in the entire Bible to support this teaching. I will explain this more in a bit. We have confused being born again and salvation for a long time. How were you born in the natural? Were you born because you or your parents believed in something or someone, or confessed something with their mouths? I don't think so.

You were conceived and born by the seed, or sperm, of your father? You had no involvement in your conception or birth. Nobody could have determined that time or your gender. It was a supernatural act of God. So is spiritual birth.

A person is born again through a supernatural act of God. It cannot be managed or controlled by a person or a particular method or system. Just as you were naturally born by a natural seed, you are born again by a spiritual seed, the seed of God, which is the Word of God. That is why Jesus did not tell Nicodemus on how to be born again.

A lot of preparation by God goes into you to prepare you before He releases that word to you. Sometimes it can take decades to prepare us, like it took eighty years for Moses. The problem with many is they are out there trying to make things and life happen and they miss it. Total and absolute yielding to God is required to receive that word from Him.

The seed gives life. No one can be born naturally without a sperm and an egg. Similarly, No one can be born again without the Word and the Spirit of God. It's impossible. That is why Jesus said that His words were spirit and they are life (John 6:63). Instead of telling

Nicodemus on how to be born again He said, "If I have told you earthly things and you do not believe, how will you believe if I tell you heavenly things?" (John 3:12). By earthly things Jesus meant the natural birth and by heavenly things He meant spiritual birth.

Peter tells us that a person is born again through the Word of God.

> Having been born again, not of corruptible seed but incorruptible, through the word of God which lives and abides forever. *(1 Peter 1:23)*

How are we born again by the Word of God? How does it happen practically in the real life? A person is born again when the Word of God comes to that person regarding their destiny. When God releases a word concerning their destiny or an assignment He wants them to accomplish, suddenly that person's spirit comes alive and they are born again. They begin to see something in the spirit realm concerning their destiny. What they see is the blue print of their future.

When the word of God comes to you, you will know it in your spirit. This is what we describe as hearing the voice of God. We sometimes say: "God spoke to me today." Your spirit man will come alive and something will change, or shift, inside you. You cannot remain the same after that.

When a woman receives a seed into her womb, others may not notice the change immediately, but something definitely happened in her. It will show up outwardly in the days to come.

> Whoever has been born of God does not sin, for His seed remains in him; and he cannot sin, because he has been born of God. (1 John 3:9)

What is the seed of God? It is the Word of God. The word used for *seed* in Greek in the above verse is *sperma,* from which we get our English word *sperm*.[4]

WHY DOES GOD USE THE WORD TO REBIRTH US?

Adam and Eve were spiritually dead because they *listened* and acted upon the words that the enemy spoke to them (Genesis 3:1–5). Wrong words killed them spiritually and resulted in all the destruction we see today. If sin and death entered the planet and mankind through believing and acting on demonic "words," salvation and life also come through believing and acting on "words": the Word of God.

God uses His Word to bring us back to life. That is why the Bible says He sent His Word and healed them (Psalm 107:20). God does everything through His words. Jesus is the Word that became flesh. We can trace this theme from the first chapter of the Bible to the last. In Revelation, we read that Jesus will destroy the enemy by the sword of His mouth, which is the Word (Revelation 19:15). God uses His Word to restore us to His original intent.

Now the question is this: How does the Word of God come to us? It can come to you in a multitude of ways. Nobody can predetermine when or how that is going to happen, just as our natural conception and birth could not be predetermined.

When that Word comes from the Lord concerning our destiny, something happens to our spirit man. It comes alive. The Bible calls it a born-again experience. We suddenly see something we never saw

---

[4] James Strong, "G4690 – sperma" *Strong's Greek Lexicon (KJV)*, Blue Letter Bible, April 14, 2020, https://www.blueletterbible.org/lang/lexicon/lexicon.cfm?t=kjv&strongs=g4690

before in our spirit man with the eyes of our spirits. Jesus calls it seeing the kingdom of God.

From then on, a person's spiritual status and position changes. They are no longer mere humans.

> If He called them gods, to whom the word of God came (and the Scripture cannot be broken).
> *(John 10:35)*

The above verse says God called them gods to whom the Word of God came. That means that before the Word came, they were not called gods.

Becoming born again is unique and different from person-to-person. One size does not fit all in God's kingdom. Religion wants everybody to do the same thing and look the same way. I don't read about anyone in the Bible who was born again by raising their hands in a meeting.

The kingdom will not work that way. This is just one reason why people who grew up in religion have a hard time understanding the kingdom and how it operates. How did, and when did each person in the Bible believe in God or Jesus? How were they saved? Each experience and occasion was unique and different.

It happened to them when the Word of the Lord came to each one of them. We just assume from our religious understanding that Jesus and Paul had crusades and led everybody in a prayer at the end to receive Him. If you look at the church today, most people get saved through an altar call. However, there is no mention in the Bible of Jesus or the disciples leading people in prayer to receive Him in this way.

Nicodemus asked Jesus how this born-again thing actually happened. Jesus told him this:

> The wind blows where it wishes, and you hear the sound of it, but cannot tell where it comes from and where it goes. So is everyone who is born of the Spirit. *(John 3:8)*

You are born again by the Word, or the seed, that is brought to you by the Holy Spirit. He is the only One who knows the blueprint of God for your life—your spiritual DNA. That blueprint is written somewhere in the Word of God. Your *seed* contains your DNA: both in the Spirit and in the natural. The natural seed contains the DNA of your natural life, and the seed of the Word of God by which you are born again contains the DNA of your spirit man, which is your destiny or calling, your assignment in the kingdom.

We were created by His word when He said, "Let Us make man in Our image and likeness in Genesis 1:26. Then He breathed His Spirit into us. We are a combination of God's word and His Spirit. His word is our DNA which describes and contains our purpose, and the Spirit empowers us to live and fulfill that purpose. The word He used to create us is our spiritual DNA. The word directs us and the Spirit empowers us.

The DNA of your spirit contains your destiny. That Word (that could be a verse or chapter of the Bible) by which you were born again is your life source. You need to hang on to it for the rest of your life.

In the gospel of John, people came to John the Baptist and asked him who he was. They wanted to know whether he was the Messiah or one of the prophets, like Elijah. It is important that we note his reply. He answered with his spiritual DNA.

> He said, "I am 'the voice of one crying in the wilderness: "Make straight the way of the Lord,"' as the prophet Isaiah said." *(John 1:23)*

You can read the whole story in John 1:19–23. John quoted Isaiah 40:3 as his mission statement. That means long before John was born, his blueprint (his spiritual DNA) was written in the Word of God by a prophet. That is the seed by which John was born again. Through it, his spirit was born and the mission for which he was sent to accomplish on the earth was revealed.

In the same way, your spiritual DNA was written somewhere in the Bible hundreds (and maybe thousands) of years before you were born. Only the Holy Spirit knows which part is yours.

When that word is spoken to you by whatever means God chooses, your spirit man will come alive. Suddenly you will know why God sent you to this planet. Your destiny (kingdom assignment) will become clear to you. That's when you see the vision for your future and that is when you are born again and the Bible calls it seeing the kingdom of God. It could come through preaching, while you are reading the Bible, or through any other means God chooses to communicate with you.

God can use any number of methods to speak His Word regarding your destiny. I will mention ten ways He speaks later on in this book. That Word that comes to you is your spiritual DNA, or the calling of God on your life. Never take that lightly—because your very life depends on it!

Jesus said the same thing. Because there is so much written about Jesus's birth, life, and destiny, it is difficult to separate it. After all, the entire Word is about Him (Hebrews 10:7).

David wrote that everything concerning his life was written in a book before he was born (Psalm 139:16). Everything on earth and in heaven consists in Jesus. He is the Alpha and the Omega. We were all created by Jesus and for Jesus. He is the Beginning and the End.

WHY MUST WE BE BORN AGAIN?

> For by Him all things were created that are in heaven and that are on earth, visible and invisible, whether thrones or dominions or principalities or powers. All things were created through Him and for Him. And He is before all things, and in Him all things consist. (Colossians 1:16–17)

When Jesus was born, there had to be a seed and the Spirit working together. That is what the angel told Mary. He said the Word would become flesh when the Holy Spirit came upon her (Luke 1:35; John 1:14). There has to be a seed and the Spirit, just like in the natural there has to be a seed and an egg. In Jesus's case, God provided the seed (the Word). It did not come from a human being.

Now the question is this: If we are all originals, how can billions of people's spiritual DNA be written within the sixty-six books of the Bible? Is there a possibility of any duplicates? There could be others who carry the same spiritual DNA as you have, but their assignment in the kingdom will be different.

For example, John the Baptist was the forerunner for Jesus. There was only one John the Baptist in the entire history of mankind. His spiritual DNA was Isaiah 40:3. There will be others who carry the same DNA, but they won't be forerunners of Jesus as John was. Their assignment will be different.

The Bible says John came "in the spirit and power of Elijah" (Luke 1:17). This means they both had similar spiritual DNA, but their functions were different. John did not perform any miracles like Elijah did (John 10:41). That is the way it works in the kingdom. If someone else comes today in the spirit of Elijah, he will do something entirely different than Elijah or John did.

That is why when you meet someone with the similar spiritual DNA as you have, something resonates in your spirit about that person.

You will feel an immediate connection with them. It will have the similar feeling of meeting a lost *family* member. Usually we say we are of the same spiritual lineage.

There is no need for envy or jealousy in the kingdom. Everyone has their place and their own unique assignment. Envy and jealousy are rampant in the church because most people have not discovered their place and their assignment in the kingdom. When they see someone flowing and flourishing in their assignment or gifts, they want to take their place or copy them and try to have what they have. That is not kingdom living. They do this because they did not recognize what they saw in the kingdom when they were born again.

According to Jesus, the whole purpose of being born again is to restore our ability to see the kingdom of God, as Adam saw it in the beginning, so that we can rediscover the purpose and plan of God for our lives and this planet. Why does God want us to *see* His kingdom? So that we can go back to the original task He entrusted us with when He created the human species, which was to expand and establish the kingdom of God on earth.

Unfortunately, most people who are born again do not pick up on the plan God has for them. They were taught that they were born again to go to heaven when they died or to join a particular type of church. That is not what Jesus or the apostles taught. In fact, He mentioned being born again only once in His entire recorded teachings in the four Gospels.

Our spirit man is set free by God's Word so we can fulfill our destiny on earth.

> For we are His workmanship, created in Christ Jesus for good works, which God prepared beforehand that we should walk in them. *(Ephesians 2:10)*

WHY MUST WE BE BORN AGAIN?

A common theologically-debated question is whether the Old Testament believers were born again? The common answer is that they were not because they did not believe in Jesus or because Jesus had not yet shed His blood. I also preached and wrote that because that is what I was taught.

Based on 1 Peter 1:23, which says we are born again by the incorruptible seed of the Word of God, I now believe the Old Testament saints were born again because the Word of the Lord came to them directly, unlike any of us. Most of the time we hear from God by reading the Word that the Old Testament saints received and wrote down for us, or by hearing someone else preaching from what they wrote.

Many of the saints in the Old Testament received the Word directly from God. Once you have such an experience with God, you cannot remain the same. Your spirit man will not remain dead. How can that be possible? John 10:35 says that those to whom the word of the Lord came were called gods. He was talking about Old Testament saints.

When the Word of the Lord came to them concerning their destiny, they were born again and saw the kingdom of God, means they saw what they were called or created to do and fulfilled their kingdom assignment. We read about what they did in the Bible.

The salvation we receive and experience through Jesus was not available to them. They had to wait for the death on the cross and Jesus took their souls with Him when He ascended to heaven (Ephesians 4:8). We know they did go to heaven because the Bible refers to them as clouds of witnesses in Hebrews 12:1.

Another misunderstanding we have is that they were born again *after they died* and were waiting in purgatory, and that after Jesus died, He went to hell (or wherever they were) and preached the gospel to them and that is how they were born again (or saved).

I don't believe that, because if that happened like that back then, couldn't it happen again? Couldn't those who are dead now without Jesus hear someone preach the gospel again after they die as some churches teach? I don't think so. Scripture says this:

> It is appointed for men to die once, but after this the judgment. *(Hebrews 9:27)*

> For this reason the gospel was preached also to those who are dead, that they might be judged according to men in the flesh, but live according to God in the spirit. *(1 Peter 4:6)*

The above verse says the gospel was preached to the dead, not so they could be saved but so they could be judged righteously. Then they could be without excuse. Note that the verse begins with: "For this reason." What reason? You need to read the verses before that to understand its context. Peter was talking about people who were living in sin and indulging in a party lifestyle.

Additionally, there is this aspect to be considered: Jesus is the Word of God and the Word made flesh. If a word was ever spoken by the mouth of the Lord, that is Jesus Christ in Word form. The Bible says:

> In the beginning was the Word, and the Word was with God, and the Word was God. *(John 1:1)*

I have never seen any reference in the New Testament that says the saints of the Old Testament were not born again. Also, there isn't a passage in the New Testament that says you need to "believe" in Jesus to be born again. Instead, it says that we must believe in Jesus to be saved. Or to have eternal life. Our salvation is a lifelong process that begins when we recognize our need for Jesus as our Savior and firmly confess our belief in His saving power.

We are supposed to be saved and born again at the same time. But it does not always happen. A person is born again by the partnership between the Word of God and the Spirit of God. This happens when a person's eyes are opened to their calling, and from then on, they *see* the kingdom of God. Let's explore that further.

WHAT DOES IT MEAN TO SEE THE KINGDOM?

When you were born in the natural and opened your eyes for the first time, you might have seen all kinds of things and people around you, but you did not recognize them. You might have felt like you were dreaming or it might have scared you. I think this is the reason most babies cry when they come out of their mother's womb.

When they see the bright light or people moving around them, their little eyes and brain have no idea how to cope with it all. They were in the dark comfort of the womb for more than nine months.

At birth, we may have seen lights, equipment, parents, nurses, part of the bed, and so on. We might have wondered about the strange world we came into. The whole time we were in the womb, we were preparing for that moment. We were not made to live in the womb forever.

That is what happens to us when we are born again. The moment you are born again, God puts a vision in your heart about your future and life. It exists in the invisible realm. What you see is the part of the kingdom (or an aspect of the kingdom) God wants to manifest on the earth through you.

What you see might shock you or seem unbelievable. Some cry because of the weight and size of the vision God has for them. What you see when you are born again is the clue to your calling. You see what you are called to do with the rest of your life on the earth.

You may not understand or have a complete picture at that time, just as the baby does not. The baby grows and begins to understand more about what they saw when they were born. The same thing happens to us. What you saw the moment you were born again will be completely different when you look back at it after ten or fifteen years. Your understanding of what you saw will change and mature. What you saw was only a glimpse of your future. God will add more of the pieces and bring clarity as you walk it out.

If you ask a child when they are five years old what they saw when they were born, they will not have a clue, but they know they saw things. As they grow, they will learn what light actually is and what a bed or blood is. It is the same with us when we are born again.

In the same way, seeing the kingdom is like seeing a country. The kingdom of God is a country. I came to the United States twenty years ago for the first time. When I went back to India, I told people I had seen the United States, but I had not seen the whole country. I had only seen the parts of the country that were connected to my assignment there. After twenty years, I have yet to see the majority of the United States.

When we are born again, we won't see the whole kingdom. We will only see the part that is connected to our calling. God will only show you what you can handle at that time. Your vision unfolds and manifests in seasons. A baby cannot handle or manage an airplane or a building. He will start with small toys.

This is why Jesus said that if we are faithful with a little, He will allow us to manage bigger things and positions (Luke 16:10).

The vision you saw has the power to bring everything you need into your life. Your food, clothing, and shelter will come as part of that calling. You don't need to worry about anything. Though we will worry and complain on the way, we need to mature and grow out of that childish behavior.

WHY MUST WE BE BORN AGAIN?

A newborn baby cries for milk. That baby thinks he or she is not going to get any milk without crying, but the mother knows that her baby needs milk even before they start crying for it. As children grow older, they stop crying for milk and food. This works the same way in the kingdom between God and us.

When you are born again, the eyes of your spirit are opened and you see something that you never saw before. You will not see anything different in the natural or any manifestation immediately, but you will know in your spirit that there is something in the spirit world that is as real as what you see in the natural. To be honest, it will be even more real than what you see in the natural.

If the vision is huge and global, God will put the same picture in the spirit of more than one person. If it is a movement of what God is doing in the "now," then the same picture will come into the spirit of those in different parts of the earth who are supposed to be part of that movement or carry the same spiritual DNA. Each one will have a slightly different function in that movement than the rest.

When the Israelites came out of Egypt, God promised them a land that flowed with milk and honey. These are people who had been slaves for hundreds of years. They did not own any land or property. When they were saved from bondage, God drew a picture of what He had in store for them in their spirit and imagination through His Word.

The picture of Israel coming out of Egypt was the Old Testament example of our salvation that we experience in Christ Jesus. Everyone who came out of Egypt heard the Word; they *saw* in their spirit the land that flowed with milk and honey. That was their born-again experience. Everybody had an equal opportunity to believe and receive the blessings. Although everyone was excited about it in the beginning, only a few had the patience to endure hardship and inherit the promise.

Every child of God who is born again sees the kingdom. This means they see a picture of what God has in store for them, but only a few will believe to receive it. Most disregard it or ignore it. They do not believe it because of fear or unbelief. Since the plan God shows them is beyond their ability, and over and above their natural capacity and the resources available to them at that time, it takes crazy faith to believe what God has in store. If you want to play it safe and live an ordinary life, then kingdom living is not for you.

I am not sharing a "dream big" philosophy. That is humanism. God never told anyone to dream big. *God has a very specific plan and assignment for you.* You cannot add anything to it or take anything away from it. Within the limit of your calling, you are free to dream big. Like Jesus said, we cannot add to our stature by any means at our disposal (Matthew 6:27).

When God called Abraham, we see the same principles in place. With the call came a promise to inherit a land that God was going to show him. Abraham saw a territory. That was the kingdom assignment he saw when he stepped out to obey the call of God. Each of us will see the aspect of the kingdom God wants us to manifest on the earth, or the assignment God has for each of us. What we see will differ from person to person.

That is why the Bible says,

> But as it is written: "Eye has not seen, nor ear heard, nor have entered into the heart of man the things which God has prepared for those who love Him."
> *(1 Corinthians 2:9)*

Many stop here, but the next verse is so important. It tells us how we will see what God has prepared for us.

> But God has *revealed them* to us through His Spirit.
> For the Spirit searches all things, yes, the deep things
> of God. *(1 Corinthians 2:10)*

This begins to happen when we are born again and will continue until we die. God will keep unfolding what He has in store for us.

Each new season in our kingdom living will begin with a word from the Lord. In the same way that there was a prophetic word written about the various stages of Jesus's life (from His conception, birthplace, early life, ministry, and everything else), we will receive words from God that precede each season of our lives too.

Jesus did the same thing when He called the disciples.

> Then He said to them, "Follow Me, and I will make
> you fishers of men." *(Matthew 4:19)*

That was the first Word by which they were born again. That was the picture He drew in their spirit about their future to begin their life in the kingdom. Most of the time, what you see comes in the form of a promise, vision, dream, or picture in your spirit about your future.

We see the same principle throughout the Bible. When God called Jeremiah, He gave him a promise (the assignment) He had in store for him (Jeremiah 1:10).

What did you see, hear, or sense in your spirit when you were born again? Do you remember? When was the first time in your life, you knew for sure God spoke to you or you heard from God? What was the Word that came to you which brought your spirit man alive? When you felt your spirit "moved" inside you. Can you go back and try to remember? Usually what you saw when you were born again will not go away from your spirit. It remains with you for life. God will not take it away from you. It is part of your inheritance as His child. It is your assignment in the kingdom.

If you did not see anything when you were born again, there is still a way for you to find it again. Go to a place where the real and *rhema* Word of God is being preached. Seek Him and He will answer you. God is faithful to communicate His plan and calling to you.

Most of the time, people say they didn't see anything because they are comparing the born-again experience with the salvation they received. Nobody really taught them about what the born-again experience is and how it happens. If a person is born again, they have to see the kingdom of God.

If you are saved, you are called. What you see, hear, or sense in your spirit when you are born again is your *calling*. In my book *Purpose, Calling, and Gifts*, I explain this in detail.

Your calling comes with your born-again experience. What you saw when you were born again is the calling you need to fulfill, so it is very important that you take what you see, hear, and sense from God very seriously. Your whole life depends on what you do with that. It is your mission on earth.

Everything you need for the rest of your life, including your financial blessings and provision, is included in that calling. How you live in this life as well as in eternity is based on how well you fulfill your calling. Even in the new earth, you will be doing what you are called to do now, but at a different level.

In the beginning, you may not understand all the small details about your calling, and you may have more questions and doubts than answers. Usually you will only see the Big Picture, not all its parts, in the same way that God told the Israelites about the Big Picture: He was going to take them to a land flowing with milk and honey. He did not tell them how many days it was going to take them to reach it, or how exactly they were going to inherit it, or what they would be required to do. None of those steps were revealed until later.

When God called Abraham, He only told him to travel to a land that He was going to show him. Abraham was called to be a father of many nations. To establish a nation, the first thing you need is land and then people. God promised that his children would be like the sand of the sea and the stars of heaven. He did not tell Abraham the location or the size of the land, how long it would take to get there, and when exactly he was going to possess it. None of those things were mentioned when the call came.

If someone for any reason misses God and walks away from what He has shown them when they were born again, they may have missed a good chunk of their life by now. However, God is gracious and merciful. He will give you any chance possible to fulfill your calling because the call and gifts of God are irrevocable (Romans 11:29). This means He will not cancel or take back your calling or gifts once He has given them to you.

God is more interested in you fulfilling His calling than you are. Your success expands His kingdom. That's why He put you here. If it seems too late to go back and change anything or start anything new, you could at least help someone else fulfill their calling with the time and resources you have left.

HOW IS A PERSON SAVED?

Now that we know how a person is born again, let me tell you how a person is saved. Salvation comes by faith.

> That if you confess with your mouth the Lord Jesus and believe in your heart that God has raised Him from the dead, you will be saved. *(Romans 10:9)*

The Bible teaches that being born again and salvation are two different experiences, but I believe both are supposed to happen at the same time. When the Word of the Lord comes to you, that's when you are born again and feel the conviction of God in your heart. Then you receive Him into your heart and are saved.

We have mixed both of them together for a long time and didn't understand the difference between them. That is why we have so many saved saints who are alive, but do not know why they are here. They do not know their purpose or what they are called to do. They are waiting to go to heaven.

Now the question is this: Can a person be saved and not born again, and vice versa? Normally we associated the born-again experience with getting saved. That is not what the Bible teaches. Is a born-again person saved? Is a saved person born again? I believe it is possible. The only requirement Jesus set forth to have eternal life is to believe in Him (John 3:15–16).

Being born again is an instant experience, but being saved is a lifelong process. When you believe in Jesus, this initiates the process of salvation. If that person dies immediately, he or she will go to heaven. But that is not all there is to salvation. Salvation came because of the fall of Adam. When we are saved, we are supposed to receive what Adam lost when he fell. Otherwise it's not salvation; it's just a ticket to heaven.

The restoration of everything we have lost can go on for generations—and might take generations to complete it. It could take generations to fulfill a word God speaks. For example, God's promise to Abraham and David is still being fulfilled, and some are yet to be fulfilled. Salvation begins in a moment of time, but it doesn't end there. Each generation has a role to fulfill in completing that process. You may not see the fulfillment of everything in your lifetime.

I have been writing about the kingdom for years, but I may not see the complete fulfillment of everything I write and the fullness of the kingdom in my lifetime. I am a forerunner. The kingdom process is being initiated in various places and in many people's lives during my lifetime. This has already started. The process will go on for generation after generation, but I see it by faith, just like Abraham did in the Old Testament. By faith and through the Spirit, Abraham saw the days of Jesus (John 8:56).

Salvation is the restoration of everything we lost when Adam fell. It is up to each person to decide how much of what they lost they want to get back in this life. If you do not initiate the process of restoration in your lifetime, the next generation will not have anything to receive and continue on with.

They will have to start the process all over again from the beginning—from the kindergarten of salvation. Many generations just waited around for rapture and went into eternity without initiating this restoration process. They didn't hear and understand the whole gospel, so the generation that came after them felt stranded and without a purpose and clear picture.

Many destroyed their lives by walking away from church and Christianity. They didn't feel like they belonged anywhere. They didn't know where to start or have anything on which to build. Some of them had dreams, but lacked the resources to fulfill them because the previous generation had not fulfilled their part. The enemy used that opportunity to confuse, strangle, and destroy them.

This is one of the reasons why Christianity began to die out in the western world. If you ask majority of the population, you will find they have some kind of Christian root in their background. But they don't want to do anything with it now because they inherited a skewed view of church and God.

The enemy stole their destinies and used the resources that could have been theirs and their children's to build his kingdom. That's what he has been doing all this time. Everything the enemy uses belongs to us.

Remember that before David died, he collected all the wealth, gold, and materials that were required to build the temple and gave it to his son, Solomon. He finished his assignment and passed the baton to the next generation. That is the way each generation should be living. What if David had not fulfilled his destiny? Solomon wouldn't have accomplished what he did. Abraham did the same for Isaac, and Isaac did the same for Jacob.

Solomon was called to do something different than David. Each individual is different and unique in the kingdom and in their calling. But Solomon did not leave a good example. However, if we look at the church today, almost everyone is doing the same thing. Most ministers look the same and do the same old thing.

Moses brought the people of Israel to the Jordan, and his assignment finished there. After that, it was Joshua's task to take the people into the Promised Land. With every generation, there should be progress. We are supposed to be going from glory to glory. Even so, the church has not made much progress in the last five hundred years. The church has been operating in a *spiritually arrested developmental state* for many generations. We have been circling the same mountain—waiting for the rapture.

We increased in number, but because of the lack of proper vision, we became irrelevant to our cultures and began to depend on the world for everything. We sing in church that we don't want the world and that this world is not our home; however, we live dependent on the world for even the smallest things like a pencil or a pin. If the people in the world did not produce any food, the church would starve to death in many parts of the world.

I encourage you to initiate the process of restoration in your life by living out what you are called to do. Fulfill your kingdom assignment and pass the baton to the next generation. Through these books, the

Lord is laying the correct foundation for generations to come. Then they can build on this, and take it to the next level.

They don't have to start from scratch or feel stranded, because now they have a blueprint laid out for them. Paul said that each one should consider how they are going to build. If we do not build with the right heart and right material it will be burned or will be tested with fire (1 Corinthians 3:10–15).

There are many verses in the Bible that define salvation as an ongoing process. Below are a couple of them:

> And you will be hated by all for My name's sake. But he who endures to the end shall be saved. *(Mark 13:13)*

> Therefore, my beloved, as you have always obeyed, not as in my presence only, but now much more in my absence, work out your own salvation with fear and trembling. *(Philippians 2:12)*

> Who are kept by the power of God through faith for salvation ready to be revealed in the last time. *(1 Peter 1:5)*

> But, beloved, we are confident of better things concerning you, yes, things that accompany salvation, though we speak in this manner. *(Hebrews 6:9)*

Salvation and being born again are supposed to happen at the same time, but because so many get saved to go to heaven, it does not happen that way. We were not taught correctly. For the purpose of this book we will deal with those two subjects differently. According to Jesus, when a person is born again, he or she must *see* the kingdom of God. Otherwise, that person could be saved, but not born again.

We have many saved people in church who have not yet seen the kingdom. They have no clue about their purpose or their calling. The only thing they know is that they are going to heaven when the rapture takes place.

I believe that being born again is the first step to salvation. When a person hears the Word of God, his or her spirit man comes alive. For the Word of God to manifest, the Spirit of God needs to be involved. The seed of God enters his or her spirit and connects it with God. From that point on, that person is able to relate with God once again on a child-and-Father basis.

My question is this: When did the disciples and others during the time of Jesus become born again? We do not read about Jesus giving an altar call at any time for them to receive Him into their hearts. Neither is there any reference to Him leading them in any confession.

When Jesus called them to follow Him, that was the moment the Word of the Lord came to them. It was at that moment that they saw the blueprint for their future. He told them "Follow Me, and I will make you fishers of men" (Matthew 4:19). That was the Word by which the disciples were born again. Later more promises were added to them by the Lord as they walked out their kingdom assignment.

LIVING BY THE WORD

We are born again by the Word of God, and that Word is the source for our lives and the blueprint for the rest of our lives. That is what the below verse means.

> That He might make you know that man shall not live by bread alone; but man lives by every *word* that proceeds from the mouth of the Lord. *(Deuteronomy 8:3)*

We have two options: either we can live by the Word (following God's plan) and His blueprint for your life, or by doing a job (based on our educational level) that depends on the world to provide bread for us. In the above verse, *bread* means something we make or produce.

It is important to note that God said we can live by every word that "proceeds" from His mouth. Every word that proceeds from the mouth of God is a blueprint for someone's life. This refers to the *rhema* word, or the word that is spoken. When that word comes to an individual, it reveals their destiny.

From that moment on, they are supposed to be living by the word they received. When they do that, the provision they need will come to them, just as God provided manna in the wilderness. The Israelites started their journey by hearing God's promise of a land that flows with milk and honey.

When we are born again, we inherit whatever is in Jesus Christ. Those who are born of God are the children of God. His holiness becomes our holiness; His righteousness becomes our righteousness. Whatever He owns becomes our inheritance. We are coheirs with Christ (1 Corinthians 1:30; Hebrews 1:2).

When we are born again, our spirits are born again to live the life God wants us to live. Just as we inherited Adam's nature through our natural birth, we regain our spiritual nature and likeness through our spiritual birth in Jesus Christ. Just as one man's disobedience made all sinners, one man's obedience made all righteous (Romans 5:19). Just like you and I were in Adam when he disobeyed God, we were also in Christ, the last Adam, when He obeyed God.

That is why Jesus had to be born as a man: so He could restore everything we lost. *If Jesus can do something, I can do it, too.* If He has received all the authority in heaven and in earth, I have received it, too. Once you are born again in your spirit, you are entitled to receive everything you lost because of the fall.

> Therefore, if anyone is in Christ, he is a new creation; old things have passed away; behold, all things have become new. *(2 Corinthians 5:17)*

Once we are in Christ, we don't live by what we inherited from Adam. Instead, we live through the inheritance of our new nature from Christ, which is the original nature that we had before the fall.

In conclusion, how does a person become born again in a practical manner? If someone comes and says they want to be born again, what do we do? Do we lead them in some special prayer? Usually when a person says they want to be born again, it means they want to be saved. They are asking us to lead them in the prayer of salvation based on Romans 10:9.

Becoming born again does not happen through repeating a prayer. We cannot intentionally lead someone in that experience, just as we cannot intentionally cause someone to be born naturally. If we have a word from the Lord for their lives, we can share that with them. If the word we share resonates with their spirit man, they might get born again and see the kingdom and receive a vision for their future. If not, we trust the Lord to do His job—when He chooses and in the way He chooses.

We cannot say when a person will be born again. When the Spirit and the Word work together in a person's life, they suddenly see the kingdom of God and the blueprint for their destiny. The wind blows wherever it wishes, and so are those who born of the Spirit.

CHAPTER 5

SEEING THE KINGDOM OF GOD

Jesus answered and said to him, "Most assuredly, I say to you, unless one is born again, he cannot see the kingdom of God." (John 3:3)

There are three steps to manifesting the kingdom of God. The first step is to see the kingdom; the second is to enter the kingdom, and the third is to inherit it (or, as I refer to it in this book, to "manifest" it). We are going to see how each one is accomplished in the light of the Holy Scriptures.

As we have learned, according to Jesus, the first thing that needs to happen to a person when they are born again is that they see the kingdom of God. We were taught that we needed to be born again to go to heaven or become part of a particular type of church. We give altar calls in crusades for people to become born again, but we forget to tell them the purpose of it.

God has given me this book to deal with that subject. We have already dealt with what it means to be born again in the last chapter. Now we will explore what it means to see the kingdom. When we see the kingdom of God, what does it look like? After we see the kingdom, what are we supposed to do next?

UNDERSTANDING OUR PURPOSE

In order to understand this, we need to go back to the beginning once again. We need a firm understanding of why God created this planet and put mankind here. I cover this foundational question in almost in all of my books because it is critical. Everything we do and believe in life has to be based on this single truth.

If we do not understand the purpose of God for creating the earth and mankind, then nothing else will make any sense and deceiving spirits can lead us astray without any difficulty. That is what has happened in the church for a very long time. We are like the blind men who went to see an elephant; each one came back with a different opinion.

In the church, everyone is trying to establish their own viewpoint about God and the kingdom. In the same way that those blind men tried to convince each other about the appearance of the elephant, each viewpoint does not have the full picture. Only when we understand the whole picture can we fit the pieces where they belong.

God created the earth to be an extension of His kingdom. He wanted to see His kingdom, His will, and His rule and reign be established here. To accomplish that task, He created a species in His image and likeness and entrusted them with that task. That is the Big Picture of His purpose and plan for the earth and mankind. Everything else must be defined in the light of that purpose.

God created Adam and Eve and put them in the garden of Eden, which was the physical manifestation of God's kingdom on earth. It was the nucleus or the prototype of the kingdom. Man's responsibility was to protect, duplicate, and expand it until the entire earth looked like what God showed him in the garden.

THE IMPORTANCE OF TREES

The Tree of Life was in the garden. Why was a tree connected to life? What does a tree have to do with life? Why didn't it say the microchip of life was in the garden or the coffee of life was in the garden? No, it said the Tree of Life. There is a specific reason for it.

When we study trees, we find something very interesting. Trees sustain life on earth. If there were no trees or plants, then there would not be any life. The oxygen we breathe (and that every other creature breathes) comes from trees. Even fish need oxygen to survive in the water. The food we eat also comes from trees and plants. Even if you eat meat, those animals were fed food that came from plants. All life on earth is dependent on trees and plants.

The economy of a nation depends on trees. Agriculture is the foundation of any thriving economy. The paper we use to print money comes from trees. The cloth and shoes we wear came from trees. Even if some parts comes from an animal, those animals depend on trees. Even education depends on trees, because every book ever printed came from trees.

Mankind's original food was trees and the food that came from them.

> And God said, "See, I have given you every herb that yields seed which is on the face of all the earth, and every tree whose fruit yields seed; to you it shall be for food." *(Genesis 1:29)*
>
> And out of the ground the Lord God made every tree grow that is pleasant to the sight and good for food. The tree of life was also in the midst of the garden, and the tree of the knowledge of good and evil. *(Genesis 2:9)*

We also read about the Tree of Life in Revelation 22:14.

Trees play a major role in the ecosystem we live in and the weather around us. The more trees we have, the better the overall quality of life and air. Trees reduce pollution dramatically.

Drought and famine come when there are not enough trees. Many parts of Africa are currently going through drought. Planting more trees is the permanent solution for this problem. That's why God planted trees in the garden. Each one of those trees represented an aspect of His kingdom.

If there was a Tree of Life, I believe every other aspect of life was also represented by trees. I assume there was a tree of government, a tree of education, and the list goes on and on. I believe God met with Adam under different trees each day dependent on what subject or aspect of the kingdom they were going to discuss that day. It was a kingdom cabinet meeting.

Throughout the Bible, trees represent different aspects of life. God appeared to different people by different trees. I believe God follows the same principle or protocol like He did in the garden. People and events are compared to specific trees. For example, in the life of Abraham a specific tree is mentioned throughout his journey. The tree, sometimes translated as the terebinth, was actually a stately oak tree. The reason that particular tree is mentioned several times is because of what it stands for. It stands for governmental alliance, endurance, strength, or power.

> Then one who had escaped came and told Abram the Hebrew, for he dwelt by the terebinth trees of Mamre the Amorite, brother of Eshcol and brother of Aner; and they were allies with Abram.
> *(Genesis 14:13)*

FINDING OUR PLACE IN THE KINGDOM

The garden of Eden was the prototype of the kingdom of God on earth. All twelve components which comprise a kingdom were evident in it. It was Adam's responsibility to multiply what he saw and expand it throughout the earth.

When we are born again, each of us will see our calling in one of the twelve components of the kingdom or a subcategory of them: kingdom, government, *ekklesia*, army, people, territory, economy, education, technology, media, industries, and agriculture. These are the twelve components of a kingdom, and our calling will be in one of them. God will show it to our spirit man when we are born again. That is our life's assignment, vision, calling, or a dream. It is the aspect of the kingdom God wants to manifest on the earth through us.

Everything a kingdom has was present in the garden. There was a kingdom economy in the garden. God talked to Adam and Eve about the precious metals and stones; they were part of the kingdom economy (Genesis 2:10–14).

Kingdom agriculture had its place in the garden of Eden. God told man what to eat and what not to eat. He came down to earth and planted a garden; He was the first Farmer on earth. God knew food was important to mankind and He wanted them to eat the right kind of food, so He Himself came down and planted that garden. He did not want any weeds or junk growing in it.

This was God's plan from the beginning. Food was to be our medicine. We see that in the first chapter of the Bible and in the last chapter (Genesis 1:29, 2:9; Revelation 22:2). In Isaiah 55:2, God tells us to listen to Him and eat what is good.

Kingdom government was in the garden. It was God's idea to govern man and earth, and that mankind would be led by His Spirit. God wanted to be our King and King of the earth. He never intended that we be governed by any other form of government or by wicked people (Proverbs 29:2). God wasn't happy when Israel asked for a king (1 Samuel 8:7). This action showed that the people had rejected Him.

Kingdom education was also active in the garden. God came down and met with Adam and Eve every day. Kingdom education is founded on answering the three age-old questions: Who am I? Where did I come from? Why am I here? It is based on identity, purpose, and your source, and then developing gifts and skills.

God was the Source of their knowledge and wisdom. They could have learned anything they wanted from Him. He is still the Source of all true knowledge and wisdom. All the treasures of wisdom and knowledge are hidden in Him (Colossians 2:3).

In this same way, we are supposed to learn from Jesus. He is our Shepherd, and we are supposed to hear His voice on a daily basis (John 10:3, 27). He told us to come and learn from Him (Matthew 11:29).

Kingdom family existed in the garden. The first family was established in the garden, as was living in the kingdom of God. When God made Eve, He did not speak to her. It was Adam's responsibility to impart to his wife what He heard from God. That was God's original design for family life.

The feminist movement and men acting like women comes from the devil. These things are happening because of the misunderstanding of the different roles and functions God gave to men and women. God did not create women to do everything men do, but to do things men cannot do.

The purpose of every person born after Adam was to see an aspect of the kingdom based on their calling and gifts, and then expand that particular area and further the rule and reign of God on earth.

Thus manifesting the kingdom of God. When the entire human race fulfilled their kingdom assignment, the entire planet would be filled with His kingdom and glory. That was the original plan.

A PROTOTYPE AND A BLUEPRINT

Through planting the garden, God was modelling a *prototype* of His kingdom and how it was supposed to function. He was showing us how the kingdom of God looked in a practical way and in its physical state. That is why He came down and planted the garden. This garden was not just a place with flowers and plants. It was the blueprint of His kingdom. We need to look at it and duplicate it or expand it on the entire planet.

The word used for "planted" in Hebrew is *nata,* which means "to plant, fasten, or establish."[5] In a literal sense, it means God came down and *established* His kingdom on earth and put the man He created into it. This is why He had to come to establish and plant it and He did not send any angels to do it. He wanted to make sure it was done exactly as He desired. It was His kingdom.

When it comes to kingdom business, God gets personally involved. When you are interested in learning about and expanding His kingdom, God will take a strong personal interest in your life. We were supposed to expand and grow His kingdom on the earth. That is why He said if we sought His kingdom first, He would provide everything we needed. He is very serious and cares about His kingdom. However, if you only sing to Him on a Sunday morning, you might go hungry or have to work on your own to feed yourself. We need to return to our original place of work.

---

[5] James Strong, "5193. Nata," Strong's Hebrew: 5193. נָטַע (nata) — to plant (Biblehub), accessed April 17, 2020, https://biblehub.com/hebrew/5193.htm)

God will show us everything He wants us to do. First, He will show us His blueprint for our mission in life, just like He showed Adam the blueprint of His kingdom in the garden, and how Moses received the blueprint of the tabernacle that God wanted him to build. God had to take Moses up to the mountaintop and show him the plan for it (Exodus 25:40). The Bible says that there are *scrolls* in heaven about everything that pertains to life. There is a place in heaven where all these scrolls are stored. This is mentioned in the Psalms.

> Your eyes saw my substance, being yet unformed. And in Your book they all were written, the days fashioned for me, when as yet there were none of them. *(Psalm 139:16)*

> You number my wanderings; put my tears into Your bottle; are they not in Your book? *(Psalm 56:8)*

There is a book (or blueprint) in heaven for my life and yours. Every day of our lives is recorded there. We should be praying that what is written on each page would be made manifest in our lives each day. We are not supposed to be living randomly, but purposefully and intentionally.

The responsibility of each human being born after Adam was to look at the garden and expand each aspect of the kingdom based on each one's calling and gifts, until the entire earth became part of God's dominion. That is why God says the entire earth will be filled His glory.

THE KINGDOM WITHIN

Unfortunately, Adam fell, and lost the garden. He lost the kingdom of God. We lost the blueprint for life on earth. God put guardian angels at the entrance of the garden, so mankind could not go back and try to enter again, and eat from the Tree of Life and remain in their fallen state forever.

Through Jesus Christ, the door to the garden (or the kingdom) of God was reopened. He is the door. As we learned from the other books in the *Discipling Nations* series, the kingdom has been restored to us. When we are born again, God restores our ability to see His kingdom, so we can manifest His purposes again.

That is why Jesus said the kingdom of God is within you (Luke 17:21). We see His kingdom in our spirit man that is inside us. He put the kingdom inside each believer, not so we could sing about it, but so we can manifest it to the world through the works we do based on our calling.

The kingdom we see will differ from person-to-person. What I see in the kingdom will be different than what someone else sees. Why? Because each one of us was created with a unique calling and for a specific assignment. Each one of us is called to do something different.

Adam had two roles to play in this. One was to duplicate the garden and expand the original blueprint of everything as it is in heaven. The materials to accomplish this were on the earth. The second role he had was to see what God was doing in heaven and manifest that on earth. In other words, Adam was to receive a glimpse of heaven and manifest it here regularly. God's work is progressive, and the Lord is always doing something new.

That is why Jesus said the following:

> I speak what I have seen with My Father. *(John 8:38)*

> Then Jesus answered and said to them, "Most assuredly, I say to you, the Son can do nothing of Himself, but what He sees the Father do; for whatever He

does, the Son also does in like manner. For the Father loves the Son, and shows Him all things that He Himself does; and He will show Him greater works than these, that you may marvel." *(John 5:19)*

I can of Myself do nothing. As I hear, I judge; and My judgment is righteous, because I do not seek My own will but the will of the Father who sent Me. *(John 5:30)*

If Jesus could not see what His Father was doing, He could do nothing. Jesus depended on His Father. That was also the way it was for Adam, and like them, it should be this way for each one of us. That is why we need to see the kingdom and be born again, and not just believe in Jesus and be saved.

WHAT IS YOUR GLIMPSE OF THE KINGDOM?

As I mentioned earlier, seeing the kingdom is similar to seeing a country. Each one will see something different based on their specific calling and assignment from the King.

If you came to the United States for a business purpose, you will see places and buildings related to that business or any other assignment. If you came there to sell art or study art, you will see museums and institutions related to art.

I have visited some places in the United States with my family and friends. You will get to visit other parts of the kingdom of God through the callings of others. When they come to minister and share the revelation God gave them, you will receive a glimpse of those kingdom areas that pertain to their calling. God will open portals in the Spirit that enable you to see. This is very deep, and I hope you understand what I'm saying.

Similarly, when you are born into the kingdom, you will not see the whole kingdom. The kingdom of God is a nation, a territory, ruled by God that is bigger than the entire universe. There is no way a person can see everything in God's kingdom. It will take eons to discover it all!

It makes sense, then, that you will only see the part that pertains to your calling. If you are called into business, you will see something related to kingdom business. If you are called into ministry, you will see something related to that. If you are called into government or politics, he will give you a vision for something related to that.

What Moses saw was different from what Joseph saw. Once you see the part of the kingdom that is connected to your life, you have to take hold of it and never let it go. Every decision you make after that should be supportive to the vision you saw. If not, you will get off track—even derailed—and may wreck your life.

What you see when you are born again is the aspect of the kingdom God wanted to manifest through you if Adam had not fallen. You will see the original plan God had for you. You will see with the eyes of your spirit what He planned for your life from the beginning, as though the fall of man had never taken place, or get a plan to restore something to its original state, usually an area that became broken as a result of the fall. That is the purpose of being born again.

EXAMPLES OF THOSE PEOPLE SEEING THE KINGDOM (CALLING) WHEN THE WORD CAME TO THEM

According to the Bible, we are born again by the Word of God. This refers to the time when the Word of the Lord comes to a person regarding their destiny, and they receive a picture of the future assignment God has for them. It is drawn in their hearts. We normally call that a vision, and the Bible calls it a calling.

When the Word of the Lord came to Abraham, Abraham *saw* a land and a nation. God promised him land as his possession and the possession of his descendants. It was kingdom territory and the building of a nation.

When the Word of the Lord came to Noah, he *saw* an ark that saved him, his family, and the entire human race. He did not see the garden like Adam because his assignment was different. The ark was a kingdom invention. Noah designed and built something that had never been made before. The ark was used to save and preserve the human race.

When the Word of the Lord came to Joseph in a dream, he *saw* himself gaining great authority, so much so that his whole family respected him. It was kingdom government. He became the prime minister of Egypt.

When the Word of the Lord came to Moses at the burning bush, he *saw* the deliverance of God's people from Egypt. It was kingdom deliverance, which included economy, army, and nation building. When they came out of Egypt, they plundered the Egyptians.

When the Word of the Lord came to the people of Israel in Egypt, they *saw* a land that flowed with milk and honey. It was kingdom territory and the building of a nation.

When the Word of the Lord came to David, he was anointed as a king of Israel. It was again kingdom government.

When the Word of the Lord came to the disciples, they saw themselves as fishers of men. It was kingdom *ekklesia*.

When the Word of the Lord came to Saul (who later became Paul), he saw himself witnessing to kings and people of influence. It was kingdom *ekklesia* and government.

Sarah and Elizabeth saw a son that would be born to them. That was kingdom family.

The list keeps going on of people and the aspect of the kingdom they saw with the eyes of their spirit based on what God promised them. That was their *born-again* experience; it was how they saw the kingdom of God. Later they manifest in the natural what they saw.

When you are born again, you should also see an aspect of the kingdom of God, which you were sent to manifest on the earth. One person might see an aspect of kingdom government, which means he or she is supposed to be involved in things related to government or politics on some level. Everyone cannot be a president or prime minister, but there are a plethora of jobs available in different sectors of government.

Another person may see something related to kingdom economy, ministry, education, business, or agriculture. Your calling could be bee conservation as part of the kingdom agriculture. It could be any one of a million things by which a kingdom functions. Whatever that person sees is based on the assignment God has in store for them. This is the work God has prepared for us to do before the foundation of the earth. God did not create any duplicates; each of us are originals. We cannot copy someone else's vision. If we do, we cancel out our calling in the kingdom.

YOUR CALLING WILL STAY WITH YOU

My question to you is this: What did you see when the Word of the Lord came to you when you were born again? Write that down in very clear and plain language. That is your destiny, your spiritual DNA—the blueprint for your life. Everything else will unfold from then on to enable you to fulfill that blueprint.

Everything God does in your life from then on will be to help you to fulfill that vision. Each and every thing that occurs next will be

God unfolding His plan to help you fulfill that assignment. If you do things contrary to what God showed you, life won't be easy. It will seem like you are fighting against God.

From that day onward, we should be following the blueprint we saw with the eyes of our spirit man. It is an inspired imagination that won't go away. It is like our shadow; it follows us closely wherever we go. We won't be able to get rid of it. Did you ever try to get rid of your shadow or run away from it? You can't.

In the same way, the vision you receive from God will remain with you until the day you die. You will grow in it, and as you do, more portals or rooms will be opened, but the foundation will remain the same.

It will expand and change with each season in your life. For example, David was a shepherd first, and then he became a musician, a warrior, a fugitive, and finally, a king. We also go through different seasons until we reach our final destiny or destination, which is our Promised Land.

Joseph did not reach the palace in one day or even one year. First, he was sold as a slave, and then he ended up in prison. From there, he was promoted to the palace. However, each season was important to fulfilling the Big Picture; each one played an important part.

As you begin to walk out the calling on your life, God will continue to add more promises to your life. It will be like adding more rooms (or an extension) to the original blueprint. It will never end, but will continue until the last day of your life.

It is very important for us to listen to the Holy Spirit each and every step of the way. He has been sent to help us fulfill our assignment. His job is to see that His Word is fulfilled in our lives. That is His primary job. He is the only One who knows that blueprint from the very beginning to the end because He is the One who drew that out by Father's direction. He is the Designer of the Godhead.

Father God is the Originator or the Creator, and Holy Spirit is the Designer or the Life-giver. Jesus is the Word of God. He is the One who accomplishes it.

CARNAL CHRISTIANS LIVE BY FEELINGS

Most people live their Christian life based on their feelings. Their relationship with God depends on how they feel at any given moment. They come to church to feel something. If they do not feel anything, they think God is not there. We have been taught to sing in order to feel God. I was in that state for many years. If I didn't feel the presence of God, I thought God had left me or did not love me anymore. If I didn't feel His anointing when I preached, I thought it had not gone well. It was a miserable time in my life, and it lasted many years.

I was a *feeling Christian* for a very long time. The Bible calls such people carnal Christians. I did not know how to go from feeling to seeing. There are four levels of experiencing God. We begin with feeling, and then we go to knowing. The third step is to see, and the fourth is to manifest. Unfortunately, most people don't even graduate from the feeling level to the knowing stage.

Knowing comes from believing what God says in His Word or taking God at His Word. If He says He will never leave us nor forsake us, then we need to believe it and not wait for a feeling that corroborates that. Jesus said that where two or three were gathered in His name, He is present. We need to believe and learn to act up on that and receive Him when He comes.

The main reason Christians do not graduate from the feeling stage is because of their lack of understanding of who God is and what His purpose is. Add fear and insecurity about whether God loves us and whether or not we will lose our salvation when we do or say something wrong, and the majority will never graduate from that stage, either. They will live a secluded and unproductive life, trying to protect themselves from the world and protect the salvation they received.

God never asked anyone in the Bible how they felt about something or if they felt His presence. He did not ask Moses, "Do you feel like going down to Egypt to deliver My people?" He did not ask Jeremiah how he felt either. The same is true of every prophet. He did not ask them how they felt. He asked them what they *saw*!

Our responsibility is to follow what we saw when we were born again. Now that we have seen the kingdom of God and recognized what we are called to do, what are we supposed to do next?

CHAPTER 6

LET YOUR EYE BE SINGLE

> *The light of the body is the eye: if therefore thine eye be single, thy whole body shall be full of light. But if thine eye be evil, thy whole body shall be full of darkness. If therefore the light that is in thee be darkness, how great is that darkness! (Matthew 6:22–23 KJV)*

I did not understand the verse above for a long time. Before I received the revelation about seeing the kingdom, I thought we were supposed to pluck one of our eyes out when we became believers if one of our eyes caused us to stumble (Matthew 5:29).

Jesus was saying that when both our natural eyes and our spiritual eyes were in alignment and had become one, we would truly see. We would not be in darkness anymore. Too many people limit themselves to what they can see in the natural. They have no clue about the supernatural (or spiritual) sight. The Bible says that spiritual things are more real or permanent than natural ones (2 Corinthians 4:18).

God has given us natural eyes to lead our bodies in its path, but not to decide the destiny of our spirit. He has given us spiritual eyes to lead our spirit, and our bodies should be following our spirit. We are supposed to live by what we see with our spiritual eyes.

A SHIFT IN SIGHT

The devil's number one attack is against your vision. If he can distort your perception, he can get you to act in a manner which is contrary to God's Word. He doesn't want you to see what God wants you to see. *Both the devil and God are after your vision*: one wishes to distort and destroy it and the other One wants to restore it.

Every trouble began with someone seeing something and acting upon what that person saw. The first temptation was about sight. The enemy promised Eve that she would see something she never saw before. When the serpent came, he told Eve that if they ate from the Tree of the Knowledge of Good and Evil, they would not die, and that instead, their eyes would be opened and they would be like God, knowing good and evil.

> Then the serpent said to the woman, "You will not surely die. For God knows that in the day you eat of it your eyes will be opened, and you will be like God, knowing good and evil." *(Genesis 3:4–5)*

What did the serpent mean by "their eyes will be opened"? Adam and Eve were not blind. Their sight was spiritual; they were focused on what God was doing in heaven, so they could manifest it on the earth. They were not conscious of their nakedness or anything in the natural.

As a result of the enemy's words, Eve *saw* that the fruit of the tree, from which God said not to eat, was good for food. That is what happens when the devil influences our vision: What God says is deadly and forbidden suddenly looks good and attractive. That's what happens in our culture today. Our culture and its demonized people and media present evil as good for us. People taste it and are stuck with those consequences for the rest of their lives.

> So when the woman saw that the tree was good for food, that it was pleasant to the eyes, and a tree desirable to make one wise, she took of its fruit and ate. She also gave to her husband with her, and he ate. Then the eyes of both of them were opened, and they knew that they were naked; and they sewed fig leaves together and made themselves coverings. *(Genesis 3:6–7)*

Eve was deceived through her sight. The first reaction of disobeying God was seeing something they shouldn't see. That's how powerful our sight is. If you do not learn to see correctly, it will jeopardize your destiny.

The moment they ate the fruit which God told them not to eat, their eyes were opened. What does that mean? Had they been blind before? We know they could see before this. It means their fleshly eyes were opened. From then on, they were able to see only in the natural and the things of the flesh. That is why they immediately recognized that they were naked, and then they were afraid.

When Adam and Eve ate from the forbidden fruit, there was a shift in what they saw. They could not see with their spiritual eyes anymore. They became like mere earthly creatures that only saw and lived by what they saw with their two fleshly eyes.

There was no longer an alignment between their hearts, spirits, and minds. Now they saw their nakedness instead of seeing God and the kingdom. There is a big difference in seeing your nakedness instead of the kingdom!

Imagine that you are suddenly going blind. How would you feel? That is how Adam and Eve felt inside them, after they ate the forbidden fruit. Before that, they could see into the spirit realm and they were one with the spiritual and the natural realm. There was no separation between the two for Adam and Eve. Once they ate the fruit, everything went suddenly dark inside them and they felt separated from God's realm for the first time. They felt ashamed and terrified.

To be naked has multiple meanings. From that time forward, Adam and Eve only saw what was wrong with them, what was missing in them—their weaknesses, defects, what was lacking, and what was temporary. They could only see into the natural realm and only what their fleshly eyes could see.

Man was not missing anything in the garden. They had everything they needed. When they lost their clothing—which was the glory of God—they sewed fig leaves and made aprons to cover themselves.

God originally created mankind with the ability to see into the spirit world. They could see into the heavens before the fall. They could see angels and God and His kingdom. After the fall, they lost that ability and the eyes of their spirits were closed.

After the fall, when God came down into the garden, they only heard the "sound" of Him walking in the garden, and they could no longer see Him (Genesis 3:8). Before that, they could see Him and communicate and fellowship with Him in person.

The devil wanted to blind Adam and Eve from seeing the spirit world, heaven, and God's kingdom. He did not want them to manifest that kingdom on earth. He wanted them to become mere physical creatures operating out of their fleshly senses and living for the gratification of their flesh. If he can blind us, then he can steal from us easily. This was the result of his deception.

This is the reason the Bible says Jesus was anointed to recover sight for the blind (Luke 4:18). Note the word *recover*. That means that at one time they could see, but they had become blind. It is referring to the original blindness that came upon humanity with the fall of Adam. It is not talking about natural blindness. This means that *everyone is spiritually blind until they are born again. Everyone needs the recovery of their sight.*

One of the first things God does to a person when they are born again is correct (or restore) their vision. He restores the eyes of our spirits to see into the spirit realm as Adam could before the fall. A loss of vision was the first thing affected when mankind fell. God wants His children to see what He sees and does in His kingdom, so they can manifest that here and now. Restoration of vision is the first thing that happens when a person is born again.

That is why Jesus said He spoke about what He saw His Father doing. Jesus was on earth and His Father was in heaven, but He could see into the heavenly realm. In the same way, each born-again believer should be doing the same thing during their lifetimes on earth. This is part of the birthright of each child of God.

An encounter with God or the devil affects our vision first. One will affect us for the better and the other for the worse; both are after our vision. Adam and Eve had an encounter with the devil, and their vision was forever skewed.

When Jesus was tempted by the devil, he tried to use the same old trick. The devil took Jesus to a very high mountain and showed Him all the kingdoms of the world and offered them to Jesus. Jesus could have taken them from him right then or followed the path (or vision) His Father had for Him instead (Luke 4:5–6).

The devil wanted Jesus to make a choice based on what He saw with His natural eyes. However, Jesus was led by His spiritual eyes and by the vision His Father gave Him for His future. It was not natural. Either we are led by our natural eyes, or we are led by our spiritual eyes. We were created to be led by our spiritual eyes, thereby walking in God's vision for us.

Throughout the Bible, we read of incidents in which people saw into the spirit world. Your journey in the kingdom begins with seeing something you never saw before: the kingdom of God. God opens your spiritual eyes to see into the spirit world. You are led by your "sight" until you discover your "vision" in the kingdom of God.

However, we have a problem: Our natural (fleshly) eyes are still, open and we see things as they are or used to be; we see our circumstances and limitations. We are as aware of all that as we are of our skin and teeth. We have been programmed to walk by what we see in the natural since our natural birth. The purpose of all the marketing, schooling, pictures, colors, movies, and flashing screens is to keep us distracted, limited, and tied to what we see with our natural eyes and think with our natural mind. Even supposedly "higher" education has been designed to veer us away from anything spiritual.

The culture we live in bombards us with images constantly every few seconds either on your phone or TV or the computer screen. They keep changing screens and sceneries before our eyes, so that we live our lives in a mesmerized state.

Our brains are programmed and addicted to the glitter—and most of us don't even think beyond it all. This is a great danger to this generation. They are constantly focused on their own entertainment and need something colorful flashing in front of their eyes. Otherwise they are programmed to think life is boring.

They can't see what God has in store for them. Their natural sight overpowers the spiritual and nullifies their God-given vision. They live only as physical creatures, constantly looking for something to gratify the lusts of their flesh.

Once we are born again, we start to be trained to walk by what we see in the spirit, and not by what we see in the natural. This is called "walking by faith and not by sight." It won't happen automatically. An *unlearning* process is required. We will learn more about that later in this book.

God started training Abraham by *showing* Him a land that he had never seen with his natural eyes. Abraham often became discouraged about his circumstances and limitations (what he saw with his natural eyes) and complained to God about it, as we all do (Genesis 15:2).

Abraham was well aware of his age and the condition of his and Sarah's bodies. All the land Abraham could see was already occupied by other kings and kingdoms at that time. He couldn't see any land that would be his, so he moved from one place to the next, looking for this piece of land that God had promised him. In the end, all the land that he walked upon by faith would one day belong to him and his descendants.

When Abraham complained or became discouraged, God would take him outside and give him a lesson about vision again. He would tell him to look at the stars in the sky and number them, or He would take him to the seashore and ask him to count the grains of sand. Abraham would gaze at the vastness of the sky and the innumerable stars and the countless grains of sand and listen as God told him that his children would be as numerable as the stars and sand (Genesis 15:5, 22:17).

God also told Abraham to lift up his eyes and look to the north, south, east, and west. He told him that all the land he could see was promised to him (Genesis 13:14-15).

By seeing what God wanted him to see and hearing the promises of God, Abraham's faith in God was refreshed. Abraham continued this process until what he saw in the natural did not affect what he saw in the spirit. He became convinced that what he perceived in the spirit was greater than the situation or circumstance he was experiencing in the natural. In other words, his eyes became single. In time, his sight (both natural and spiritual) were united in one with the spiritual presiding over the natural.

When God called Jeremiah to his prophetic ministry, the first thing He taught him was to see into the spirit. God asked Jeremiah what He saw. He said He saw a branch of an almond tree. Jeremiah was seeing into the spirit; he wasn't viewing a physical tree next to where he was (Jeremiah 1:11). God said Jeremiah saw it well, and that He was ready to perform His Word (Jeremiah 1:12). The moment we see in the spirit what God wants us to see, He begins the process of accomplishing His work in and through us.

The sooner we learn to see into the spirit and then live by what we see there, the faster it qualifies us to live in the kingdom of God and manifest it on the earth.

God will continue to train us until what we see with our spirit and our natural eyes become one (or single) with our spiritual eyes. This means there won't be any conflict between what you see in the spirit and in the natural. We need to reach a place in the spirit in which our natural circumstances do not affect how we think and live, where what we see with our natural eyes loses its influence over what God shows us in our spirit.

We need to become aligned with the vision of God with our whole being. When we are, everything else will become dim and unimportant, no matter what happens in the natural. That is why the psalmist says this:

> Therefore we will not fear, even though the earth be removed, and though the mountains be carried into the midst of the sea. *(Psalm 46:2)*

The psalmist had reached a place in his spirit in which whatever happened in the natural no longer affected how he lived. That is the only way he could have written this. Many people are stuck with what they see in the natural; all they talk about is what is limiting them. They ignore what God has shown them because that vision seems too far out or impossible or even scary to them.

Whenever God shows you something, it will seem impossible in the natural. God's plans are big; His vision is enormous. You will not have the ability or resources to complete His assignment. You will need to continually trust in Him and His provision to complete the task. And that is fine because *God's resources are limitless.*

Jesus said, "If therefore thine eye be single, thy whole body shall be full of light" (Matthew 6:22, KJV). As already mentioned, when our eyes are single, it means that what we see with the eyes of our spirits and our natural sight become one or single. We will have *univision,* not double vision.

The people of Israel couldn't enter the Promised Land because of their double vision. What they saw in their spirit and what they saw in their immediate circumstances was not united as one. Their natural fears and inclinations overpowered their spiritual vision and cancelled it out. They could not make progress. They kept going around the same mountain for forty years.

Have you asked someone how they were doing, and they replied that they were going through the "same old thing"? They mean that they have not made any progress in the last several years. They are still circling the same old mountain.

The Israelites saw a land that flowed with milk and honey, but every time they encountered a circumstance that was contrary to that vision, they could not control their emotions and their bodies and bring them into submission to the vision God had showed them.

Instead, they complained and murmured and became angry at God and Moses. God gave them many chances to bring their natural sight and emotions into alignment with their spiritual sight, but they failed each time. As a result, they perished in the wilderness without inheriting the promises of God.

This could happen to us today, too. If we do not train our sight and submit to the vision of the kingdom we were given when we were born again, we will miss what God has for us. That is why the Bible says we do not walk by sight, but by faith. Christians should not walk by what they see in the natural, but by what they see with the eyes of their spirit (2 Corinthians 5:7).

To be honest, when God calls a person and puts His vision in him or her, their immediate circumstances will be in total contradiction to what God has showed them. This will happen to everyone, so you are not alone. Every single person God has ever used had to go through this training.

In the garden of Eden, Adam and Eve saw into the spirit. They could see what was happening in heaven so they could manifest that on earth. That was God's original plan and something Jesus repeated in the Lord's Prayer: *As it is in heaven, so be on earth*. God wanted things on earth to be exactly as it is in heaven. He has never changed His mind concerning this, and He never will.

Our responsibility is to follow the vision God gave us with our whole being, without doubting and questioning. We will all have doubts and questions now and then, but God will keep sending people and incidents to encourage us to keep going. That's why you are reading this book. God wants to encourage you and tell you that what you saw is real and that it is possible and accessible.

There are different individuals we read about in the Bible who saw into the spirit world. Elisha saw the army of God surrounding the mountain where he was staying. His servant could not see them, so he prayed to God to open the eyes of his servant so he could see them (2 Kings 6:14–17).

That needs to happen to each one of us. That is what should happen when a person is born again. Jesus told Nathaniel that he would see the heavens opened and the angels of God ascending and descending upon the Son of Man (John 1:51).

Stephen saw into the heavens before he was stoned to death. He saw Jesus standing at the right hand of God (Acts 7:56). May the Lord open our eyes to see what He wants us to see! May we not walk and live by what we see with our natural eyes, but by what we see in the spirit instead.

Everything and everyone around you may endeavor to steal what you see in the spirit. The enemy comes to steal, kill, and destroy, so he will try to steal the vision God showed you first thing. That is what he stole from Adam and Eve first. The devil wants people to live as a mere human being like an animal that lives only by what it feels and sees.

Once the enemy steals our vision, we are dead spiritually, and once we are spiritually dead, we are the same level as an animal. God and His kingdom will not receive any benefit from our existence—we are just taking up space and using God's resources in vain.

Paul was so stuck in what he saw and who he was in the natural (his education, his race, and his prominence in Jewish society) that Jesus had to blind him for three days to correct his vision. His pride and ego was that lofty!

Jesus had to strike him down to the ground (Acts 9:3–4).

While he was blind for that time period, something powerful happened inside of him. God was painting His vision into Paul's spirit and heart. He sent a man named Ananias to lay hands on him to impart the Holy Spirit into him, and with the Holy Spirit came the blueprint for his destiny.

When his natural eyes were opened three days later, what he saw in the spirit was more real than what he used to see in the natural, and Paul immediately began to preach about Christ (Acts 9:20).

When a person has an encounter with Jesus, which is what needs to happen when a person is saved and born again, it is impossible for that person to remain the same and return to an ordinary life like everybody else or what they used to do. If they do, then I question the legitimacy of their born-again experience.

When you are born again, God removes the veil from your heart and the eyes of your spirit and allows you to see into His kingdom. You will see a glimpse of what He originally planned for your life. This is the reason He created you and your mission in life.

From that moment on, you are supposed to follow what you saw, ignoring every limitation and distraction and overcoming every challenge you may experience in your immediate circumstances.

God has given us natural eyes to see our surroundings, and vision (which I call the eyes of the spirit) to see into the invisible. In the beginning, what you see with your natural eyes and your spiritual vision will be two different things. They will be in contradiction to one another. When God gives you a vision, your immediate surroundings will look like the exact opposite of what He has promised you.

We need to train our hearts and minds to not depend on our natural sight for guidance, encouragement, and hope. If we depend on the natural, we will be disappointed and left without any hope. We need to train ourselves to rejoice in the hope of our vision in the spirit. Until our natural sight and spiritual vision become aligned and one, we will remain ineffective for the kingdom of God.

The best way to explain this is to think about how a guide dog leads a blind man. The man sees the place he wants to go in his imagination and tells the dog to lead him there. The dog has the natural eyes and leads the man where he wants to go. The dog doesn't decide where the man should go. The man does that, even though he doesn't have natural eyes. That dog plays the role of our physical eyes. In the same way, our natural eyes should be guided by the inner sight of our spirit. Too many are led by their natural eyes and end up in the wrong places in life.

Once you are trained by God, you will reach a place in your life in which your immediate circumstances have no effect on how you live. You will be guided by what you see in the spirit, and in time, your circumstances will begin to line up with the vision you saw.

That is what happened to Abraham and Sarah. When God gave them the promise, their bodies were old and they didn't have the capacity to bear a child. Over time, their faith became stronger than their circumstances and their bodies began to align with that they saw in the spirit. The Bible says their bodies received strength (Romans 4:19–20). From where did that strength come? From the faith they put in the promise of God.

Their faith in the promise of God became stronger than their situation in the natural, and things in the natural began to change and take shape according to their faith. That is what needs to happen to each one of us with what God has shown us concerning our lives.

We need to get to a state of faith in which there is no longer any conflict between the heart and head, between the spirit and mind, and between natural sight and the vision God gave us. When that occurs, our whole being will be in alignment with the vision God has given you. Your body will be full of light.

You will be reconciled with things in heaven and things on earth. There won't be any more conflict in you about what God has called you to do. Your outside circumstances will have no more negative influence over where you are going in the spirit. That's how you overcome this world and its influence.

This is what Jesus meant when He said our eye would be "single" and our whole body "full of light." If it is not single, we will be like everyone else who is walking in darkness. May the Lord give us the grace to go through the process of aligning our vision with His.

PART II: ENTERING THE KINGDOM

CHAPTER 7

SEEK GOD'S RIGHTEOUSNESS

And he believed in the Lord, and He accounted it to him for righteousness. (Genesis 15:6)

The second part of seeking the kingdom of God is seeking His righteousness. Seeking God's righteousness is as important as seeking His kingdom. One will not work without the other. Even if you seek the kingdom and see it, you cannot enter it without discovering and receiving the righteousness of God. Most people do not benefit from the kingdom because they walk in self-righteousness instead of the righteousness of God. Most do not realize they do this. I didn't for a long time.

SELF-RIGHTEOUSNESS: THE OTHER RIGHTEOUSNESS

If God tells us to seek His righteousness, it tells us that there is another kind of righteousness out there that is not His. Self-righteousness is the result of depending on our own religious works, abilities, and qualities. It is difficult for most humans to admit total helplessness; we all try to find some "goodness" or "merit" in ourselves and try to defend our behavior.

Many believers are wounded, fearful, sick, anxious, and depressed—sometimes more so than people in the world. They're not sure if God loves or even likes them. They're not sure if God accepts them. They're not sure if they're saved or if God has forgiven their sins, so they "get saved" again and again. They repeat a prayer after the preacher Sunday after Sunday. Neither the preacher nor the people are sure if they are saved yet or not. They have a religious appearance, but point their finger at each other. They have a form of godliness, but no power.

Some Christians say that Jesus is their Lord, but they haven't given Him ownership of anything in their life. When He requires something from them, they throw a temper tantrum or hesitate in yielding. They think they have surrendered to Jesus because they sang "I Surrender All" the other week, but they try to control everything around them, including their life and those they know. Sometimes they even try to control God. Insecurity, self-pity, guilt, regret, and condemnation are eating them alive, so they are not confident in God.

Most live in fear of losing their salvation. The only reason they do not sin is their fear of going to hell. Fear of losing salvation should not be the reason we choose to lead a righteous life. You live right because you have been made righteous in Christ, have peace with God, and are dead to sin; it has no more dominion over you.

I'm not trying to point my finger at anyone; this was my story, too. I was the most religious and self-righteous person on the planet. I was as blind as a bat. I was a tongue-talking Christian, yet I judged and criticized everyone. In the flesh, I considered myself the most righteous person on earth, but in the spirit, I was as weak as a dry leaf.

I judged and criticized others because I was living under the law and I didn't like myself. I always fell short of my own expectations—and God's, too. I had this internal struggle with rejection. Insecure people feel better when they criticize or talk about someone else's weakness or failure. We do this because it deflects our attention off our own weaknesses and makes us feel better about ourselves.

When I received the revelation of the grace of God, I knew I had no right to judge anyone else. I knew that, in the sight of God, I was equal to everyone else. In Christ, you and I have the same *amount of righteousness* imputed to us. The religious spirit has done much damage by stealing every good thing God has given us to enjoy and making our lives miserable. Everyone needs the law *until* they receive the revelation of the love, righteousness, and the grace of God; otherwise, this world would become rotten with sin.

> But by the grace of God I am what I am, and His grace toward me was not in vain; but I labored more abundantly than they all, yet not I, but the grace of God which was with me. *(1 Corinthians 15:10)*

GETTING SAVED AGAIN AND AGAIN (AND AGAIN)

Many believers act like God's love for them depends on what they *do* and how *spiritual* they are. They act as though they have earned their salvation by confessing *all* their sins, even the minutest, and feel that one mistake has the power to ruin the whole thing and force them to start all over again from square one.

They live in a cycle of being righteous every morning and a sinner by sundown. They feel holy on Sunday morning and live like sinners the rest of the week. They have no confidence in their faith or in their relationship with God. They have a love-hate relationship with Him instead. Many never grow beyond this. As a result, they will not fulfill their purpose, only showing their pretty faces in church on Sunday morning and giving a *tip* to God once in a while.

We blame non-believers for the way they live and what they do because we are not happy with ourselves and don't like ourselves. We think that if the people in the world would just get their act together and come to church, then all our problems would be over. Well, we were those people in the world once, doing the same things they do, and we came to church. Did everything change overnight for us?

The religious spirit always causes people to blame someone else for their problems. They will not admit they are wrong; it is always the other person's fault: "If they would just act right and get their life in order, then I would be fine," or "I am not happy because so-and-so is making my life miserable. They are not holy enough or living right." Let me tell you, that is a religious and controlling spirit.

The Pharisees were the best example of this. They could not see their own wrong. They always pointed their finger at the sinners and at Jesus, while the plank was in their own eyes. One of the most important lessons I learned as a Christian, which also happens to be one of the most difficult to practice, is emotional responsibility: taking responsibility for what I feel and how I act.

SELF-RIGHTEOUSNESS AND THE LAW

Self-righteous people end up being extremely religious and conservative, but they never become holy. They are always searching for what they should add to their religious-duty list so they can earn another trophy. They will do prayer walks, hospital visitations, prison ministry, caring for the elderly, and anything else that will make them feel better about themselves. Meanwhile, their hearts are miserable or they are irritated with themselves and others because no matter how much they do, it is never good enough. They always feel like they have to do more to make their God happy.

Self-righteous people believe their righteousness is attained through, and dependent on, the works they perform. In truth, they are still under the law. They will not admit it because one part of their head believes they are saved by grace, but they never understood what that means. With the other part, they are still trying to obey the law. Still others are saved by grace, but they believe they can only remain saved by keeping the rules of the Old Testament.

They go back to the law. Let me tell you, if you go back to the law, the curse of the law, which is poverty and sickness, will begin to manifest in your life.

If any of these are operating in your life, it means you are not living in the grace of God, but in self-righteousness that comes by keeping rules and regulations.

Self-righteous people can be very disciplined and perfectionistic. If there is a prayer meeting at the church at four in the morning, they are the first ones there. Then they will tell ten other people about it that day, so they can feel superior and more spiritual than others. The people who listen to them will feel bad because they are not as spiritual. This heightens their sense of guilt and loss because they did not pray at four in the morning.

Self-righteous people have a set of rules and disciplines they observe about everything, and they do anything they can to keep those rules. They believe God's love for them and the blessings they have are founded on keeping those rules. They will try to impose those rules on others. They believe that if everybody just did what they do (and did everything *the way* they do), then this world would be a perfect place. But if anyone breaks one of those rules, they will be out of their favor that week (or maybe even forever).

They live like this because that's how their relationship with God works. They are walking on a tightrope with Him. If they fall even once, they have to repent and confess all their sins one more time. So they take their "list of sins" or their "special prayer pill" (some call it confession) that hits the "right spot" in God, and go through it all over again.

A SPIRITUAL PHARISEE

I used to be a spiritual Pharisee. I was extremely religious, unusually insecure, with zero confidence in my faith in God or in His love for me. Outwardly, I appeared spiritual, but inwardly, I did not believe I was even saved. Why? The salvation I had received was based on my good works, not on what Jesus had done on the cross. I believed that if I bent over the wrong way, my salvation would fall out of my pocket. Then I would be lost again, and have to wait until the next Sunday to get saved again and start all over again. If the rapture came before that, I was out of luck!

I could lose my salvation every few minutes on any given day and kept getting saved over and over again. I stayed in that religious rut for almost twenty years. I didn't know salvation was a gift I received by faith. I thought I had to earn my salvation through my good behavior, and keep it safe by being perfect.

I was living on the basis of righteousness by works and not by faith. Sometimes I hid or would not go to preach when people invited me because I didn't feel spiritual enough. I'm sharing this with you so if you are stuck in that religious rut, you can be set free. There is nothing more miserable than getting stuck between the law and the grace of God: between self-righteousness and the righteousness of God. If you are, you will be in a state of constant spiritual constipation.

God tried to reach out to me many times, but I could not accept His offer because it didn't look religious enough for me. Similarly, Jesus tried to reach out to the Pharisees, but they refused His offer because they would not accept His lifestyle. To them, Jesus was not spiritual enough and not holy enough. They thought this way—even though they were actually dead in their sins!

I knew there was something wrong in my life, but I wasn't quite sure what it was. I began searching to pinpoint the problem and find the solution. I read books about spiritual warfare, deliverance, and generational curses. I attended seminars and conferences by so-called "specialists," but found no answers. Instead, I grew increasingly more frustrated and discouraged.

I thought that if I could meet the most anointed person in the world, it would help me. If they would lay hands on me, I would be delivered and anointed, and then my ministry would explode. I fasted and prayed for God to connect me with the right person—some famous preacher—so I could launch "my ministry" under their umbrella and influence.

Well, God did not send the most anointed person. In fact, He had *already* sent the most anointed person into my life, and His name is Jesus. I will get to that in a minute. Many people laid hands on me, but there was no change. I spent almost five years in counseling rooms, but still there was no peace in my heart. Nothing was good enough for me.

When I heard the personal stories of these so-called "specialists," I found that their problems were the same as, or worse than, mine. I attended a special meeting with one of them and I wanted to sit as close as I could to the front, just in case the anointing jumped off him and might fall on me.

However, I found that these people had others with them (people with money and pastors of large churches) who followed them or were their wealthy partners; only this group got to sit in those front rows. I didn't have that kind of money, and I wasn't a pastor of a large church. My place was all the way up in the balcony, where I had to use binoculars to even see the person on the stage.

GETTING SICK AT A HEALING MEETING

In one instance, I had to speak in "Christianese" to get through the security lines and find a seat in the third row. I told them I was a minister from India. I said to myself, *This is the day. He's going to snap his finger and call me up to the platform to lay hands on me and prophesy over me. I'm going to fall on the floor under the power of God; and when I get up, I will be free and anointed. Everyone will see what happened to me on television and my worldwide ministry will begin tomorrow!*

I sat there looking pious and holy, and never took my eyes off the "specialist" on the stage. If he snapped his finger at me, I didn't want to miss it; I thought this was the chance of a lifetime. All of a sudden, I began to feel uneasy inside. I began to feel pain in my body like never before. I became so sick that I didn't hear a thing the preacher said.

It felt like thousands of needles were piercing through my skin from my head to my toes; the pain all over my body was excruciating. I had never been sick like that before or since. I thought I was going to die. I couldn't wait for the meeting to be over—and since I had "worked" my way so close to the front, I didn't feel comfortable getting up and walking out.

I was so happy when the meeting was over. I ran to my hotel room, confused and disappointed, and confessed all my sins *once again,* crying out to the Lord for His mercy.

I believe I got sick because my focus was on a man instead of Jesus. The specialist is not the Author and Finisher of my faith, Jesus is. Later, I learned that all I needed to do was to look to Jesus and the Word to know what He had done for me. When I repented, I was healed immediately. I was probably the only one who ever got sick in a healing meeting! From that point on, I stopped looking to the specialists. I knew that all I needed had to come from Jesus alone.

YOU HAVE THE ANOINTING!

All this time, I had been running around trying to receive from people what I already possessed: the anointing.

> Now He who establishes us with you in Christ and has *anointed us is God*, who also has sealed us and given us the Spirit in our hearts as a guarantee. *(2 Corinthians 1:21–22)*

> But the *anointing which you have received from Him abides in you*, and you do not need that anyone teach you; but as the same anointing teaches you concerning all things, and is true, and is not a lie, and just as it has taught you, you will abide in Him. *(1 John 2:27)*

According to the New Testament, every New Covenant believer is equally anointed! That might surprise you, but it is the truth. I didn't receive a small portion of the Holy Spirit and someone else received a bigger portion. These verses do not say, "Well, I am Paul, so the anointing on my life is greater or more special than what you have."

John didn't say, "You know we are original apostles, so you need to receive your anointing and blessings from us. When we come, we will do an anointing service and lay hands on each of you so be ready with a thousand-dollar special offering." Have you heard this kind of thing in your life anywhere before?

Instead, the apostles and Paul both said this: "*God anointed you. The anointing you have received from Him abides in you…the same anointing teaches you concerning all things.*" It's time for the body of Christ to believe God and His Word. We all are equally anointed, but we are not all called to do the same thing.

In the early church, they had a clear understanding of what each one was called to do. In Acts 6, we see the apostles appointing believers who were full of the Holy Spirit (anointed) and wisdom to serve at the table. They did not receive this anointing from the apostles; the apostles merely acknowledged the anointing that Jesus had given these men, and delegated them to their area of function.

The reason we are running after someone to anoint us is because we don't understand that we are already anointed, and we have not grasped what we are supposed to do with our lives. Therefore, we think that if we can get his or her anointing, we can do what he or she is doing. Before we can discover our *destiny*, we need to first discover our *identity*. We are different members of the same body *with different functions*.

We all received the same Holy Spirit and are all equally anointed. The same blood and life that runs through my head also runs through my feet; the blood and life I have in my head isn't more valuable or different than that in my feet. We all have the same life and the same blood, but different body parts with different functions.

That's the way it works in the body of Christ, so stop looking at someone else as super-anointed or more special than you. Find your place (calling) in the body and let the anointing that is in you flow to other members. Then you will realize that you are special, too.

Since the anointing and the life you have comes from the Head (Jesus), that means the same anointing you see working in the person you admire is also in you. Stop thinking that another person is more anointed than you are; they are simply anointed to do a different task than you—that's all. They may have begun functioning (by exercising faith) in that anointing earlier than you because they understood that possibility sooner. Now it's time for you to start!

FINDING PEACE WITH OUR ANOINTING

Another misconception that renders the body of Christ ineffective is this: Many believe that if someone is really anointed, they should be able to perform miracles and signs and wonders. To try to do this, some tap into spiritual power that is not of God, and we have many false apostles who do signs and wonders by demonic powers.

Everyone is not anointed to do the same thing. Joseph was anointed to be a prime minister, but he did not perform any miracles. Abraham, the father of our faith, was anointed, but he did not cast out any demons. Isaac and Jacob were anointed, but they did not heal the sick. I don't think they ever preached a message or wrote any books, either.

Bezalel was anointed by God with the spirit of wisdom, knowledge, and understanding to imagine and create things (Exodus 31:3). Esther was anointed to influence the king of Persia. Moses laid hands on seventy elders, and the anointing came upon them. Unlike Moses, they did not do any miracles, but they were anointed to govern and solve problems.

Daniel was anointed to be a statesman. Not everyone worked miracles in the New Testament, either. John the Baptist came with the spirit of Elijah, but he didn't do any miracles (John 10:41). In the early church, anointed people served food for widows. Joseph of Arimathea was a rich man and a disciple of Jesus. He did not perform any signs, but he was anointed to make money and influence governments. He was a prominent council member.

You need to find what God anointed you to do and find peace in that—instead of comparing yourself with what someone else is doing and yearning to have what they have. Imagine what would happen to our feet if they compared their function with our hands and tried to do what our hands do instead. The Bible says that God anointed us with the Holy Spirit. He *abides* in us. He did not come to visit; He came to stay.

Can you imagine how many people run around trying to receive a word or some kind of anointing from other people? These people often use the example of Elijah and Elisha, but they are not interpreting that correctly. Could Elijah have laid his hands on anyone he wanted (maybe after a special miracle service)? No! God specifically told Elijah to meet Elisha and anoint him. Neither Elijah nor Elisha initiated this process (1 Kings 19:16–19).

If God tells someone to anoint you, they will come to you. God knows your address. You don't need to run after anyone. It is not God who drives you to do that; it is your ignorance and insecurity. Through my works, I was trying my best not to lose my salvation, which I had not earned in the first place. I was trying to receive an anointing that I already had. The devil kept me in ignorance and strung me along for a long time, until the Holy Spirit began to open my eyes to what the Bible really says. My problem was that I didn't know where I fit in the body of Christ.

People who are saved but still living under the law of the Old Testament have difficulty understanding the grace or the love of God. To them, grace means loose living, sin, and being out of control. They don't like the message of grace because they fear sin and losing their salvation through a misstep. But to those who understand grace, sin is not a problem because they are already free from the bondage of sin and are dead to it. Sin has no more power or dominion over them.

If someone is *living* in sin and says they are under grace, they are deceived and they may not be saved yet. They are still in the kingdom of darkness. They might say they are saved, but once you are saved, you are free from the dominion of sin. As long as you are living in grace, you will not choose to sin. We sin when we slip away from grace and move under the law. As the Bible says, those who are born of God do not sin.

> Little children, let no one deceive you. He who practices righteousness is righteous, just as He is righteous. He who sins is of the devil, for the devil has sinned from the beginning. For this purpose the Son of God was manifested, that He might destroy the works of the devil. Whoever has been born of God does not sin, for His seed remains in him; and he cannot sin, because he has been born of God.
> *(1 John 3:7–9)*

According to the New Testament, no one becomes righteous by good works. We do not earn righteousness. We receive it as a free gift. The reason is this: We did not become a sinner by committing sin; we were born sinners. We inherited sin from Adam by birth, and that is why we sin. In our salvation, we inherit righteousness from Jesus Christ, the last Adam (Romans 5:12–18).

That is why the Bible does not call the believer a sinner. It is against the birthright in Christ of a kingdom citizen to call themselves sinners. Once we receive the free gift of righteousness (through new birth), we do good works because we are born righteous, not the other way around. When we receive the righteousness of God, we are no longer poor sinners saved by grace. Instead, our confession should be, "I am a child of God and the righteousness of God in Christ Jesus by faith." Jesus did not become sin for us so we could continue to live in sin. He became sin for us to set us free from sin, so that we could be the righteousness of God (2 Corinthians 5:21).

A LESSON ON GRACE

"So," you may ask, "What is the solution?" I want to share with you a little bit about how God saved us through Christ and what He did for us. It has nothing to do with what we did or what we do; it is all based on what Christ did on the cross. For religious people, it is difficult to comprehend.

Though we think we understand this, many do not. It's a process. The good news is that you are not alone in this. The majority of believers are in the same boat. They are under the influence of a religious spirit. That is why the world is in the shape it is, so do not feel bad about it or think you are the only one who has to go through this. You are not alone.

It is unfortunate that today we look at people who are operating in the gifts of the Spirit and think they are superheroes who have attained a spiritual height that we could not. In the Bible, this was the *first* practical lesson the disciples had (when they were still carnal) in their Discipleship 101 class. Using their gifts came *first*, not after graduation.

Today, we have this lesson last and as the highest degree anyone could achieve, and that is why most people do not operate in their spiritual gifts. And so our Christianity remains only in word, but has no power to prove it.

The religious church has set the bar so high that no one is able to reach it. We have been praying (in fact, some people attend at least one prayer meeting a day), fasting, spitting, rolling, shaking, and speaking all kinds of gibberish—but are not able to *do* anything.

What is the solution? We need to be reeducated in the Holy Scriptures. We need to unlearn everything we learned about God and life and start fresh from Genesis. We need to understand the grace of God.

How are we saved?

> But God, who is rich in mercy, because of *His great love with which He loved us,* even when we were dead

in trespasses, made us alive together with Christ (by grace you have been saved), and raised us up together, and made us sit together in the heavenly places in Christ Jesus, that in the ages to come He might show the exceeding riches of His grace in His kindness toward us in Christ Jesus. For by grace you have been saved through faith, and that not of yourselves; it is the *gift of God*, not of works, lest anyone should boast. *(Ephesians 2:4–9)*

It is the way of all great kings to display their wealth, glory, and military power to other kings and kingdoms. They hold demonstrations and organize parades to show off their wealth and might. Even today, nations have military exercises to show off their weapons and firepower to other countries. This verse says that God, who is rich in mercy and grace, shows off the exceeding riches of grace in this: *in His kindness He saved us*. It has nothing to do with us. All we need to do is believe and receive it.

Do you know why God loves us with such a great love? There is only one reason; He *is* Love. Do you know how many believers are stuck in their life because they made some mistakes and do not feel worthy? Or feel like they lost their calling or their salvation? Too many!

Let me tell you, my friend, God didn't call you because you didn't make any mistakes.

God knew what He was getting into when He called you. God knew every mistake you would ever commit before you were born. This is not a surprise to Him; it's a surprise to us. When God bought us with such a high price, He knew the defects that came with the product He was getting! He was not cheated or misguided by the sales guy, as some seem to think.

Salvation and the forgiveness of sins are gifts of God to sinners, not rewards for good behavior to perfect or religious people. Now the question is: "How do I remain saved? Don't I have to do all the right things to keep my salvation?" No, not if it was a gift. The gift was not given based on how good you were. It was free. It's hard to believe, but it's the truth. The Bible says that once we are saved, we are kept by the power of God.

> Who are kept by the power of God through faith for salvation ready to be revealed in the last time. *(1 Peter 1:5)*

What keeps us from stumbling or falling?

> Now to *Him who is able to keep you from stumbling,* and to present you faultless before the presence of His glory with exceeding joy, *to God our Savior,* who alone is wise, be glory and majesty, dominion and power, both now and forever. Amen. *(Jude 24–25)*

RIGHTEOUSNESS IS A FREE GIFT

Again, you did not become a sinner by sinning. We all became sinners because of Adam's transgression. That means it is unfit for God's justice system to punish us. It is unreal for God to demand that we do everything right when He knows it is impossible for fallen humans to do this. So He decided to forgive our sins and make us righteous in spite of who we are and what we did.

> For if by the one man's offense death reigned through the one, much more those who receive abundance of grace and of the gift of righteousness will reign in life through the One, Jesus Christ. Therefore, as through one man's offense judgment came to all men, resulting in condemnation, even so through one Man's righteous act the free gift came to all men,

> resulting in justification of life. For as by one man's disobedience many were made sinners, so also by one Man's obedience *many will be made righteous.* (Romans 5:17–19)

You do not need to look or act pious in order to receive the free gift, because it does not depend on your behavior. It depends solely on what Jesus did on the cross.

SALVATION IS A GIFT

Just as righteousness is a free gift, salvation is a free gift. You do not need to crawl on the floor or climb any hill to be saved; just believe and receive.

> For by grace you have been saved through faith, and that not of yourselves; it is the gift of God, not of works, lest anyone should boast. *(Ephesians 2:8–9)*

We are not saved by prayer or baptism, but by simple faith in Christ Jesus and what He did for us. That's it!

EVERYTHING ELSE GOD GIVES US IS FREE

God gave everything to Adam for free, and He does the same for us.

> And the Lord God commanded the man, saying, "Of every tree of the garden you may *freely* eat." *(Genesis 2:16)*

> He who did not spare His own Son, but delivered Him up for us all, how shall He not with Him also *freely give us all things? (Romans 8:32)*

> Now we have received, not the spirit of the world, but the Spirit who is from God, that we might know

> the things that have been *freely given to us by God.*
> *(1 Corinthians 2:12)*

> As His divine power has given to us all things that pertain to life and godliness, through the knowledge of Him who called us by glory and virtue.
> *(2 Peter 1:3)*

There's nothing we can earn from God by our good works or through keeping any law. He has already blessed us with everything we need. It was given to us as a free gift. The only thing we can do is receive it with thanksgiving.

CHAPTER 8

ENTERING THE KINGDOM

> *He has delivered us from the power of darkness and conveyed us into the kingdom of the Son of His love. (Colossians 1:13)*

It is very important that we understand this verse. Our deliverance is already done and we are in God's kingdom right now. However, we may not yet experience this fully or feel it in the natural. There are two possible reasons for this. The first is the deception of the enemy, and the second is that we have not yet appropriated deliverance in every area of our lives.

Similarly, although God forgave the sin of the whole world in Christ, not everybody believes and enjoys the benefits of that action yet. This verse doesn't say God delivered us and brought us into a religion or a particular type of church. It says He brought us into His kingdom.

Once we arrive in God's kingdom, it is our responsibility to learn how it operates. In His kingdom, everything works opposite from the country of our birth. The culture, language, food, economy, and everything else is different than what we were taught growing up in our country.

Unfortunately, most believers don't learn how the kingdom of God operates. Instead, they continue to live their lives based on the culture, economy, and so on of the country of their natural birth. As a result, they miss everything God has for them. Instead, they go to church, sing about what they are going to have in heaven after they die, and listen to sermons every Sunday. They wait to experience in heaven what God intended for them to have on earth.

If a person needs to understand the kingdom of God, God has to reveal that to him or her. It is more *caught* than *taught*. I have spent months sharing about the kingdom of God with people, and at the end, they still have no clue what it is because it has been hidden from them. As long as the religious spirit is operating in a person, there's no chance of that person understanding the revelation of the kingdom of God.

ENTERING THE KINGDOM IS A PROCESS

How does a person enter into the kingdom of God? Is it by just saying a sinner's prayer?

The moment a person is born again and sees the kingdom, God immediately begins the process of equipping that person to enter His kingdom. That's why the excitement of being born again doesn't last too long.

To enter the kingdom, we must qualify to fulfill our kingdom assignment, which is to restore the marred image and likeness of God in us. When we complete that process, God will take us to the place where our destiny needs to be fulfilled. It could be a place on this earth or it could be a state in our soul. Many people have to move to a different location to fulfill their destiny. Entering the kingdom does not mean entering or going to heaven.

To the people of Israel, it was the Promised Land. Entering the Promised Land was entering the kingdom of God for them. Before they could enter, they had to complete the wilderness journey to qualify. What happened to them during the wilderness journey will happen to us as we go through the process of entering the kingdom. That process is completed by the work of the Word and the Spirit of God in us.

This does not mean the same exact incidents will happen to each of us. I'm talking about the spiritual principles (1 Corinthians 10:6, 11). We will learn more about it later in this book. Just because the Israelites entered the Promised Land didn't mean they inherited it. Once they entered the Promised Land, they had to defeat the giants who lived there before they could possess it. We will have to overcome giants in the spirit (demonic spirits) to fulfill our destiny too.

Every mindset and stronghold that exists in our minds against the Word and kingdom must be pulled down and destroyed. This process is not easy. It might be the most painful experience we will ever go through. It's a battle between life and death, and flesh and spirit.

VISITING VERSUS LIVING

To enter any country, you need to meet some requirements. You need to qualify. Some countries require a visa, or at least a passport. I have traveled to many countries. The process to obtain a visa to some countries is not that easy. It is the same way in the kingdom. To enter God's kingdom, we need to meet the requirements He has put in His Word.

There's a whole new level of requirements you need to fulfill to live or get resident status in a country. Visiting or entering are different from *living in* a country. The kingdom of God is also a country. You are created to not just visit it, but to live in it.

When the Bible speaks of entering the kingdom of heaven, it is not referring to going to heaven when we die or going to church on a

Sunday morning. I believe it is possible for people to make it to heaven without entering and experiencing the kingdom God wants us to experience here on earth.

Unfortunately, the majority of believers have not entered the kingdom of God. They are living in the world, wholly dependent on it for their sustenance. They visit a church and they believe they are in the kingdom or living for God. That is far from truth!

The majority of the people of Israel who left Egypt did not enter the Promised Land. Just like them, we have to qualify ourselves to enter the kingdom of God. That is what we will be learning about in this chapter.

When it says Jesus is the Door to heaven or the kingdom, it doesn't mean we step on Him and walk over Him to enter through an actual door. It means that in order for us to enter the kingdom, we need to have the same nature and likeness that He has. This was the same image and likeness Adam had when God created him.

As long as Adam had that nature, he lived in the kingdom of God. When sin entered his being, he could no longer function in the image and likeness of God. As a result, he lost the garden, which was the kingdom of God.

THE SEVEN ENTRANCES TO THE KINGDOM

There are seven principles in the New Testament that we need to apply to our lives so we can qualify to enter God's kingdom again. I call these principles the "Seven Entrances" to the kingdom of God. Jesus mentioned five of them in the Gospels, and the sixth and seventh ones are mentioned by Paul in Acts and Peter in his epistle. I will go into detail about these principles later in the book. When we apply these seven principles and live by them, we will qualify to enter God's kingdom.

When we complete this process of entering the kingdom, we will unlearn everything the enemy kingdom (this world system) has taught us through family, religion, culture, education, and political background since the fall of Adam. We will be free from racism, the caste system, self-centeredness, poverty, pride, and everything else that came into and upon us because of the fall.

When we apply these seven principles, we will be led by the Spirit as we were originally designed to be, and our mindset (our thoughts) will be formed and operated by the Word of God. The image and likeness of God will be restored to us. You will enter your place of destiny and the rest will be history.

That is why the Bible says the whole creation is waiting for the manifestation of the sons of God (Romans 8:19). There are many Christians on the earth today, but very few sons and daughters of God who are functioning in the image and likeness of their Father as Adam did before the fall, or Jesus did while He was on the earth.

God wants more sons and daughters who are mature to administer and manifest His kingdom on earth. God has no benefit in having more converts, more members in a church, or by having everyone in heaven. He wants His kingdom to come to earth and His will be done here as it is in heaven.

ENTERING THE KINGDOM

To deliver us from the world's system and bring us into the kingdom of God, God begins a process in every believer from the moment they are born again. That process is called "entering the kingdom." To change our mindset and form a kingdom mindset in us, we all need to go through various deliverance processes.

These processes are not easy, and most people don't complete them. As a result, they die without inheriting the promises of God or the kingdom. Similarly, most of the people of Israel who came out of Egypt did not enter the Promised Land. They did not yield to the process of God in the wilderness. As a result, they all died in the wilderness unfulfilled.

God did not bring us out of Egypt (darkness) to die in the wilderness. He has a destiny for us: He wants us to inherit the kingdom of God and fulfill His assignment here on earth.

The place of our destiny is the kingdom of God. True kingdom living is flowing in our calling and functioning in the gifts God gave us. When we think according to the Word of God, we will be transformed into the image and likeness of God again.

Once we have truly repented and renewed our mind, we will think like Adam thought before the fall about ourselves, God, and the world around us.

Seeing and entering are two different things, so the process to obtain both experiences is also different. We learned about *seeing* the kingdom in an earlier chapter.

In the natural, when a baby is born, that baby has a spirit, soul, and a body. When we are born again, our minds and bodies remain the same, and we will feel the influence of the old nature as we used to. Similarly, when the Bible talks about being born again, it is not just talking about our spirit. Jesus didn't end with the spirit. He went on to talk about our minds and bodies as well.

When you want to buy a house, you call a realtor to ask about the houses for sale. Then you go and *see* the house you like; you *enter* the house to see whether that is the one you are looking for, and if you like that one, you buy it and *inherit* it or possess it. Just because you saw the house doesn't mean you enter it, and just because you entered it doesn't mean you own it.

The process for our minds and bodies to become born again is called entering the kingdom of God. Being born again and *seeing* the kingdom is a momentary experience, just like the conception of a baby, but *entering* the kingdom of God is a process in which our souls and bodies are being transformed into a new creation in Christ, and this can be a lengthy process.

To be born again, first the seed of the Word of God needs to be deposited into our spirit, and then it will begin to grow. The more the Word grows in us, the more the influence of the old nature and the flesh is lessened. The more the Word is in us, the more we will be transformed into the image and likeness of the Son of God.

I used to think (like many others) that entering the kingdom was a momentary experience or something that happened after we died. Many people mistook going to heaven with entering the kingdom of God. They are two very different experiences.

My wife and I have three children, and I was with her in the birthing room when she gave birth to all of them. None of those experiences was a "boom" experience. I remember the months and weeks of preparation, expectation, and the labor pains my wife went through to give birth to each of our children. It didn't happen quickly; it was a process.

My children entered this world through pain and discomfort. It was not easy for them; and to be honest, they didn't want to come out of the comfort of the womb. They didn't come out smiling and excited to see this world. Their first reaction was crying their lungs out.

The same thing happens to each believer. Entering the kingdom is a painful process, but once we do, we will be happy we went through the process. It is as if you are going through the birth canal for a period of time. Imagine what a baby must feel when they are in the birth canal. It is a life-and-death battle. It would be like going through the eye of a needle.

You will cry for your life and try to run away if possible from everything and everyone. Leaving the pleasures, comfort, and the ways of this world is not easy, and many are not willing to sacrifice them. Entering the kingdom means leaving this world and its ways and entering a new country. It terrifies some. Similar to what a baby goes through in the birthing process, you won't know what the other end looks like until you get there.

Normally, a woman doesn't go through any pain to conceive a baby. It is the same with becoming born-again. It is an exciting experience to see the kingdom, but the journey necessary to enter it is not comfortable to our flesh. It is not comfortable for a baby to come out of the womb into this world, either.

To be born again in our spirits is an easy job, but to be transformed in our minds and our bodies (letting both come under the guidance of the Holy Spirit) can be a painful experience. During the process of entering the kingdom, we sometimes scream, shout, and even lose hope, just like a woman giving birth. But unlike that woman, we don't know exactly why we are going through certain difficult situations.

THE COMPONENTS OF THE KINGDOM

Since the kingdom of God is a country, it has everything a nation has, but it's ruled by a king. Before we start the process of entering it, it's good to know what's on the other side. The kingdom of God has everything any other nation has, but works differently.

For example, the country we were born in has a culture, and so does the kingdom of God. To migrate from our natural culture into kingdom culture is not easy. We need to purge ourselves from the culture we were brought up in, so we can learn and operate in the culture of the kingdom.

The kingdom of God is a place. Right now, it's a spiritual place or territory. When it says "enter" the kingdom, it does not mean you will walk through a physical gate or door and enter some physical kingdom somewhere.

Most of these experiences happen internally in our spirit man or in our soul. When something is real inside us, it will automatically manifest on the outside. The reason nothing good is manifesting outside now is because there is nothing good inside in our soul. We prosper as our souls prosper (3 John 1:2).

KING

When you are born again, you are born into a kingdom. This kingdom has a king, and His name is Jesus. Regardless of the type of government you grew up with, you now need to learn to how a kingdom operates to enter it. God's kingdom is a theocracy. It is not easy for many to switch from a democratic mindset to a kingdom lifestyle.

From the moment you are born again, you belong to Him and Him alone. You live to serve Him with your life and for the glory of His name. Not just on a Sunday morning. With every breath you take and every second of your life, you are supposed to live for Him. Most don't do that. They give the best of their strength and life serving the world system for money.

If we accepted Jesus as our Lord, that means He owns us. He purchased us with His blood. We must be living for the One who bought us and redeemed us (1 Corinthians 6:20, 7:23).

The New Testament believers and ministers were blamed for preaching and serving another King other than Caesar (Acts 17:7).

GOVERNMENT

As already mentioned, the kingdom of God has a government. Our patriotism should support the kingdom of God and His government first, regardless of the country in which we live and the flag or constitution we are pledged to serve. Our first allegiance must be to the government of God, not to any earthly system of government or a country.

If an earthly government issues any laws not in agreement with the kingdom government, we must obey God our King and not the earthly system (Acts 5:27–29).

Kings are not voted into power, and their governments do not allow protest. The opinion of a subject is of no consequence in regard to what the king has ordered. The king's decree must be carried out without questioning.

CULTURE

Similarly, every country and kingdom has its own culture. Culture is composed of traditions, belief systems, manners, and a way of thinking and living. It also includes our language, ethnicity, and prejudices. We need to put them aside and accept and learn the culture of the kingdom of God in their place.

Most do not die to their own culture and learn the kingdom's in its place. They bring their racism and prejudices into the church instead, and continue to judge, criticize, and marginalize other people based on their language, ethnicity, or color.

After introducing the kingdom, the first thing Jesus presented was the culture of the kingdom in Matthew 5–7. To learn the culture of the new country (God's kingdom) of which we are part, we need to renounce and tear down every stronghold created by the culture of our natural birth, replacing it with kingdom culture.

LANGUAGE

When we are naturally born, the first thing we learn is our mother tongue. It takes a while to learn our language. We begin by saying "ma-ma," "da-da," and simple sounds like that. It takes a couple of years for children to learn to pronounce words and sentences. We have fun with our children and smile at their childish attempts to practice language. I still remember some of the funny things I said when I was three years old, but I don't speak like that any longer because I became an adult.

When you are born again, you begin learning the language of the kingdom of God. You don't learn it in a day or two. It takes a while to learn the kingdom language—possibly longer than it took us to learn our native tongue. Many of the things we learned culturally, including our language, needs to be unlearned to speak kingdom language.

What would happen to you if you did not speak the language of your country? You would not be able to relate or communicate; and it would be extremely difficult to find a job or benefit from the resources of that country. Your experience and your quality of life will be very limited if you do not know the common language.

It works the same way in the kingdom. One of the main reasons most believers are not benefiting from the kingdom is because they do not speak the language of the kingdom. Without learning the language of the kingdom, your ability to experience and benefit what the kingdom has to offer will be extremely limited.

What is the language of the kingdom of God? *Faith is the language of the kingdom.* Most of the world is used to speaking negativity. This varies depending on the family we grew up in and the climate of our homes. If we grew up in a negative atmosphere or with a lot of criticism, then it is more difficult to learn the language of the kingdom. This is the same if we grew up in a poverty mindset.

Our minds (thinking patterns) and our hearts get programmed by the words we speak repeatedly. To undo that (or reprogram them) will take time and effort. The more we learn and practice speaking faith, the easier it will get. We must begin by practicing with our lips. For a while, our minds and hearts will fight against this. Expect that.

We need to persist until what we say with our mouths is one and the same as the thoughts in our minds and the feelings in our hearts; that's when the miracle will begin to happen. Our internal communication needs to come into alignment with the words of our mouths and the thoughts of our brains. That's when we will begin to walk by faith and not by sight.

Many people give up speaking faith. Their mouth will say one thing and their hearts continue to believe and speak in a totally opposite manner. We need to break and destroy those strongholds. One of the best ways to destroy strongholds is by declaring or commanding—in short, by speaking in faith.

> For assuredly, I say to you, whoever says to this mountain, "Be removed and be cast into the sea," and does not doubt in his heart, but believes that those things he says will be done, he will have whatever he says. *(Mark 11:23)*

Note the connection between the words of our mouths and what we believe in our hearts as stated in this verse. Our words and our internal communication have to align and become one. Then we will begin to see breakthroughs happening.

If we do not speak faith-filled words, nothing much will happen. Not much will change. God's kingdom is governed by words. If you choose to speak negativity instead of faith and blessing, you will attract curses and cancel out your purpose and calling by your own words.

People blame the devil for a lot of things he is not responsible for. Much of the harvest we reap is the result (or the fruit) of our own words (self-imposed curses). Other problems could be the result of our own wrong choices and lack of knowledge and understanding.

ECONOMY

Just as we are born into the economy of our nation, we are born again into the economy of the kingdom. Your outlook has been affected by the economy of your country and the family you grew up in.

Lying, cheating, and being stingy, as well as covetousness, selfishness, and greed are part of the world's economy. Living to make money and working for money is part and parcel of the world system. In the kingdom, we don't work for the purpose of making money. Instead, we live to fulfill our purpose and calling; in turn, God supplies what we need, and we are blessed financially.

We need to learn God's economy. In the kingdom, we give to receive. I have written a whole book on this subject called *Kingdom Economy*. You can find the information at the end of this book to order a copy.

EDUCATION

This world's educational system is set up to produce slaves to serve its system, like cogs in a machine. After we complete our education, we secure a job, on which we are dependent for the rest of our lives. That is not the way the kingdom of God works.

When we get an education, it means we become the master of something. That's how you know if you are educated or not; you understand something and have a thorough knowledge of it. A kingdom education is different from a worldly one. Kingdom education is geared toward fulfilling four goals. First, it establishes your identity;

it answers the question of who you are. Second, it helps you discover your purpose. Third, it helps you discover your calling, and fourth, it helps you identify your gifts and master them.

Once you go through all four, you will be unstoppable and will no longer experience any financial problems. People will come and pay you for your services because you have mastered your gift, and people will need the benefit of the gift you have.

AGRICULTURE

As we have discussed, God introduced His kingdom through a garden. God knows food is important to us. When He established the nation of Israel, He gave them very specific dietary rules. He told them what they should eat and what they shouldn't to keep them healthy and strong.

Some believers think that because they are under grace, they can eat whatever they choose. That is not so. We are supposed to be led by the Holy Spirit in everything we do, and that includes eating. Holy Spirit will tell you what is good for you and what is not.

Paul said all the creatures of God were good if we received them with thanks (1 Timothy 4:4). That doesn't mean we need to eat everything we see, though. In times of emergency or scarcity, we might eat something that we normally would not. Paul also said that all things are permissible or lawful, but that not everything was helpful (or edifying) (1 Corinthians 6:12).

MEDIA

The devil is called the prince of the power of the air. The reason the media is so powerful is because of the spiritual force working behind it. One of the weapons the devil uses against us is wrong information presented as truth. Lies presented as truth are powerful when people have received (and believed) them.

When we enter the kingdom, we need to decide whose report we are going to believe. Will we believe what God says in His Word or what we hear from the many different media outlets?

TERRITORY

The earth and its fullness belong to the Lord. We don't teach much about the earth in our churches. We are programmed to neglect it because we believe it is being kept to be burned with fire. When you come into the kingdom, your attitude toward the earth will change (or needs to change). God wants to establish His kingdom on the earth. The earth is kingdom territory.

God created us to take care of the earth. But the religious spirit has deceived us by saying we don't belong here. That allows the devil to occupy the whole planet. Your purpose is connected to the earth in this life and in the next. That's one of the reasons that every parable Jesus shared had something to do with the earth.

PEOPLE AND NATIONS

Every people and nation belong to the Lord. They have been deceived by the enemy and they are serving him now. When kingdom citizens arise in every nation and take their rightful place to possess and occupy that land, they will establish the kingdom and will of their Father, the King.

ARMY

The kingdom of God has an army that is standing ready to carry out the orders its King and citizens declare 24/7. Angels are the army of the kingdom of God. We need to learn how to work in cooperation with the angels of God to accomplish God's will on earth.

INDUSTRIES

In every country, God's children should be the most productive group of people in every level of society. We have been focusing only on the "spiritual" for too long. As a result of our neglect in the area of developing industry, we have lost our nations to the devil and his children. We need to start factories and manufacturing hubs everywhere. We need to be more creative, industrious, innovative, and productive than the people in the world.

SCIENCE AND TECHNOLOGY

Science is not an anti-God or anti-kingdom element. True science is supposed to work in support of the Scriptures. The enemy has stolen this area and used it to advance his kingdom. Technology must be used to advance God's kingdom instead. We need to learn kingdom science and technology.

The Bible says we should "enter the kingdom." This means we need to start appropriating each aspect of God's kingdom into our lives. It is not referring to having some spiritual experience in a meeting. Now that we understand this, we are going to look into how the process of entering actually works.

CHAPTER 9

THE PROCESS OF ENTERING THE KINGDOM

> *This is the gate of the Lord, through which the righteous shall enter. (Psalm 118:20)*

In John 3:5, Jesus said we needed to be born of "water and Spirit" to enter the kingdom of God. In this verse, *water* represents the Word, and *spirit* represents the Holy Spirit. He didn't say Spirit and water. He is so much smarter than we are. He knows what He is talking about. Through renewing our minds with the Word of God, our souls will be aligned to our born-again spirit. Through surrendering our bodies to the Holy Spirit, our bodies will do the same.

When mankind fell from his original position, one of the first things that was damaged was our minds. Before the fall, our spirits were in charge of our lives. When that spirit died, the mind didn't know what to do, so it took control and began to tell us what to do. However, we are spirit beings and are supposed to be led by our spirits and God's Spirit.

After we see the kingdom, God starts working on our soul, preparing us to enter His kingdom. Everyone's mind is damaged until they begin to think like God thinks about them. Everyone struggles with some form or level of mental *illness or dysfunction*. This is only healed when we renew our minds with the Word of God.

When we try to handle spiritual things on our own with our damaged mind, we have confusion, spiritual barrenness, division, spiritual depression, and so on in the church.

It was no accident that when Jesus began His public ministry, the first thing He announced was to change the way we think.

It was like He was saying, "Hey, people, what you have been thinking about yourselves and God is wrong! In fact, the way your mind works is just the opposite of the way I created it to function. Just stop for a minute, and I will help you change. I will restore it to its original state!" Jesus didn't come preaching about tithes, the rapture, and prosperity. If you listen to most preachers these days, their subject is probably one of those.

> Repent, for the kingdom of heaven is at hand. *(Matthew 4:17)*

The Greek word for *repent* used here is *metanoeó*, which means to put a complete stop to the way you are thinking, what you are doing, and where you are going.[6] It means to forget the past and start all over again, so there has to be a night-and-day difference between life before and after repentance. If there is no difference, then we have not repented—we have only "confessed."

THE TRANSFORMATION OF OUR SOULS

The transformation of our souls doesn't happen in one day. The Bible calls it sanctification, and it is an ongoing process. It doesn't happen

---

[6] James Strong, "3340. Metanoeó," Strong's Greek: 3340. μετανοέω (metanoeó) — to change one's mind or purpose (Biblehub), accessed April 23, 2020, https://biblehub.com/greek/3340.htm)

automatically when we say a prayer. No, it is a daily fight, and we need to renew our minds with the Word of God so we can exchange the old for the new. We were created by the Word; it is the original "software" by which our minds operated until sin entered. After we are born again, we need to restore our minds to think like Adam thought before the fall.

The Word is the only tool that can renew our minds. In the natural, our thoughts are opposite to what the Word says. The natural mind that we inherited from Adam says to hate our enemies and do evil to those who treat us badly. Jesus, the living Word, instructed us to do the opposite.

The new mind that we inherited from the second or last Adam told us to love our enemies and do good to those who persecute and despitefully use you. It is our decision to choose from which mind we are going to operate: the mind of our spirit, which is the mind of Christ, or the carnal mind (Romans 8:7). God will not force you, and Holy Spirit will not push you. You need to make the correct decision by using your brain and your own free will.

How do we know whether or not we have renewed our minds? When our minds are renewed, we will begin to think like Adam thought before the fall in the garden. He did not worry about his food or about tomorrow. There was no jealousy, envy, fear, or hatred in him. There was no doubt about God's love for him. He had the mind of Christ.

Jesus told us in John 15:7 that if we abide in Him and His words abide in us, whatsoever we shall ask, He will give to us. The Word is called the water because we use water to clean ourselves and quench our thirst. Once we are born again in our spirit, we need to use the Word to wash and cleanse our minds to live a life that is productive and pleasing to the Lord.

We can also see our reflection in water. God wants us to look into the water of His Word and see the person He has mirrored there.

Through His Word, our identity is revealed to us, and the distortions the enemy has taught us will fall away.

Our minds need to be transformed by the Word. The true Word does not divide people; it unites them. The church has been divided into thousands of pieces—all based on different and faulty interpretations of the Word. For their own personal gain, deceitful leaders, directed by the devil, have divided the body of Christ.

When you see a leader who is trying to build an "island" or an "empire" and segregating a group of believers and does not have a vision for the unity of the body of Christ in that city or town, that person is a deceitful worker. It doesn't matter how many miracles he or she performs or what event he or she can predict. That person is shortsighted and blind. Such work will not last for more than a generation. Most of those empires will disintegrate with the death of the founder.

If we let the Holy Spirit interpret the Scripture for us, do you think He would tell us contradictory things? He is not the spirit of confusion, but truth. One notable pastor told me that he could not come to the meeting that I was arranging because I did not belong to the same denomination as him. Another friend of mine told me that his church would cancel the meetings if they knew ahead of time that an unbeliever was coming to that meeting. Can Christianity get weirder than this?

Dear saints of God, I am not making this stuff up; these incidents are true. When our minds are transformed by the Word of God, we will begin to see the image and likeness of God in every human being. Jesus saw this when He was in public ministry. The Pharisees brought Him a prostitute to be stoned, but Jesus didn't see her as a prostitute; He saw her as His daughter whom He had made in His own image and likeness.

The Pharisees divided people into different groups: tax collectors, Samaritans, fishermen, and so on. Jesus saw everyone as the children of the same Father. What kind of world would it be if all Christians began to see the image and likeness of God in each other? I don't think we will enter the kingdom of God if we don't change our attitudes and get back into the Word. We look at people and treat them based on what they believe: Pentecostal, Baptist, Catholic, Charismatic, non-Charismatic, and so on—just as the Pharisees did.

Jesus is the Door to the kingdom (John 10:9; Revelation 4:1). Many come to the Door of the Kingdom and spend their entire life around it. They see the kingdom—*but never enter.*

We were made by the Word, and we need the Word to repair and renew our old life. God gave us the Word in written form so we can come to Him every day and repair our damaged parts. This is not a one-day project, but an ongoing lifestyle. We are changed from glory to glory and from faith to faith day by day. Every area of our lives that is not in line with the Word of God will need to be changed and be conformed to the Word of God.

The Word is the key to entering the kingdom of God. Everything in the kingdom works according to the Word of God. If we are not familiar with the Word, we will not receive much from God.

When temptations knock at our door, who answers the door—the Word or our flesh? Jesus was full of the Word. He was the Word. When He was tempted of the devil, the Word answered the door, and the devil was defeated! The kingdom of God operates by the principles of the Word of God. Everything in it works according to the Word of God. So in order to enter the kingdom, we need to pass the test of the Word of God. Unless the Word operates through you, you will not be permitted to enter the kingdom (Psalm 105:19).

RENEWING THE MIND

Once you are born again in the spirit, the real work starts in the mind, or soul. What good is a born-again spirit imprisoned by a darkened and ignorant mind? Your spirit by itself cannot do anything. Your spirit gives suggestions and impressions, but unless your mind receives those suggestions and makes the right decision, nothing will work out well. Unless we renew our minds with the Word of God, we cannot make right decisions.

Originally, we were led by our spirits. The mind and body worked in submission to the spirit. After the fall, our spirits were dead, and we were led by the soul and body. When a spirit is *dead,* it means it is no longer in the driver's seat in a person's life. It is unable to connect with God. It doesn't mean it is completely lifeless. If that were the case, the person wouldn't be alive, either.

When we are born again, the spirit is released from prison and able to connect with God once again. Seeing the kingdom is the first evidence we have that our spirits have come alive in God. Once we are born again, the process begins that will reverse and restore us to the original plan God had for us. The training of our souls and bodies to submit to the Holy Spirit begins.

Your mind and spirit need to come into alignment. Your mind needs to believe the same thing you have in your spirit, as well as who you are in the spirit. Your mind is supposed to tap into what is in your spirit and manifest that through your body and what you do day by day.

The kingdom of God is in our spirits (Luke 17:21). We carry the kingdom of God, Jesus Christ, Holy Spirit, and the government of God in our spirit man. I don't think it is outrageous to say that we carry heaven (or the government of God) within us in our spirits.

Your mind needs to be trained to obey your spirit and the Word. Your unrenewed mind is an enemy to your spirit and God. Many have a born-again spirit, but their mind has not been born again yet. When you are born again, your entire being needs to be born again. In the natural, when someone is born, it is not just their spirit that is born, but their mind and body, as well.

Your soul is comprised of your will, emotions, intellect, desires, and memories of past experiences. These areas need to be transformed into the image and likeness of Jesus Christ. Know this: The purpose of salvation and the born-again process is not to join a church or a denomination and sing some songs and hear sermons.

God has given us another chance to become His son, just like Adam was His son in the beginning. To God, salvation means to become like Adam before the fall or to become like Christ on earth and do what they did. Entering the kingdom is a process to reprogram our minds to think and act like sons of God. We live on the basis of the knowledge we have (2 Peter 1:3), but wrong knowledge produces wrong thoughts, and wrong thoughts produces wrong results.

When God created the earth, He gave it and everything in it to Adam, His son, to manage. Every treasure and all its resources and riches belonged to Adam. It should be the same today. Everything on the earth should belong to the sons of God. The Bible says all things are ours: things present, things to come, the world, and everything in it (1 Corinthians 3:22).

If the Christian walk is not doing any good for your life and to the planet earth, then you may have received some wrong information when you came to Christ. You might have even heard the wrong gospel (2 Corinthians 11:4). If your salvation experience didn't change your life, then you are not saved. If the faith you have is not producing the result that you expected, then you have the wrong kind of faith.

If your soul is not being healed from all past negative experiences, wounds, traumas, and mindsets, the anointing that will flow out of your life will not be pure. Every sin and hurt that wounded your spirit leaves emotional garbage in your soul, which clogs and defiles the new man you became in Christ. When we come to Christ, our souls (including our will, emotions, and consciousness) do not change. We have to cleanse our minds and the depth of our being from all emotional debris left over from our past experiences.

With the Israelites, God worked from the outside to the inside. He started from their bodies and then worked into the soul and spirit.

In the New Testament, it is reversed. It begins within and works from the inside out. God starts with the spirit, and then works out from there to the soul and body. The Israelites were made free in their bodies, but their souls were bound by the ways of Egypt. They saw more miracles from God than any of us, but they couldn't submit their souls and bodies to Him. In Egypt, they had been controlled by taskmasters, and all their decisions were made for them.

In our lives, emotional strongholds that were formed before we were born again came into the kingdom with us and they act as our taskmasters. Those strongholds must be destroyed intentionally. Each of us has those strongholds, and they must be addressed. Otherwise they will sabotage our journey into kingdom living.

The Israelites didn't know how to make choices for themselves. Even though they were free of the Egyptian taskmasters, the mindset they had formed in Egypt was still in operation. They were not in charge of their lives. They were tossed to and fro like a ship on the ocean, going this way and that, depending on their feelings and their circumstances (Psalm 107:26–27). The Bible says their spirit was not steadfast with God (Psalm 78:8).

Many people come to Christ, but they never submit their soul and body to the lordship of Christ. Their soul is controlled by different taskmasters of their past life. These may be anger, lust, pride, greed, rebellion, abuse, rejection, fear, insecurity, and the list goes on.

I don't believe they will reach or fulfill the destiny God has for their lives. Paul says that we should run our race "according to the rules" so that we may not run in vain (2 Timothy 2:5).

Jesus said that in the end many will come, saying:

> "Lord, Lord, have we not prophesied in Your name, cast out demons in Your name, and done many wonders in Your name?" And then I will declare to them, "I never knew you; depart from Me, you who practice lawlessness!" *(Matthew 7:22–23)*

It is possible to cast out demons and heal the sick without knowing Christ! What a terrible day that would be! What is the goal of Christian life? I believe it is to be transformed into the image and likeness of Jesus, the Son of God, so we can accomplish God's will on earth.

The goal of Christian life is not just to reach heaven or have the gifts of the Holy Spirit operating in our lives. Jesus never preached the gospel in that way. The total sum of all His teaching was focused on character change in the here and now. He wanted us to enter, live in, and manifest His kingdom now, not when we get to heaven.

Many have made it their goal to speak in tongues or flow in one of the gifts of the Holy Spirit. Once they do that, they feel they have *arrived* at their destination. That is a deception. It is very unfortunate that we have had so many healing and prophetic schools, but few kingdom schools. We should be teaching people how to live in God's kingdom.

Everyone has faith. Even the heathen has faith in their stuff, but faith based on wrong knowledge produces wrong results. I grew up in church, but I was one of the most miserable people in the whole world. I believed everything others told me to believe and did everything that I saw everyone else do.

In time, I realized that it was not just me who was miserable. Everyone who went to church with me was miserable, too. They just kept doing what they knew, hoping that one day life would get better. No one dared to question why they did things as they did; they didn't know any better and had no other choice. Most lacked the guts to question the established church practices. They were afraid that if they didn't do what everybody else did, God would punish them, or those in the church would label them as heretics.

It's not easy for a person who has been raised up in the world's system or a religious church to change the way they were trained to think. God allows us to go through challenges to train us to think differently. When we go through a trial or a challenge and come out of it, we often say, "Oh, I didn't know it worked that way," or, "I didn't realize that before," or something similar. This just means that we learned something we didn't know before, and as a result, we learned to think differently. That's the purpose of everything we go through after we receive salvation.

God is teaching us how to think differently and how life works in His kingdom.

Once we are trained to think according to the Word of God, become mature in the things of God, and understand how He operates, He no longer has to allow us to go through tribulations like we did when we first began our walk with Him. Sadly, most people never learn and mature so they die in the wilderness, just like the people of Israel—without seeing the fulfillment of His promises.

Understanding this enables us to count it all joy when we go through various trials and temptations, as James says to do (James 1:2–4). They all work for our benefit—even though we may sometimes feel like we are going to die in that process.

In Deuteronomy 6:7, God said we are supposed to talk about the Word when we sit in the house, when we walk by the way, when we lie down, and when we rise up. Imagine if we lived with our children like this, instead of filling their minds with kids' movies and cartoons.

All born-again believers should and could inherit the kingdom of God in this life, but in reality, it is not that way. If it were, all the people who came out of Egypt would have inherited the Promised Land. Only two did. In the same way, only a few of the born-again people today truly inherit the kingdom of God. They can see what is available for them, just like the people of Israel saw and tasted the grapes from the Promised Land, but only a few might enter and taste its blessings.

TRANSFORMATION OF THE BODY

Your body also needs to be rebirthed. The Spirit of God is the solution to the problems that you have in your body.

> Your body is the temple of the Holy Spirit who is in you. *(1 Corinthians 6:19)*

Your body, not your mind or spirit, is the temple of God's Spirit. The third step to entering the kingdom is to be "born again" in your body, which means bringing your body into alignment with your spirit.

To do that, we must crucify the desires of our carnal bodies and submit them as living sacrifices. Unless we do this, we will die like Moses did. He only saw the Promised Land from Mount Nebo, but did not enter it. Dear saints of God, God wants us to not only see the kingdom, but also enter and inherit it.

When you are full of God's Word, you will be led by the Spirit. When you are full of yourself and have five pity parties a day, you are not allowing the Holy Spirit to lead you. When you are led by the Spirit, you will not fulfill the lust of the flesh. When you are not led by the flesh, you will inherit the kingdom in its fullness. This is why we must yield our bodies to the Lord.

Our body was given to us to provide a "house" for the Spirit of God. This provides God, who is Spirit, the legal right to operate in the physical world.

Once we are born of the Word of God and abide in the Word, we will be led by the Spirit of God.

> For if ye live after the flesh, ye shall die: but if ye through the Spirit do mortify the deeds of the body, ye shall live. For as many as are led by the Spirit of God, they are the sons of God. *(Romans 8:13–14 KJV)*

Our bodies are a gift from God. They don't belong to us.

> You are not your own. For you were bought at a price; therefore glorify God in your body and in your spirit, which are God's. *(1 Corinthians 6:19–20)*

God is Spirit. He needs a physical body to operate on earth.

Earth is governed by natural laws, and everything that dwells here must have a material body. Earth is made of material substance, and our bodies are made from the earth. God made our bodies so that His Spirit could dwell in us. We are His agents on earth who will do His will *on earth as it is in heaven.*

Once we surrender both spirit and soul to Him, God will start working on our bodies. In the Old Testament, God dwelt in the temple, which was made by hands. He also dwelt in the praises of His people (Psalm 22:3). He couldn't dwell in people because they were not yet saved by the blood of Jesus. In the New Testament, He chose our bodies as His dwelling place, which was His original intent.

> Do you not know that you are the temple of God and that the Spirit of God dwells in you? *(1 Corinthians 3:16)*

We spend a lot of time taking care of our bodies because we want to look good in front of other people. How much time do we spend presenting ourselves to the Holy Spirit to whom our bodies belong? We forget the purpose for which our bodies were given to us. We all desire to have the power of God in our lives, but how many realize that He wants to dwell in us? Furthermore, the only hands and mouths He can use are ours; through them, He wants to bring healing and comfort to hurting people.

When we use our bodies for other purposes than the reason for which they were created, they get sick and becomes a burden instead of a blessing. It's like an automobile. If you don't take good care of it, your body will break down and will not run properly. When we use our bodies only to gratify the lust of the flesh or personal ambition, we will feel pleasure at first, but later it will bring pain and grief (1 Corinthians 6:13b).

God will allow us to go through difficult times until we reach the place in which we say what David said in Psalm 63:

> Oh, God, You are my God; early will I seek You; my soul thirsts for You; my flesh longs for You in a dry and thirsty land where there is no water.
> *(Psalm 63:1)*

When our spirits are born again, the Holy Spirit comes to our spirits, but He will not manifest His power through us yet. (He may manifest to some all at once, but usually it happens over a period of time.)

Only when a body is yielded to the Holy Spirit will His power begin to manifest. When we are born again, the Holy Spirit comes inside us. When our minds are renewed, we will begin to be led by the Spirit. When our bodies are yielded to Him, He comes upon us and the power of the Spirit will begin to manifest through us. Only when all three of these are accomplished will we walk in the destiny God has for us in His kingdom.

We need to train our minds to think and act according to the Word of God. Then we will be ready for God to pour out His Spirit upon us. Jesus said:

> You shall receive power when the Holy Spirit has come upon you. *(Acts 1:8)*

We have the power of God only when the Holy Spirit comes upon us, not in us. There is a difference between the Holy Spirit coming in you and upon you. He comes *in* when we surrender our spirits to the Lord, and He comes *upon* us when we surrender our bodies to Him. God's Spirit is a "holy" Spirit, and His dwelling place needs to be holy. God's power is available to anyone who needs it. The only requirement is that He needs a body that is totally surrendered to Him. The Bible says God's eyes run to and fro over the earth to find people whose heart is perfect toward Him, so that He can show Himself great on their behalf.

Giving our bodies as living sacrifices to God is called our "reasonable service." The most reasonable thing we could do for God is to give our bodies to Him (Romans 12:1).

The world around us is hurting and dying without the love and power of God. The only solution to this chaotic situation is the power of God. We are the only people God can use if He needs to touch someone. Without the power of God, we are greatly limited.

We need the power of God to inherit the kingdom of God and defeat the enemy who is holding our inheritance hostage. The Israelites reached the Promised Land, but they needed to drive out the inhabitants before they could possess the land. The inhabitants were very strong and outnumbered them, but they were defeated because of the power of God. In the same way, when we surrender our bodies to the Holy Spirit, there is no enemy that will be too strong for us to defeat.

There won't be any wall too high for us to jump over. There won't be any challenge that we can't overcome. As the Bible says, all things are possible with God. When we surrender our lives, it is no longer we that live, but God living through us. We exchange our weakness for His strength, and everything He has become ours. The kingdom of God is an unlimited kingdom.

We can take this world for Christ. God was convinced of that, and that is why He started the church. He knows that we can do the impossible through Him, but the question is: Do we know what He knows about us? He didn't start a weak church. He started a triumphant church, and He is coming to receive a triumphant church without spot or blemish.

DEFEATING THE SEVEN GIANTS

There are giants in the spirit that are holding us back from inheriting the kingdom of God. Our destiny is the Promised Land for each believer. You need to overcome these giants by the power of the Holy Spirit.

There are seven "giants" each believer needs to overcome, in the same way that there were seven nations the people of Israel needed to overcome to possess their land. We do not face a natural enemy like they did. We fight against forces of darkness. Below are the seven giants each believer needs to overcome if they are to enter and inherit the kingdom of God:

i. Lust of the Flesh
ii. Fear
iii. Anger
iv. Selfish Ambition
v. Love of money
vi. Unbelief
vii. Pride

Each of these emotional (spiritual) giants represents the natural giants the Israelites faced and overcame.

Out of the six hundred thousand men who left Egypt, only two finished the race and reached the Promised Land. What kept them out? One of the "giants" I mentioned above. Physical factors like the giants in those nations might have caused those conditions inside them to overpower their faith. The Bible says the majority did not enter because of unbelief (Hebrews 3:19). Moses couldn't enter because of his anger. He made it to heaven when he died. Which *giant* is keeping you from inheriting the kingdom of God?

The Bible says we need to be in the group that receives the promises by faith and patience, and not among those who perish through unbelief (Hebrews 6:12; Hebrews 10:39). Great and wide is the way to destruction, and many are traveling on that road (Matthew 7:13–14).

> Know ye not that they which run in a race run all, but one receiveth the prize? So run, that ye may obtain. *(1 Corinthians 9:24 KJV)*

Though all run, only one obtains the prize. Unless we reach our promised land, our running is in vain. Unless we enter the kingdom, all the Christian and church stuff we do is absolute dung. It's just religion. Our promised land is the destiny God has promised us. It is not heaven, as some think and teach; the promised land is a land right here on this earth. It is our kingdom inheritance.

THE PROCESS OF ENTERING THE KINGDOM

Our promised land is the "place" or "land" or "condition of our heart" that is God's destiny for us; it is the destination in which He will fulfill the promises He has made to us. It could be a physical place on this earth or a spiritual state that we will arrive at in our hearts.

Just like the Israelites, today only a few inherit the kingdom or fulfill their destiny. Many see it in their spirits, but do not pay the price to enter and inherit it. As I said before, we need to overcome the lust of our bodies to inherit the kingdom of God. We cannot obtain the promises of God with our own might and in our own strength. It is His Spirit that leads us into our kingdom inheritance.

Once the spirit, soul, and body are born again, we will inherit the kingdom. We can make it to heaven by just getting saved, but that does not accomplish anything for God and His kingdom here on earth.

Jesus did not save us just so we can make it to heaven. He wants us to make the place we possess on this earth (our domain) like heaven before we leave it. He wants us to get a glimpse of heaven and make it a reality here on earth. God's will *on earth as it is in heaven* is our mandate. The following verses show us who will not inherit the kingdom of God.

> Do you not know that the unrighteous will not inherit the kingdom of God? Do not be deceived. Neither fornicators, nor idolaters, nor adulterers, nor homosexuals, nor sodomites, nor thieves, nor covetous, nor drunkards, nor revilers, nor extortioners will *inherit* the kingdom of God. *(1 Corinthians 6:9–10)*
>
> Now the works of the flesh are evident, which are: adultery, fornication, uncleanness, lewdness, idolatry, sorcery, hatred, contentions, jealousies, outbursts of wrath, selfish ambitions, dissensions, heresies, envy,

> murders, drunkenness, revelries, and the like; of which I tell you beforehand, just as I also told you in time past, that those who practice such things will not *inherit* the kingdom of God. *(Galatians 5:19–21)*

> For this you know, that no fornicator, unclean person, nor covetous man, who is an idolater, has any inheritance in the kingdom of Christ and God.
> *(Ephesians 5:5)*

If you are still struggling with any of the abovementioned behaviors in your flesh, know that you will by no means inherit the kingdom of God in this life. Again, people misquote those Scriptures and think they are talking about people going to heaven. They are not referring to going to heaven. They specifically speak about inheriting your kingdom assignment and fulfilling your destiny *here on earth*. To help us overcome these behaviors, the Lord takes us through an *un*learning process, which is the topic of the next chapter.

CHAPTER 10

THE UNLEARNING PROCESS

> *Thus says the Lord: "Do not learn the way of the Gentiles; do not be dismayed at the signs of heaven, for the Gentiles are dismayed at them." (Jeremiah 10:2)*

Once we see the kingdom, the process of entering it begins. In order to enter the kingdom, we have to go through a series of *unlearning* lessons to understand how the kingdom of God operates. The kingdom of God works opposite from our culture, nation, and the religion or church we grew up in.

From the moment we are born again, we are enrolled into the Kingdom University and start this *unlearning* process. I hope you noted the difference in what I just wrote. Most people join a university to *learn* new things, but in God's university, we will need to *un*learn what we already know before we learn the new.

Most won't be willing to let go of what they have and what they know—what took them years to accumulate and learn. So a conflict begins in them.

GOING THROUGH THE WILDERNESS

To help us with this process, God takes us to the *wilderness*. By "wilderness" I don't mean a literal place, but a state in the spirit in which God, through His infinite wisdom, will use our circumstances in the natural to bring out everything that is in us that does not belong to His kingdom and to our original nature. God wants to detach us from our dependence on this world and its systems so we can depend on His kingdom for everything instead.

This is similar to the detox process we go through in the natural. Every fiber and cell in our being needs to be reprogrammed according to the ways of God. Even our DNA will get reprogrammed. That is why the Bible says that if anyone is in Christ, they are a new "creation." A new creation cannot have old DNA.

You will go through a thousand deaths and feel like you won't make it to the next day. All you need is simple trust in God and in His Word. He will make it happen and carry you through. The only thing we must do is make sure we do not step out in our flesh out of frustration and anger, and sin. If we do, we will delay the process even longer or we may not make it to our promised land. We simply need to keep our eyes on Jesus and trust Him.

We will go through the refiner's fire. His holy fire and His Word will test every fiber of our being. Every intention of our hearts, including our thoughts, motives, prejudices, ambitions, desires, dreams, and attitudes, will be tested seven times. If they do not belong to the kingdom, they will all have to go. If we fail a test, then we will have to take it again and again until we pass it.

We will go through the test until we are conformed to the image and likeness of God, which we originally had. The reason God takes us to the wilderness is to seclude us, so that it will be just us and God.

THE UNLEARNING PROCESS

There are no shopping malls or swimming pools in the wilderness. God will provide us with what we need to survive—the daily manna. There is no abundance in the wilderness. It is a place of survival. Living there is denoted by a period of isolation; people won't recognize what you are going through inside.

The wilderness is like boot camp in the army, in which the new recruit unlearns the old ways and is trained in the new ways of the kingdom. The more we cooperate with God, the faster the process will go. It does not become easier. There is nothing easy about this, but cooperating will shorten it.

In this process, God decides who will be among the chosen ones. The Word says that many are called, but only a few are chosen. Only a few will complete this unlearning process successfully and learn the new ways of the kingdom. Once you complete this, from then on nothing can destroy you. The enemy's onslaughts will not defeat you.

Every single person God used in the Bible (and in our time) went through this process. Some try to take shortcuts and end up short-circuiting their destiny. Some go after opportunities to make money or commit adultery and shipwreck their lives (1 Timothy 1:19). Others pursue the gifts of the Holy Spirit and try to become famous, and the end of their lives is miserable and tragic.

God's school and system remain the same, but circumstances differ from person to person and place to place. His principles and ways remain the same for all eternity.

In truth, God wants us to unlearn everything we learned from the other kingdom before we learn anything from Him. Otherwise, what we learn from Him will get choked by the old and will not produce the fruit it is supposed to bear.

RENEWING OUR MINDS

Why must we unlearn everything? Because everything we were taught before wasn't based on His kingdom; it was based on another kingdom, the kingdom of darkness. This unlearning process is called the renewal of our minds.

There are only three subjects in this university: trials, tests, and temptations. We will learn everything else that we need in the course of *taking* the above subjects, which means that we will learn while we are going through those trials, tests, and temptations.

This is why the Bible tells us to count it all joy when we go through various trials (James 1:2). Trials are sent to help us unlearn, not to destroy us. We might feel as though they are going to destroy us, but they will not. Once we finish the process of unlearning and then learning God's ways, we will reach a place in which we lack nothing, as it says in James 1:4.

Everything we know now was intentionally or unintentionally taught to us by others; that include our culture, education, religion, and entire life experience. We did not come into this world with any know-how. We only knew how to cry when we came out of the womb. When we are born again, we get a fresh chance to learn God's ways and about His kingdom. The problem is that we already know a lot of incorrect information that we need to get rid of.

That is why the Bible instructs us to desire the pure milk of the Word like newborn babes (1 Peter 2:2). This verse is very important. When we come into the kingdom of God, we need to look at the Scriptures and start learning from them as if we were only babies and don't know anything. It says we need to learn from it (or *drink* it) like a newborn drinks their milk.

A newborn baby does not ask any "deep" questions. They don't ask where the milk came from or where their daddy and mommy came from. They do not question the origin of God or wonder who Cain married. When a new believer asks these types of questions, they stem from the inaccurate information they received from somewhere else about God and His Word.

Let me tell you something very important: Once you become mature in the spirit, you won't have these kinds of questions anymore. You will just know things in your spirit and these types of questions won't bother you. Why? Because you "know" God in your spirit; you do not just know *about* Him in your brain. When you know Him on such a level, nothing else matters. He will answer all the questions you have. Once you know Him, even if this whole world falls apart, you won't be shaken by it.

LEARNING GOD'S WAYS

Earlier in my life, when things did not work out as I hoped and I was depressed and disappointed, God directed me to go to Genesis and learn afresh. That is exactly what I did. I had to get rid of almost everything I knew about church and Christianity prior to that time. I have been writing about the first two chapters of Genesis for the last twenty years and I still haven't exhausted them yet.

From the moment you meet Jesus, He takes you on a journey of unlearning. Through that unlearning process, you will also learn the ways of God. It's a simultaneous process. Everyone whom God used had to go through this process.

God had to send Moses into the wilderness for forty years to unlearn everything he learned in Egypt during his first forty years. He was a very smart guy, a prince of Egypt, but that wasn't enough for the kingdom of God. He spent the next forty years in the wilderness unlearning everything he learned in Egypt. Then when God knew he was ready to do kingdom work, He appeared to him in the burning bush.

We all grew up in different cultures and religious backgrounds and had good and bad experiences in our upbringing. They all have to go so we can learn God's ways and how to trust Him as our Father. Moses was taught and trained in all the wisdom and skills of Egypt, but none of those skills helped him lead God's people out of bondage and through the wilderness.

Moses had to be completely "emptied" of all that he knew before God could release him to his destiny. For most of us, our worst enemy is what we already know. We don't know what we are supposed to know. We just know bits and pieces of many things. We often spend more time feeling confused and stuck than feeling on track, being productive and accomplishing our tasks. That's because of the upbringing we had. We were not taught about anything properly.

God wants to empty us, but we are actively trying to fill ourselves with more stuff. Almost every believer I know has a book by their side. On any given week or month, they find a new book and get excited about it. That excitement lasts only until they find the next one.

This has been going on for decades, and they have not made much progress in any area of their lives. They are constantly learning—but that learning is not benefitting them because they have not unlearned their old ways yet. Until they do that, nothing will change in their life for the better.

As the Word says, new wine cannot be poured into old wineskins. Wineskins represent our past experience and learning, or old mindsets, religious systems, traditions, and practices. They have to go if we are going to receive anything new from God.

It took forty years for Moses to do that. Most of us don't make it through the process. Many will not even begin the process. They just continue through life and die without entering the kingdom, even though they may have gone to church all their life. It took me twenty years to complete this process in my life.

Sometimes people come to me after reading one of my books and say they want the kingdom. I am thankful for that because it means they are seeking God's plan for their lives right now. However, too often the next thing they want is a ministry position with me, and they want to know how much I will pay them. That is when I realize that they do not truly understand my message.

I don't run a business, and my mission is not to make money or provide employment for others. My mission is to help more people discover God's kingdom and their assignment in it. And that is exactly what each of them needs to do: Seek God first and listen as He opens up their destiny in His kingdom.

THE EXAMPLE OF THE ISRAELITES

When the Israelites came out of Egypt, God took them to the wilderness. Why? He had to remove everything they learned in Egypt as slaves before He could take them to the Promised Land. That is why He took them to the wilderness. It took them forty years, as well. That is the whole purpose of the wilderness experience. Everyone has to go through it.

The Promised Land represents the kingdom of God. Egypt represents the kingdom of darkness, or this world system in which each of us grew up. We will not fulfill our kingdom destiny with the mindset formed in us as we grew up. Their journey to the Promised Land was the process of them seeking God's kingdom. That's how we seek God's kingdom. What happened to them is an example for us (1 Corinthians 10:6, 11).

Once you start the journey of seeking God's kingdom and His destiny in it for you, He will begin to supply what you need as He did for the people of Israel. We will have to trust His ways, as it may not come the way we expect, want, or are used to.

The Israelites were not willing to unlearn the ways of Egypt. They thought God was fighting against them by allowing them to face difficult circumstances. Every time they faced a challenge, they complained and murmured against God. They thought God left them, or that He was against them, or that He brought them to the wilderness to kill them. Have we ever felt the same? In truth, God had not left the Israelites. He was giving them opportunities to unlearn the old ways and learn the new way of trusting Him for their needs instead of the system of Egypt.

As slaves, they were fed daily in exchange for the work they were doing for Pharaoh. They knew that at a certain time each day their food would be provided by their taskmasters.

When they got to the wilderness, they ran out of food after three days. They panicked. It was a scary experience for them. Because they were afraid, they began to complain and murmur. They feared they were going to die. We might feel the same.

From God's perspective, He was giving them an opportunity to learn how to be fed from His kingdom and not depend on the world's system. They did not know what to do or how to do it. Their brains were frazzled trying to figure it out.

LEAVING GOD'S RESPONSIBILITIES TO HIM

Once you commit your life to Jesus and His kingdom assignment, it is *His responsibility* to provide for you and feed you. It is not based on your job or the money you earned. Today, many commit their lives to Jesus so they can go to heaven or gain material blessings, but they never commit themselves to His kingdom assignment. They go straight back into the world to support themselves. They become slaves to the world system. Many do not know that He has a kingdom assignment for them.

Jesus promises that if we seek first His kingdom and His righteousness, all the things we need will be added to us. The experience of the people of Israel is the best example we have. They all came out of Egypt through a great deliverance, which represents our salvation in Christ Jesus.

Coming out of Egypt or getting saved is not enough. That is only the first step. He saved them for a purpose. It is the same with us; He saved us for a reason. It was not just to take us to heaven when we die, but to fulfill His kingdom assignment right here on earth.

God brought His people out of Egypt to build His kingdom. He wanted them to be a kingdom of priests (Exodus 19:6). God wanted to establish a nation so that His praise and glory would be made known to the ends of the earth through them.

It was God's responsibility to feed, protect, and provide for them. Once we are saved and commit our lives to doing His will, it is His responsibility to provide and protect us. But this is not what we have been taught; we learned to *mumble* a little "Jesus loves me" prayer and wait to go to heaven the next day. Lord, have mercy!

In the wilderness, God was helping His people transition from Egypt to His kingdom. They had to leave the ways of Egypt and learn the ways of His kingdom. This meant they had to stop depending on Egypt for their sustenance and start depending on His kingdom for their provision by believing and trusting in the promises He gave them.

This is not an easy process for us. It doesn't sound easy as I write this here. We will run for our lives when He turns off the provision of Egypt! When there's no money left in the account and no food in the kitchen, it will scare the life out of us and we will feel like kicking and screaming. It was not easy for the Israelites to go through this process, either. Each time it happened, they wanted to go back to Egypt.

But each of us has to go through this; otherwise, we will never enter the kingdom of God. We can sing all day long and do all kinds of religious stuff, but nothing will be a substitute for the unlearning process. There is no shortcut to get us through the wilderness faster. If we try that, we will sabotage the entire process and our lives.

The Israelites were very accustomed to the system and ways of Egypt. They knew when their lunch would be ready and what would be served. Everything was scheduled and regimented for them. In the wilderness, they didn't know what was on the menu, when it would be ready, or where it was going to come from. Total trust in God was needed. Their flesh fought this way of life. In truth, they were fighting for control: control of their lives, circumstances, and futures. However, only God is in charge of all that.

God gave them forty years to unlearn what they knew before and learn His ways, but the majority didn't make it through. Only two passed the test and obtained the promise. We think about their lives and feel sad for them. However, we are going through the same process in our lives.

THE DISCIPLES HAD TO UNLEARN

When Jesus called His disciples, they had to go through this process. No one is exempted. Jesus met Peter at the seashore. He was washing his nets to go home. Jesus was preaching by the shore and a great multitude was around Him.

After preaching, Jesus asked Peter to move the boat back into the water, so that He could sit and teach some more. Peter had to wait until Jesus was done. Keep in mind that Peter was tired. He toiled all night and had not caught any fish. I believe he was tired, frustrated, and unhappy and this stranger just showed up and asked to use his boat for free to preach to a crowd. He might have thought, *Nobody uses a fishing boat to preach to people.* That was the beginning of the unlearning experience for Peter.

When you are tired and frustrated, you won't feel like helping someone else, but Peter passed that test. He wanted to go home and rest because he had not slept yet. He had worked all night the previous night. He didn't want to leave his boat with a total stranger, so now he had to wait patiently until Jesus was done.

When Jesus finished His preaching, He told Peter to launch the net into the deep for a catch. This was Peter's payment for letting Him use his boat. Nobody does anything for God without receiving a reward.

Peter said, "Lord, we toiled all night and did not catch anything." There are a couple of things we can understand from that sentence. First, Peter was thinking, *Lord, I worked all night, and I did not catch anything. I am tired and sleepy. I just want to go home and rest.* The second is his honesty. He didn't say, "Lord, I toiled all night, and all I could catch was a few puny fish." He didn't try to put any trust or merits in his accomplishments, his experience, or his flesh. He made a transition from self-righteousness to His righteousness at that moment.

Peter was completely honest about his current life situation. Being honest with ourselves and with others is a big lesson and a key to learning. I meet people all the time who do not want to admit that they made a mistake or need help, or that they are not accomplishing what they hoped they would.

They will bring up an excuse or talk about some "tiny" fish they caught fifty years ago. That choice is not helping them or their family. They boast about past accomplishments or where they have been. In truth, their trust is in their own flesh.

Another major thing we need to understand here is that fishermen did not fish during the day. They went at night. Jesus was asking Peter to do something that was totally against his tradition, experience, and knowledge. He was not new to the fishing business. He had been doing this business for years, possibly even for generations. Their fathers were with them, and it is possible they were working in their father's business.

Peter did not tell Jesus, "Do you know how many years I have been doing this? I know every wave and type of fish in this lake! I have walked over every grain of sand on this shore. I grew up here. I know where the fish move and when the time is right to cast my net for a catch—and this is not it!"

Peter could have said all kinds of things based on his pride, ego and experience. He could have said, "You know, sir, we have been in this business for many generations. My great-grandfather was the one who caught the biggest trout ever from this lake. I still have his picture framed in my house holding that fish. We never go to fishing during the day. No one does! It is really stupid even to try." Have you said or heard similar statements?

And then there is the fact that Jesus was a carpenter by trade. He may not have caught even a single fish in His entire life. Here He was giving advice to an experienced fisherman about how and when to fish. However, Peter was open to receive advice. He did not let his pride get in the way. He was teachable.

Jesus helped Peter unlearn all his experiences and learning in one event. Peter answered, "Lord, at Your word, I will do this." Peter did not rely on his own strength, experience, or tradition. He was willing to do something he may have never done before. This is the key to everything in the kingdom. When God says something, when He speaks through someone, you must be open to receive and obey, not brag about your accomplishments, experience, traditions, or family names.

Peter received the biggest catch of fish in his entire life that day. But he refused anything to stop him from walking out his kingdom destiny. He left everything behind and followed Jesus.

Peter passed all the tests and entered the kingdom that day. He did not have to wander around in the wilderness for forty years. What took forty years for the people of Israel, he passed in one day. His kingdom destiny was released immediately, and the rest is history.

Many people use Peter as an example for talking too much or being impulsive. They do not realize what Peter went through and what he accomplished with his life. Those people who make fun of him are still stuck in religion.

GETTING RID OF THE FORMER LIFE

That unlearning has to happen in each one of our lives if we are going to enter the kingdom of God. Everything we are and everything we learned: Our education, pride, *churchianity*, and family heredity has to be left at the door before we can enter the kingdom of God.

Many people search for their heredity, tracing it to some dead old kings in Europe. They say they are in the same lineage of a king who lived hundreds of years ago. Many of these people are barely surviving. They do not own anything, but they take pride in being related to this dead king from the past. Meanwhile, when they were born again, they were adopted into a royal family and made *living* kings and priests by God Almighty. They do not take that seriously.

What is stopping you from entering the kingdom? What do you need to unlearn? What do you need to get rid of? Compared to the kingdom, nothing else is worth more in the end. Do not show any mercy to those things that hold you back; throw them all into the dumpster. That is what Peter and Paul did when they met Jesus. They did not worry about their reputation or how they would support themselves the next day. They threw themselves into the hands of Jesus.

When Paul met Jesus, he had to unlearn everything he knew from before. He later wrote that he considered all of it dung for the "excellency" of the knowledge of Jesus Christ. Everything he had learned up to that point became rubbish to him. It was nothing but trash (Philippians 3:8).

When you meet Jesus, everything you considered worthwhile in your former life will become trash, and trash needs to be thrown out. Nobody keeps trash as a trophy in their living room. It will stink up the whole house. Many do not get rid of it, so they never enter the kingdom. They walk around holding their trophies for many years and are not willing to let go of anything.

Why does God want us to unlearn everything? His intention is to restore us to His original plan. We are created in His image and likeness. That is how we are supposed to function. However, all the junk we learned from our upbringing, religion, school, culture, movies, and the like have brainwashed us.

We do not know how to function like God. God's image and likeness in us has been marred and distorted. Through the born-again experience, He wants to restore us to how we were created to function originally. He wants to "reset" us: That's the whole purpose for getting saved. That is why the Bible tells us this:

> Therefore, if anyone is in Christ, he is a new creation; old things have passed away; behold, all things have become new. *(2 Corinthians 5:17)*

God accomplishes this is through something I call "divine interruptions." God comes in and interrupts our normal schedules. Things we thought would work out well do not work anymore. Suddenly, things change. The income you had before disappears. The friends and people you relied on walk away from you.

Very basic things that were easy become difficult. These are the signs of divine interruptions designed to teach us His ways. We might be minding our own business and hoping to live a peaceful, normal life, but all of a sudden, situations and circumstances get thrown into our lives that totally disrupt and turn our lives upside down.

It's not easy to discern God's ways in every circumstance. Some of them are very painful and will not make any sense to our natural minds for a very long time. Do you think what Job went through made sense to him? He experienced the death of all of his children and lost everything he owned in one day! That does not appear good on the outside. There's no way to explain those things in the natural. Why do such things happen?

What if one of our children is born with a special need? How do we reconcile good versus evil? How do we decipher the goodness of God in something that is considered an act of evil? If we hang in there and do not become bitter, keeping an open ear to learn what God is trying to teach us, it will all make sense in the end.

PUT AN END TO THE OLD

The rest of Jesus's teachings in the Gospels were geared to help people unlearn what they learned from the Old Testament. That is why He would say things like this:

> You have heard that it was said to those of old, "You shall not murder, and whoever murders will be in danger of the judgment." But I say to you that whoever is angry with his brother without a cause shall

> be in danger of the judgment. And whoever says to his brother, "Raca!" shall be in danger of the council. But whoever says, "You fool!" shall be in danger of hell fire. *(Matthew 5:21–22)*

He was unlearning the old and replacing it with the new.

Unfortunately, many people come to the kingdom knowing "everything." It takes them a few years to unlearn all that through mistakes and trials, and eventually they realize that they'd better get some help. Many think that walking down the aisle of a church and repeating a prayer will get them into the kingdom. Jesus didn't tell Nicodemus that. He didn't lead Nicodemus in a sinner's prayer so he could be born again and enter the kingdom of God. There is no evidence of that in the Bible.

Jesus simply said, "Be born again!" It is a new beginning. You have to let go of everything you have learned and experienced prior to this new experience. Nicodemus knew too much about the law; he was a teacher, but he didn't know God. However, he was a wise man; that is why He came to Jesus seeking help. Others in his day perished in their pride and ignorance, even though they thought they knew God.

The first requirement for having a new beginning is to put an end to the old. If you don't put an end to the old, you cannot start a new thing. Many do not put an end to the old. Instead, they drag the old into the new, and then they can't tell the difference between the two. The Israelites did that when they came out of Egypt. They couldn't let go of their old memories and experiences of Egypt, and they got destroyed in the wilderness.

This is why Jesus said to come to Him and learn from Him (Matthew 11:29). God's ways and thoughts are higher than our ways, as high as the heaven is above the earth. Before we can learn from Jesus, we have to unlearn everything we know. God never starts a new thing until He puts an end to the old.

THE ENEMY'S DECEPTIONS

I was having lunch with a dear friend of mine and he said something that startled me. He said that most young Americans lose their mind when they are fifteen and regain it when they are thirty. What a deception! What a loss! There is nothing more demonic than that. During the prime time in which a person is supposed to focus on their purpose and develop their gifts, they are serving the devil or doing nonsense instead.

The more self-reliant and stubborn you are, the longer it takes to unlearn what you learned.

To be born again means to start fresh once again. That means everything you did and learned until that moment has to be declared null and void. You cannot depend on the old and try to navigate in God's kingdom with that mindset. It won't work because you are operating in two different kingdoms.

This world system and its ways are opposite to the kingdom of God. Nothing even comes close. The enemy will try to make you believe they are all the same, and even that maybe his ways are a little better and easier than God's. They might seem easier in the beginning, but they are not better in any way. The Bible says that there is way that seems good to a man, but its end is destruction (Proverbs 14:12).

The enemy will only show you the good side of the Tree of the Knowledge of Good and Evil. He will not show you the evil attached to it first. He will try to lure you with the good, and the end will be destruction.

Joseph had to be thrown into prison to unlearn some of his natural ways and learn God's ways. We do not learn God's ways in a school. We are taught God's ways by learning to be led by the Holy Spirit. God is trying to empty you so that there will be nothing in you to trust. The only thing you will have left to trust is Him and His Word.

THE BATTLE WITHIN

We are trying to fill ourselves, and God is trying to empty us. That's the struggle we feel. It is a battle between the flesh and the spirit. The more you allow God to empty you, the more He can fill you with Himself.

Sometimes I go into a frantic mode when I get ready to preach or minister somewhere because I have no idea what I am going to say or what I am going to do. I don't prepare messages ahead. Instead, I receive them from the Lord and deliver His words to the people for that particular meeting. I don't prepare "ready-made" sermons. Sometimes He doesn't give me anything until the last minute. As a result, the natural man feels anxious and nervous. What if God doesn't show up? What if I don't have anything to say? Will I look like a fool in front of others?

Those are all the thoughts of my natural man or the flesh. I can tell you God has never failed me—not even once. The truth is that it gets better each time in some ways, but harder for the flesh. In the spirit, we grow from glory to glory. The more you can learn to trust in God and allow Him to flow through you, the more you will experience real freedom and fulfillment and true ministry. But it's a scary place for the flesh.

The Bible says that those who trust in the flesh or men are cursed (Jeremiah 17:5). Our only trust is supposed to be in God Almighty. May the Lord help us to empty ourselves and trust Him. At the wedding in Cana when the wine ran out, six empty water pots were left. Jesus told them to fill them with water. Water represents the Word. When you fill your life with the Word, Jesus will turn it into wine that will quench other people's thirst and satisfy their souls. What a beautiful picture!

Those water pots represent us; we need to let God fill us with His Word. That's what happened to me. When I was young boy of fifteen or sixteen, I read the Word whenever I could. Today, everything I read when I was younger is emerging as wine to bless others. Remember that it takes time to make wine in the natural. In Cana, Jesus overrode the time limit and made instant wine—and it was excellent. Normally it would have taken years to produce a vintage of that quality.

Now let's see how God helps us go through this process of unlearning so we can enter His kingdom.

CHAPTER 11

SEVEN ENTRANCES TO THE KINGDOM OF GOD

She cries out by the gates, at the entry of the city, at the entrance of the doors. (Proverbs 8:3)

Why are there seven entrances to the kingdom of God? What do I mean by entrances? The fall of Adam caused significant damage to every area of our lives. This was especially true of the image and likeness of God in us, as well as our minds and how we think about God, ourselves, and the earth. In order for us to enter into God's kingdom, it is necessary for us to regain our true nature and our minds need to be renewed.

To help us with this process, God placed seven principles in His Word to which each of us needs to adhere. Each of those principles is an "entrance" back into the image and likeness of God, because the Bible uses that word in reference to each of them. It says that unless we do them, we shall by no means "enter the kingdom."

With these seven principles come seven tests to help us apply them in our lives. Each of us will be tested with seven tests in seven areas of our lives. To know more about these seven tests we will go through, please read *Keys to Passing Your Spiritual Tests: Kingdom Secrets to Your Spiritual Promotion*. I have written extensively about these tests and go through each one and how to pass them in that book. It's a manual for life.

This is not something you can learn in a classroom. You will not take a written test after hearing a lesson or get through this in a church on a Sunday morning. You will have to experience this in real life, and those tests are much harder to pass than a written test because we will face them when we least expect them.

When I say there are seven entrances to the kingdom of God, I do not mean there are seven steps to salvation or going to heaven. There are seven principles mentioned in the New Testament that we need to apply to our lives for us to enter the kingdom of God here and now. This is to restore our original image and likeness to live in God's kingdom. This is something we experience in this life.

Each of these principles are geared toward helping us overcome a negative tendency that came into us because of the fall, a tendency or a defect in our nature, which keeps people out of the kingdom of God. God is trying to reverse that process and restore our original identity and nature. Jesus mentioned five of these principles, and the sixth and seventh ones are mentioned by Paul and Peter respectively. We are going to look at them one by one.

In this chapter, we will go through six of them, and I dedicated a whole next chapter for the seventh.

I. THE SOURCE OF OUR RIGHTEOUSNESS

> For I say to you, that unless your righteousness exceeds the righteousness of the scribes and Pharisees, you will by no means *enter* the kingdom of heaven. *(Matthew 5:20)*

This says that unless our righteousness *exceeds* the righteousness of the Pharisees, *we shall not enter the kingdom*. The Pharisees were one of the most religious Jewish sects in Jesus's time. They would swallow an elephant in an attempt to filter a mosquito. That means they followed the letter of the law to its fullest but they lost the whole purpose behind it, which was to love God and show grace and mercy to people.

They believed in their own righteousness—one based on works, their appearance, and their words. They gave tithes to the temple on everything they possessed. They would not walk by a leper, fearing they should also become unclean. They lived and died the Old Testament Law like no one else could.

However, Jesus said our righteousness had to be greater than theirs to enter His kingdom! How would we do that? What does that mean? Do we have to do greater righteous works than they? Do we have to follow the Law more strictly than they did? Do we have to wear holy robes?

I do not believe any of those requirements will answer our problem. Jesus said very clearly that we need to seek first "His kingdom and His righteousness." I believe the answer is right there. Jesus said we cannot enter the kingdom if we depend on our righteousness earned by doing good works or keeping the Law of Moses. If it were so, Scripture would contradict itself because the Bible says our righteousness is like filthy rags before God (Isaiah 64:6).

The only righteousness that exceeds the righteousness of the Pharisees is the righteousness of God Himself! How do we receive it? Simple: God bestows His righteousness freely upon everyone who believes in the Lord Christ Jesus. We cannot enter the kingdom based on our works, our appearance, or by the long prayers we pray.

The Bible says that no one is justified by the works of the law, and that if anyone still depends on the works of the law, he or she is under a curse (Galatians 3:10; Romans 3:20, 28; Philippians 3:9).

> But now the righteousness of God apart from the law is revealed, being witnessed by the Law and the Prophets, even the righteousness of God, through faith in Jesus Christ, to all and on all who believe. For there is no difference. *(Romans 3:21–22)*

It is very difficult to accept the fact that God will declare a sinner righteous because He believes in Christ. Our natural mind will not accept this, and we tend to add some work to it to feel better about ourselves. It is because of our fallen human nature that we try to look good in front of others and do good things to feel better.

We naturally want to base our acceptance with God and other people on our deeds. The world's entire religious system is geared toward one thing: encouraging people to do good things so they can escape the wrath of God or the gods they believe in.

The Bible is the only book that teaches righteousness by faith. It teaches that God accepts a person not based on their *works*, but on their *faith*—and faith alone. God does this because it's not our fault personally that we were born in sin. Unfortunately, it is difficult for people to believe and receive the free gift of God.

They are ignorant of the fact that they have already been accepted by God, and all they need to do is believe (Romans 5:8, 10). Jesus came to declare the acceptable year of the Lord. What does that mean? He came to declare that God was not angry at people. Instead, He accepts them and loves them for who they are, not based on their works.

All of humanity (except Adam) became sinful not by their own choice. The Bible says that one man's disobedience made everyone a sinner, and that through one man's obedience, God declared everyone righteous (Romans 5:18). So if you want to enter the kingdom, do not boast of your achievements, or ability, or any of your personal qualifications, but receive the free gift and walk in it humbly.

> For by grace you have been saved through faith, and that not of yourselves; it is the gift of God, not of works, lest anyone should boast. *(Ephesians 2:8–9)*

Jesus did the work for us and paid the price for our freedom. What liberty God has provided for us! Does that mean we don't need to do anything good because we have been freely declared as righteous? God forbid. Good works are a foundational teaching of the Bible. What matters now is the heart and reason behind what we do. We do not do good works *to be* accepted by God; we do good works because we *are* accepted by God.

Righteous people do righteous works. Righteous works do not make an unrighteous person righteous. In Paul's letters, it is interesting to see how often Paul encourages the leaders and believers to be involved in good works. (See Romans 2:10, 13:3; Ephesians 2:10; 1 Timothy 2:10, and many others.)

If you have any questions about this point, refer back to the chapter called "Seek His Righteousness" earlier in this book.

II. KNOWING AND DOING GOD'S WILL

> Not everyone who says to Me, "Lord, Lord," shall *enter* the kingdom of heaven, but he who does the will of My Father in heaven. *(Matthew 7:21)*

Once you accept Christ and are born again, you have a special assignment from God; it is the will of God or the call of God for your life. There are three dimensions to the will of God.

The first is to obey the Word of God, which is the *revealed will of God*. This is general for all believers and there is no distinction. We are all commanded to obey the Word, regardless of our circumstances or status. God has a will for every area of your life. The Word teaches us about family, finances, raising children, and relationships. God has written about what to do and not do in everything that pertains to life in His Word. If we reject the Word, we are rejecting God, because the Word is God. When you receive the Word and respect it as God's Word, God will reveal the next dimension of His will.

The second is the *specific will of God*. We are all different members of the same body. Each member in our bodies has a specific function. Our legs cannot do what our eyes can do, and the eyes cannot do what the ears can do. It is the same in the body of Christ. We are all different members of the same body with different functions. God created each individual uniquely and with a distinctive calling and gifts.

Millions of people are out there working hard and trying to serve God. They are busy from morning till evening, weeks on end, working for God through all kinds of duties and performance. That is not what God expects from us. The only thing He is expecting from us is that we discover His will, do it, and then go to heaven when we die.

There are others who are trying hard to become miracle workers. They believe that if they can just perform some miracles, they will achieve a higher level of significance and attract people's attention and respect. They are focused on receiving offerings and building a ministry. Jesus calls them workers of lawlessness.

Some of the scariest verses of the entire New Testament are these:

> Many will say to Me in that day, "Lord, Lord, have we not prophesied in Your name, cast out demons in Your name, and done many wonders in Your name?" And then I will declare to them, "I never knew you; depart from Me, you who practice lawlessness!" *(Matthew 7:22–23)*

It is the responsibility of each person to find out what his or her specific calling is and to fulfill it. We do not see God using two people the same way in the Bible. God does not call all of us the same way or to do the same thing. Note that Jesus said the abovementioned verses after He spoke about doing the will of God to enter His kingdom. If casting out demons, prophesying, and doing wonders in His name are not considered necessarily His will, then what is His will? We will discuss that below.

The third dimension is the *eternal will of God*. God's heart is to see His kingdom to manifest on earth and for His will to be done on earth as it is in heaven. That's why Jesus said, "who does the will of My Father in heaven" in Matthew 7:21. The Father's will is to see His kingdom established on the earth

Now the question is this: How do we discover God's will for our lives? God's heart is to see His kingdom to manifest on earth and for His will to be done on earth as it is in heaven. Everything else God does is to accomplish that one single and the most important will He has. Each individual He sends to earth was sent to accomplish that single goal. However, we all do this in different ways in levels.

When we are born again, we *see* His kingdom, and He gives us vision regarding our individual mission here. Romans 12:2 says that when we completely yield our bodies as a living sacrifice to Him, we will know the good and acceptable and perfect will of God.

Our bodies were given to us to enable us to do the will of God on the earth. However, because of our sinful nature, our bodies were consumed by various kinds of lusts and passions that took them in many directions. It is often too late to submit our bodies to God as they get destroyed over time by age or sickness.

III. BECOMING CHILDREN AGAIN

> Then Jesus called a little child to Him, set him in the midst of them, and said, "Assuredly, I say to you, unless you are converted and become as little children, you will by no means *enter* the kingdom of heaven." *(Matthew 18:2–3)*

Why did Jesus say we had to be converted and become as little children to enter the kingdom of heaven? I always wondered about that. Then God gave me three precious children, and I began to learn from them. We can gain great wisdom from children. Our sinful natures get worse the longer we live on this earth. However, there is a form of innocence and godliness in most children before they reach the age of accountability and begin to know sin.

Children don't come into this world understanding mathematics. They must learn what one plus one is. We teach them that. They do not know what love or forgiveness means either. They have to learn almost everything. By the time we become adults, we are already programmed, but not according to God's kingdom and His ways.

That is why Jesus said we needed to be "converted" and become like children again in order to enter the kingdom. We have to unlearn everything we had previously learned, and replace it with kingdom ways. The kingdom doesn't operate in the same way we were raised according to our culture and family. Life in the kingdom begins by "unlearning" everything we learned. It is an upside-down kingdom. That is why He gave us another chance to be "born again."

We dealt with this in detail in the "Unlearning Process" Chapter. To understand the kingdom, we need to go back to Genesis again. We often think we know what the Bible says, but we don't. If we did, we would have understood about His kingdom from the time we first followed Jesus.

We were taught religion, not kingdom living, and we have to unlearn almost everything. When our spirit man came into our mother's womb, it came with the blueprint of our destiny. Everything concerning our lives was written in the DNA of our spirit. Instead of receiving and training our spirit, we were brainwashed by others teaching us the ways of this world, its culture, and about a religion (Christianity or another religion).

When we discover the kingdom of God, we need to undo and unlearn everything. We must begin fresh and learn the ways of God again. We rediscover the DNA of our spirits and follow God's plan for our lives. This is why Jesus said we needed to become like little children. Children are eager to learn and experience new things.

Kingdom life is more about unlearning first than learning. Sometimes we get so passionate about the kingdom that we try to learn more, but our first step when we discover God's kingdom must be to *unlearn* everything we learned prior to that before we learn anything new.

If we do not unlearn before we start learning about the kingdom, the old religious stuff in our minds will choke the word of the kingdom and it will not produce the fruit it is supposed to bear. Every time we hear the Word, we get excited, but that excitement will not last when the old junk surfaces and swallows up what we heard about the kingdom of God.

When we are born again, we are born into God's kingdom as little children. There are different words in Greek that are used for children and sons. In John 1:12, we read that to "as many as received" Jesus and believed in His name God gave the "right to become children of God." The Greek word used for "children" in that verse is *teknon*, which means "a little child."[7] We don't come into the kingdom as adults; we have a lot of growing to do.

QUALITIES OF CHILDREN

Let's study some of the qualities possessed by children to help us understand the reason Jesus said this. There is a difference between being childlike and childish. God does not want us to be child*ish*, but child*like*. Here are some of their qualities:

Innocence: Children are not judgmental of people. We should not be judging others, so that we will not be judged (Matthew 7:1–2).

Imitation: Children imitate whatever their parents, siblings, or their friends do. We need to imitate our heavenly Father as dear children (Ephesians 5:1).

Forgiving: If we offend a child or discipline them, it does not stay in their mind for too long. They forget offenses and do not keep today's offenses for tomorrow. I wish I were like that. We need to forgive others easily and not harbor the offenses in our hearts (Matthew 6:14–15).

Eager to learn: They are inquisitive. They are always open to learn new things and go new places. We need to be willing to learn new things when we come into the kingdom. Be teachable (Matthew 11:29).

---

[7] James Strong, "Teknon," Strong's Greek: 5043. τέκνον (teknon) — a child (of either sex) (Biblehub), accessed May 5, 2020, https://biblehub.com/greek/5043.htm)

Sensitive: Though they forget offenses easily, they will get offended if they are treated badly. They are tender and also sensitive to the treatment of others. We need to be sensitive to the Holy Spirit like little children are (1 Thessalonians 5:19).

Content: You can spend hours with them and they will never get tired of you. We need to be like that with our Father, and content with what we have while we are working towards the mark of our high calling (Philippians 4:11; 1 Timothy 6:8; Hebrews 13:5).

Quick to make new friends: Children have a special discernment to know people. If they discern that a person is safe, they will make friends easily. We need to be friendly and make new friends to share the gospel of the kingdom with (Hebrews 13:2).

Quick to believe: It doesn't take much to make a child believe in something. If I tell my three-year-old that there is an elephant behind the couch, she will believe it. We need to believe God's Word, just like little children believe what we tell them (Mark 5:36).

No concept of worry: Children do not worry about tomorrow; neither are they anxious about their present circumstances. We should not be worrying about tomorrow (Matthew 6:31, 34).

They are always joyful: Children are always joyful. It takes an adult to make them stop being joyful. We need to live in the culture of the kingdom, which is righteousness, peace, and joy in the Holy Spirit (Romans 14:17).

Pure and undefiled: Children speak from their heart. They don't have any concept of sin or wrongdoing. We shouldn't be deceitful, but have a pure heart toward God and others (Matthew 5:8).

Forgets things easily: We need to keep reminding a child the same things again and again. Once we confess our sins to God we should also forget them and stop keep going back rehearsing the memories

(Philippians 3:13). The Bible says we need to exhort each other daily (Hebrews 3:13) to be in faith and walk in love.

Easily excited and happy: It doesn't take much to make a child happy. When God speaks, we should be excited to listen to Him (1 Peter 1:13–15).

Needing constant training: A child needs to be taught how to live. Human beings are not born with the ability to survive as some other animals are. If a newborn does not have a parent or someone to care for them, they will die.

Kingdom living involves life-long learning. Similarly, when we come into the kingdom of God, we need to be taught about this new way of living. We come in like a little child and need to learn the ways of God in order to prosper. A new believer needs to be taught about everything when he or she comes into the kingdom of God (1 Peter 2:2).

They have no fear: Children do not have a concept of fear like adults. Their fear is superficial; when an adult tells them to do something, they will believe it and do it. The Bible says God has not given us a spirit of fear, but of power, love, and a sound mind (2 Timothy 1:7). We shouldn't fear the enemy or the people of this world.

Some say that the Bible renders the thought, *do not fear!* in different ways 365 times—one for each day of the year. I do not know if that is true, but that thread is certainly present. God is constantly comforting His people and encouraging them to trust Him and not be afraid. If there is one thing that hinders us from living the life God called us to live, it is the spirit of fear.

Children will ask for anything: They are famous for asking questions about anything and everything. They will ask for a million dollars, even though they have no concept of what it means to have a million dollars. Similarly, we are commanded to ask for anything we need in our lives. God told Jeremiah to call upon Him and He would answer him and show him great and mighty things of which he had no knowledge (Jeremiah 33:3). That promise still stands for us today. Jesus told us to ask and we will receive (Matthew 7:7). When we ask God for something, we should ask Him with childlike faith.

Children are energetic: Children are full of energy and vitality. We should live and serve God with excitement and not as a chore (Psalm 100:2).

Take some time and have a group discussion on the following points. Jot down how these common qualities found in children apply to us as God's children too.

- Imaginative
- Full of love
- Free and unencumbered
- Truthful
- They do not judge others based on their appearance
- They will are big-hearted, and will do anything you ask them to do
- They are always pretending to be somebody great
- They are fun to be with
- Very creative
- They have no concept of sin
- They are willing to share with those they love
- They need to be trained and taught constantly about everything in life
- They require adult supervision

We learned from the chapter on the unlearning process that God wishes to accomplish this in each one of us.

WE HAVE TO BE TAUGHT

Humans are the only species that need to be taught about everything. Other creatures have a natural instinct to do certain things, but humans need to be taught almost everything: how to eat, what to eat, how to walk, how to clean themselves, how to brush their teeth, and so on. When a child reaches five or six years of age, he or she goes to school for the next twelve or fifteen years to learn more. Similarly, when we come into the kingdom, we don't come into it knowing anything. Being born again gives us a fresh start.

When a child is born, he or she doesn't understand anything about their nation or their ethnicity. They learn all that as they grow up. When we come into the kingdom, we must surrender all that stuff to King Jesus.

We become citizens of God's kingdom and part of a worldwide community and family. Each of us is a "new creation" and a "kingdom citizen," and we are holy. We have been made holy unto the Lord. We no longer judge people based on their color, race, or nationality. We are all citizens of the same kingdom, members of the same family, and children of the same Father.

Everything we were taught by this world's economy is also unlearned and gives way to the kingdom economy. When the disciples met Jesus the first time, they left their boats and nets and followed Him (Matthew 4:20). That meant they had to depend on Jesus and His kingdom for their next meal and every one after that. They had to trust Jesus.

They did not ask Him for six months to go and discuss the possibility of following Him with their family. They did not go off and work to save as much money as they could until Jesus's ministry grew and could support them with a monthly salary. They were not concerned about saving to pay the bills. None of that works in the kingdom.

We either find our livelihood in God and His kingdom or we do not. Either we trust in ourselves or we trust in the God of the universe to provide for us.

All religious knowledge about the church must be replaced with a kingdom-based understanding. If we try to enter the kingdom with our old church mindset, it will backfire, and we will get hurt instead of being blessed.

That is what it means to be converted and become like little children. We will not enter the kingdom of God if we are not converted. We should be willing to learn God's ABCs.

That is what happened to me when I discovered the kingdom of God. I had to leave everything behind, as you read in the beginning of this book. May the Lord help us to know what to leave behind and the wisdom to know how and when to do it!

IV. RECEIVING THE KINGDOM AS A LITTLE CHILD

> Assuredly, I say to you, whoever does not receive the kingdom of God as a little child will by no means enter it. *(Mark 10:15)*

There are three ways to interpret this. One is that we need to receive the kingdom as a little child receives something from his or her parents. Children get excited when they realize they are going to receive a gift. They don't look at the price tag as some of us do. Little things can cause them to be excited and happy.

Children don't think about all the details. They are not concerned about where it came from and what is going to happen to that gift. They live for the moment. Life in the kingdom is unpredictable. Do you remember when Peter and his brother, Andrew, left their business and followed Jesus immediately? They did not ask Jesus what they were going to eat the next day. They did not inquire as to where they would be staying that night. They were not concerned about how much money they would make. They received the kingdom as little children received a gift. We should do the same.

God is offering us the most precious gift anyone could ever receive: His prosperous kingdom. The reward for leaving what we own and receiving His kingdom assignment is worthwhile. However, we will lose His kingdom opportunities if we are still holding onto what we have. The stakes are high.

The second way to interpret this is that when we receive *other* people into the kingdom, we have to receive them *as we receive a little child*. Children are wonderful, but they will mess things up and often run inside with dirty hands, muddy feet, and soiled clothing. We need to have patience to help people get cleaned up, just as we would help little children.

The third interpretation is my favorite. Jesus is also saying that we need to receive the kingdom as we receive a little child. Wow! When the Lord opened my understanding to that verse, I felt like shouting. A little child is full of surprises. So is the kingdom. When you receive the kingdom, it comes to you like little child, but no one likes to remain a little child forever. That "little child" actually refers to a newborn baby.

A newborn baby is full of untapped and undeveloped potential. You cannot predict everything that child will do or what that child is going to become. Kingdom life is unpredictable, too. However, it has an amazing destination in mind for each of us, and one that will fulfill us like nothing else ever could.

From the moment we receive the kingdom, we start to grow, and the kingdom begins to grow. We never stop learning, and the kingdom will never stop growing, either. The moment you stop learning and growing, you will be done with life, and will be out of the game.

I tell my coworkers that we are in a constant state of innovation. By the time they finish editing a book, I already have new version of that book within my heart. The Lord continually gives me more to add to my books. I keep learning and growing. Kingdom living is a moment-by-moment experience, not a once-a-week Sunday morning ritual.

It's not easy to bring up a child into maturity. We have to struggle and pay a price. When we receive the kingdom, we go through struggles and pain to unlearn, and then acquire the new things the Lord wants us to teach us.

It is important that we keep our minds and hearts open. The biggest enemy of God's kingdom is religion, and human or religious traditions. Every religion has its own default settings or programs on which they rely. For some reason, Christians think our traditions are superior to those of other religions. No, they are not. Our traditions are just as religious as that of the Hindus or Muslims.

Why do we sing three fast songs and two slow songs? Where is it written in the Bible that this is the way we should worship the Lord? Why do we say that this is the way God manifests? How many times have you seen God manifest in our services? I am not talking about having warm feelings.

How often have you seen a real manifestation of God Almighty in which He showed up and healed every deformity and disease? I am not talking about headaches and back pains. I am talking about the blind seeing and the lame walking. If you know of any place where this is happening, let me know. I would like to visit and be a part of it.

We need to receive the kingdom of God the same way we would receive a little child. We need to nurture it, care for it, and protect it, because the religious spirit will try again and again to steal the kingdom away from you. You need to be free from the religious spirit more than once. It will try to creep back in again after it leaves.

Jesus Himself said that when we hear the Word of the kingdom, Satan himself comes to try to steal that Word (Mark 4:15). Why does Satan come? Why doesn't he send a demon to do the job? When it comes to the kingdom of God, Satan gets involved. He does not trust any of his demons to do the job. He knows that if a person receives the kingdom of God and grows in it, he will lose his ground. He hates the message of the kingdom of God.

The church's ignorance about the kingdom of God is the only thing that is keeping the devil in business on earth. The moment believers worldwide receive the kingdom and begin to manifest it, the devil will be out of business in no time.

Satan will send a demon when he wants to afflict someone with sickness or a calamity, but he comes on his own to steal the Word of the kingdom.

Jesus shared two parables to prove how the kingdom grows and expands. One is the parable of the mustard seed.

> Another parable He put forth to them, saying: "The kingdom of heaven is like a mustard seed, which a man took and sowed in his field, which indeed is the least of all the seeds; but when it is grown it is greater than the herbs and becomes a tree, so that the birds of the air come and nest in its branches."
> *(Matthew 13:31–32)*

Like a mustard seed, the kingdom of God starts small within us and on the earth. It cannot remain the same once it is planted in a field. When the kingdom of God is planted in us, we are the field in which it is supposed to grow. When it grows, it becomes a tree and the birds of the air come and nest in its branches.

When the kingdom grows in us, others will notice and they want to become partakers of its benefit, too. They will come to learn from you and enjoy your fruit. It is impossible for the kingdom to remain the same; it is constantly expanding.

Scientists have discovered that the universe is constantly expanding, too. The Bible says that of the increase of His government and peace, there shall be no end. The moment we limit God and His kingdom, we will stop being effective on the earth for Him. The whole purpose of religion is to limit God and us. The kingdom does not do this.

The second parable Jesus shared about the expansion and growth of the kingdom is the parable of the leaven.

> Another parable He spoke to them: "The kingdom of heaven is like leaven, which a woman took and hid in three measures of meal till it was all leavened."
> *(Matthew 13:33)*

Leaven is a contagious element. Once you mix it with dough, you cannot remove it again. It will take over the whole dough just in a matter of time. That's the way the kingdom expands. Leaven expands horizontally, and a tree (think the parable of the mustard seed) grows vertically. The kingdom needs to grow vertically and horizontally until it fills the whole earth.

> For the earth will be filled with the knowledge of the glory of the Lord, as the waters cover the sea.
> *(Habakkuk 2:14)*

V. OUR WHOLE BEING NEEDS TO BE BORN AGAIN

> Jesus answered, "Most assuredly, I say to you, unless one is born of water and the Spirit, he cannot *enter* the kingdom of God." *(John 3:5)*

Jesus said unless we are born of water (the Word) and the Spirit (the Holy Spirit), we will not enter the kingdom. What does this mean? Man is a three-part being. When you receive Christ, your spirit is born again, and that is when you see the kingdom in your spirit. However, you have a soul and a body that need to be born again, too. That means they need to be aligned with your born-again spirit.

I have heard many people teach this incorrectly. Some say being born of water refers to the natural birth, as a baby comes out of the womb with water. That cannot be true here because entering the kingdom is something that happens *after* a person is born again. To be born again, a person needs to be naturally born and alive, so it is not talking about the natural birth.

A second misunderstanding is that this verse is referring to water baptism. The purpose of baptism is not to enter the kingdom. People do not enter the kingdom by being baptized. The purpose of baptism is to identify with the death, burial, and resurrection of Jesus Christ. Baptism exemplifies the burial process of the old man, which died when we were born again (Romans 6:4, 6).

Being born of water represents being born by the Word of God. The water represents the Word (Ephesians 5:26). Jesus taught on the rivers of living water flowing out of us, which is the Word of God. Once we are born again in the spirit, the next part that needs to be born again is the soul. Our souls needs to be washed and renewed with the Word of God. Our bodies also must be born again. We went over both of these at length earlier.

The moment we are born again in the spirit, God begins the process for our souls and bodies to become born again. Most people don't complete this process, just as the majority of the Israelites who came out of Egypt did not inherit the Promised Land and perished in the wilderness instead.

They were saved, but could not bring their souls and bodies under subjection to the will and plan of God. They saw the Promised Land (their destiny) in their spirits, but could not enter. It is easy to be born again in our spirits, but for our souls and bodies to come into alignment with the destiny God has for us will require that we die many deaths. We need to be crucified daily like the Bible says in Romans 6:6, as well as Galatians 2:20, 5:24, and 6:14.

Our Promised Land is the dimension of the kingdom of God we enter and experience here on earth. Our bodies need to come under the total submission and leading of the Holy Spirit because our bodies are the temple of the Holy Spirit (1 Corinthians 3:16; 6:19).

We have many believers in our churches who have been born again in the spirit, but their souls and bodies are still in captivity to the kingdom of darkness. I am sorry to say that they are not living in God's kingdom. It is not their fault; they were not taught correctly. That is why God allowed me to prepare this teaching.

As long as our minds and bodies have not gone through the process to manifest the life of the spirit, there won't be any difference between us and the unbelievers around us, except that we go to church every Sunday morning and speak "Christianese." Galatians 5:21 says that if we don't overcome the works of the flesh, we won't inherit the kingdom of God.

The lust of the flesh is not always sexual in nature. It refers to anything the natural body or the soul longs for to satisfy its longings other than God and His kingdom.

VI. TEST AND TRIALS—TAKING PART IN HIS SUFFERING

> And when they had preached the gospel to that city and made many disciples, they returned to Lystra,

> Iconium, and Antioch, strengthening the souls of the disciples, exhorting them to continue in the faith, and saying, "We must through many tribulations *enter* the kingdom of God." *(Acts 14:21–22)*

Suffering is part of what we go through in our transformation from a natural way of thinking to the kingdom way of thinking. There are three areas from which we can expect suffering and tribulation.

MENTAL AGONY AND STRESS

When we come into the kingdom, we come in with a mindset that was formed by this world. As we try to pull those strongholds down and renew our minds, we will experience pain because this is not an easy task. We are programmed to function in a particular manner. We think, speak, and act as we were trained to do. To change those into a new system will take time, practice, and much patience.

ATTACKS FROM DEMONIC FORCES

When you accept Christ and become a child of God, you will become a target of the enemy. As you become interested in the kingdom of God, his attacks will increase. The enemy will try to harass, deceive, and distract you in an effort to pull you back into the old fold. But know that you are victorious in Christ Jesus. I can guarantee that. It is a battle, and there will be casualties and days you are disappointed and feel like you want to quit. This is normal. Persist in believing and speaking in faith. Hold fast the confession of your faith.

ATTACKS FROM FAMILY, FELLOW BELIEVERS, AND UNBELIEVERS

People who do not understand you will try to oppose you and give you much pain. Always know that people are not your enemy. We do not fight against flesh and blood, but against spiritual forces. God will use everything you go through for your good in the end. As a preacher once said, "Everything in your life is either God-sent or God-used." As long as we live on this earth, we will have tribulation, but Jesus encouraged us, saying to be of good cheer because He had overcome the world (John 16:33).

Don't be deceived into believing some utopian teaching that tells you that when you receive Christ and become a child of God, you will no longer go through any challenges or trials. These deceivers will tell you that all you need is faith, and that once you are full of faith, you will not be affected by problems anymore. Such foolishness!

That teaching is not biblical. Everyone who lives a godly life in Christ Jesus will face persecution (2 Timothy 3:12). Everyone listed in the hall of fame of faith in Hebrews 11 went through enormous trials and challenges in their lives. Some died for their faith.

It has been given to us, not only to believe in Jesus, but to suffer for His name (Philippians 1:29). As long as we live on this earth, both blessing and challenges will be part of our lives. There is no way to escape this.

CHAPTER 12

THE SEVENTH ENTRANCE TO THE KINGDOM

VII. MAKING YOUR CALLING SURE

> *Therefore, brethren, be even more diligent to make your call and election sure, for if you do these things you will never stumble; for so an entrance will be supplied to you abundantly into the everlasting kingdom of our Lord and Savior Jesus Christ. (2 Peter 1:10–11)*

The seventh entrance is to make sure of exactly what you are called to do, and to know your assignment in the kingdom. These verses say we need to be diligent to make our calling and election sure. Nowhere does it say that we need to be diligent to make our purpose sure, because our purpose was already made clear by God in Genesis 1:26. Nothing can be added or changed in that.

IF YOU ARE SAVED, YOU ARE CALLED

To fulfill God's purpose for our lives, when we are born again, each of us receives a calling so we know in which sphere we are supposed to fulfill our purpose. There are various types of calling. Moses was called to be a deliverer, Peter was called to be an apostle, and Joseph was called to be a prime minister. Whatever you are called to do in the kingdom is your ministry. Ministry is not always preaching from a pulpit or helping the poor.

Everybody has a different type of calling to fulfill the same purpose God has for every human being, which is to have dominion over the earth on some level.

GOD CALLS US ACCORDING TO HIS PURPOSE

Believe it or not, there is specific call of God on your life. A *calling* is an act of God. Through it, He releases you to fulfill your destiny in His kingdom.

God calls us according to His purpose, which He decided in Christ Jesus before the world began. The Bible relates our calling with God's purpose, which means that anytime it refers to our calling, it will mesh with His purpose for mankind. We are called according to His purpose.

> And we know that all things work together for good to those who love God, to those who are the called according to His purpose. *(Romans 8:28)*

There is only one purpose for the entire human race. When God calls someone, He does it to fulfill that original purpose on some level.

> Who has saved us and called us with a holy calling, not according to our works, but according to His own purpose and grace which was given to us in Christ Jesus before time began. *(2 Timothy 1:9)*

A calling is the allotment from God that tells you which area He wants you to work in within His kingdom. It's very important to stay within the boundaries of our calling in His kingdom. If we step into something we are not called to do, God is not responsible to provide for us or protect us. *Our provision is attached to our calling.*

Callings have to do with a specific group of people and a specific geographic location. When we study the lives of the people in the Bible, we see that they were called to function at a specific location.

The reason many lack provision is because they are not functioning in their calling. Either they are operating based on our traditions, or under the influence of the religious spirit. We do not see anyone in the Bible running around trying to find a job to help themselves fulfill what God has called them to do. If there is a calling, there is provision.

> So when the Lord saw that he turned aside to look, God *called* to him from the midst of the bush and said, "Moses, Moses!" And he said, "Here I am." *(Exodus 3:4)*

God called Moses so He could fulfill His purpose through him. His purpose for him was to exercise dominion over Egypt, and his calling was to deliver the people of Israel out of slavery. His gifts were many: faith, miracles, governing, signs, and wonders.

Jesus called the disciples and Paul (Romans 1:1).

> And when He had *called* His twelve disciples to Him, He gave them power over unclean spirits, to cast them out, and to heal all kinds of sickness and all kinds of disease. *(Matthew 10:1)*

Paul prayed that we would know the hope of our calling (Ephesians 1:17–19). It is noteworthy that the people in the Bible knew their purpose. They were not religiously brainwashed, like most people in the church are about their purpose. Even today, Jewish people know why God put them on this planet. Many of them are well-versed in the first five books of the Bible. They are not running around conducting music concerts.

The verse above says that God saved us and called us before time began. That means that our salvation and calling were planned by God before we were ever born. There is a general mindset that only some people are called and others are not. That is a misconception. *Every believer is called by God.* Salvation and the call are something we receive at the same time.

Another misunderstanding we have is that after we are saved, we will receive our calling a few years down the road. That is wrong as well. If you are born again, you are called by God to do something specific in His kingdom. The primary purpose for God saving you was because He had something prepared for you to do. He saved you because He has called you before the foundation of the world.

> For we are His workmanship, created in Christ Jesus for good works, which God prepared beforehand that we should walk in them. *(Ephesians 2:10)*

I wasted many years of my life waiting for a burning-bush experience or a Damascus-road type of encounter, to make sure I was called, but nothing came. There was no lightning from heaven, nor was there any angelic appearance in my bedroom. I knew in my heart that I was called, but I was looking for assurance. I had to fight against doubt and unbelief.

If you are born again, you will know in your heart what you are called to do. Salvation and the call of God come in the same package. Not everybody is called to do the same thing, and not everyone is called into full-time ministry. God calls people to do all kinds of different things, and not just the ministry in the church that we regard as His.

To God, *everything we do in His kingdom is a ministry to Him*. Everything we do is part of our worship. Whatever our assignment is in the kingdom is a service to our King. That is our ministry. If you are called to be a hairdresser, that's your ministry.

God instructed Moses to tell Pharaoh to let His people go so they could minister to Him or serve Him. They were all ministers of God because they were called out by Him from Egypt to serve Him.

When was Paul called into the ministry? When did he receive his salvation? His salvation and calling (born again) came all at once in the same day and time. When were the disciples saved and called? Their salvation and calling came the same moment Jesus called them. Your salvation and call came at the same time, too.

God gave burning-bush experiences in the Old Testament because the people were born again through an understanding of their destiny from the word of the Lord that came to them. They weren't saved the same way we are; they needed an external experience to confirm their calling because they didn't have the indwelling of the Holy Spirit and Christ in them like we do. Please do not misunderstand that.

If people won't listen to any other means, God may still use an *experience* to call someone to do a specific task today. He is not limited, but we shouldn't wait or look for an encounter with God. Many look for such experiences because of doubt and unbelief. God is patient with us in all our shortcomings.

OUR CALLING IS VERY SPECIFIC

To fulfill your purpose, God calls you to do something specific. Everyone is called to do something different. Even if you are an apostle or a pastor, no apostle or pastor is called to do the same thing. In the 1980s, God used Dr. Cho in South Korea to establish the largest church in the world. He gave him the idea to start cell groups.

Ministers from all over the world flocked to South Korea to find out the secret of starting a large and vibrant church.

They found that the secret was the "cell system" which Dr. Cho had implemented. They took that idea and went back to their countries and churches and tried to make it work because they also wanted to have large churches. However, it did not work for them. It was a unique design that God gave to Dr. Cho.

Paul and Peter were as different in their callings and ministries as night is from day. They could not agree on many levels. It wasn't that either of them was wrong; they were simply called to do different things and reach different groups of people.

God does not create copies. He only creates originals. When you try to copy someone else, you lose your identity and calling. When God began to use Benny Hinn in a particular way, many servants of the Lord began to think, *If I'm really anointed, then I have to do ministry like Benny does*. They began to blow on people and shout "Touch!" when everybody was quiet in worship. They didn't have the same result.

I heard that some people even went so far as to "stage" the manifestations of God. They paid people to fall when they blew on them or said the word *touch*. It got out of control and many suffered shipwreck as a result. That's why Peter says we should be diligent to make sure of our calling and election. The anointing in your life is not determined by how many people fall when you blow on them in your meetings, but how many of those people rise up and fulfill their destiny.

Today, many get saved with their focus on going to heaven. No one in the Bible got saved with that intention. People get saved today to escape from hell. Nobody was saved like that in the Bible. No one gave an altar call to go to heaven or escape from hell in the entire Bible.

The Greek word for "calling" is *klésis*, which means a calling or invitation.[8] That is the root of the word *ekklesia* (or *ecclesia*). *Ek* means "out of" and *ekklesia* simply means "called out ones."[9] God calls out certain people to fulfill His purpose.

God doesn't save you and then call you ten years later. They both come at the same time. God saved you to fulfill your calling. Too many do not recognize their calling. What comes later is "commissioning."

COMMISSIONING

Calling and commissioning are two different things. Just because you are called doesn't mean you are commissioned to walk in your calling yet. Commissioning is usually done by other people who recognize your calling. Commissioning is a *recognizing* or *releasing* that allows you to walk in your calling. Most of the time, this is done by other apostles or prophets. God Himself may commission some people to do what He is assigning them to do.

Paul was saved and called through his road-to-Damascus experience. He was commissioned fourteen years later by the prophets and teachers from the church in Antioch (Acts 13:1–2).

There might be a time period between your calling and commissioning. That is why Jesus said many are called, but few are chosen. Calling gives you the right to sign up for training. Then God takes you

---

[8] James Strong, "2821. Klésis," Strong's Greek: 2821. κλήσης (klésis) — a calling, accessed April 24, 2020, https://biblehub.com/greek/2821.htm)

[9] Ecclesia (Church)," Wikipedia (Wikimedia Foundation, May 27, 2019), https://simple.wikipedia.org/wiki/Ecclesia_(Church))

through a process of preparation. Many don't make it through. Any company that hires people to work for them takes them through training. They want to make sure their employees are doing exactly what they want them to do.

In this case, the same system works in God's kingdom. Kingdom training is severe and grueling. To prepare you to pass all the spiritual tests you will ever go through and qualify for commissioning, God gave me a powerful book to help you graduate faster, which is called *Keys to Passing Your Spiritual Tests*. You can find this book on my website at www.TheKingdomNetwork.org.

TEN WAYS TO
RECOGNIZE YOUR CALLING

When a person is born again, they see the kingdom of God and discover their calling. The aspect of the kingdom we see differs from person-to-person. How do we recognize our calling in the kingdom? God can use any of the following methods to make our calling clear to us.

Since no one can see God or has ever seen Him, how do we know and hear His voice? God has made ways to communicate His calling to us. He may not use the same way for everyone, but He knows what to use for each one as He created them uniquely.

You might think, *Abraham, I did not see or hear anything when I was born again. Now, how do I discover what I am called to do?* Don't worry, God has many methods to communicate the Word of our destiny to us. We are going to check them out. He may use any one of these ways to communicate your calling to you.

I. HOLY SPIRIT

Have you ever wished God would send someone to let us know exactly what He wanted us to do? Maybe an angel, or a stranger, or our pastor—anybody. That *is* what He did. He sent a person who knows everything to be our Helper and Counselor. This super genius person is Holy Spirit—and He knows everything in all of heaven and earth.

There is only one person who knows the purpose of your existence, and that is the Holy Spirit. He is the One who made you. The Bible says in 1 Corinthians 2:11 that no one knows what is in the mind of God except His Spirit. God sent His Holy Spirit to this earth to be with us and in us, and to guide us into all truth.

But as it is written: "Eye has not seen, nor ear heard, nor have entered into the heart of man the things which God has prepared for those who love Him." But God has revealed them to us through His Spirit. For the Spirit searches all things, yes, the deep things of God. For what man knows the things of a man except the spirit of the man which is in him? Even so no one knows the things of God except the Spirit of God. Now we have received, not the spirit of the world, but the Spirit who is from God, that we might know the things that have been freely given to us by God. *(1 Corinthians 2:9–12)*

The Holy Spirit knows everything about you. He is called a Helper by Jesus (John 14:26). Whenever you need help with anything, just ask, "Holy Spirit, please help me." He will help you. The reason we do not get help is because we don't ask. He will not impose Himself upon you to help you, but He will stand beside you and wait for you to call out to Him.

The Holy Spirit is the only person who knows the will of God concerning your life. He knows the blueprint. He can communicate your calling through any of the following methods.

II. DESIRE

God most often communicates His calling by placing a desire or picture in your heart. He does that between the ages of sixteen and twenty-five. You need to recognize your calling at that time and focus the rest of your life in preparing and accomplishing it.

Desire is the seed to your destiny. God imprints an indelible desire within your heart, and it sticks with you for the rest of your life. You need to make sure it is the desire of your born-again heart, and not your head or just a feeling that comes and then goes after a few days. There is a difference between them.

The picture or vision you received in your spirit man when you were born again will not go away, but the desire of your head will change with every new circumstance or diminish over time. The Bible says we should delight in the Lord, and He will fulfill the desire of our hearts (Psalm 37:4).

When I was eighteen years old, I had only a desire to go to a Bible school. I didn't know anything beyond that point. Once I went there, God unfolded the next step. That's how He works. If you wait to know all the details, you will miss Him.

III. GIFTING

What are you good at? Your gifting can be a clue to your calling. Many people are born with a natural talent to do various things, and it could be a clue to your destiny. I didn't grow up speaking English. I knew three words in English until I was eighteen years old. Then I went to a Bible college in India, and within three months God opened my understanding and gave me the English language as a gift. I began to speak and preach in English. God told me I would need that for my future. I didn't know where my future would lead me then.

Years went by, and I became more fluent preaching in English than in my own native language. Then God gave me books to write. When He gives me a message, He gives it to me in English. Why? Because the message is primarily for English-speaking people. I even dream in English. That was a clue to my calling, but it took me a while to figure that out.

The gifts God has given you naturally or spiritually are connected to your calling, and therefore, they are clues. Sometimes God will use your natural gifting to fulfill your spiritual calling. God might help you build a business to provide for your call. Whatever your calling, God will equip you with the right gifts. You just need to trust Him and thank Him for it.

Each person has at least one spiritual and natural gift. One will provide a source of income, and the other will enable you to serve the body of Christ.

IV. PASSION

You may not know of a gift or special ability, but you have a passion to do or learn something. You need passion if you are serious about fulfilling your calling. When I was a teenager, I had this passion to learn European languages, like French and German.

Every time I saw ads in the newspaper for learning those languages, I thought, *I need to go and join that school.* But I never did, and I wish I had.

Of course, you must make sure your passion is not a "strange" one. I have seen people with passion for all sorts of weird things. You can be passionate about crazy things. Your passion needs to be based on knowledge and God's purpose for your life. It must be submitted to God and in line with His plan.

V. WHAT UPSETS YOU

You are born to solve a problem on this earth. What is the one thing that you would like see changed? What makes you angry? What makes you cry? What bothers you the most about life on earth? Those areas are clues to your calling too. After you decide what you want to do, you must get the right education to help you fulfill your calling.

A long time ago, I watched a movie about Mahatma Gandhi. Originally from India, Gandhi was working as a lawyer in South Africa. One day while he was traveling by train, he happened to sit on a seat that was only for white people. When they got to the next station, the white people threw him off the train. He was embarrassed and angry.

That experience created within him a passion for his own people. At that time, India was ruled by the British. He left South Africa and returned to India and initiated his historic fight for freedom. Eventually, his non-violent tactics worked, and he pushed the British out of India. This is an example of how God communicates His calling to an individual.

VI. VOICE OF GOD

Sometimes God speaks to you directly, through His Word or through someone else about your calling. All of a sudden, something comes alive in your spirit man. Some aspect of the kingdom becomes clear as crystal. It is suddenly more real to you than the tree outside your window.

We see that in the Bible. Sometimes God tells parents about the calling of their children. Their calling over these children was so unique that they needed an entirely different upbringing than other children. In each critical juncture of your calling, you need to hear the voice of God and make the right choices so you stay on track. Samuel, Gideon and Samson are examples of this.

VII. CIRCUMSTANCES

Where you were born and your family background plays a role in discovering and fulfilling your calling. Sometimes children take over their parents' business or ministry after their passing, but it doesn't have to be like that all the time. I have seen children taking over ministries and businesses when they are not anointed to do so. God might have someone else in mind, but because of family ties, parents tend to put their children in those positions.

You may be a woman who doesn't have a passion to do anything big. You may not have a big dream, but simply desire to be a wonderful wife and mother. That is perfectly fine. If that's God's perfect will for your life, you can be happy and content in that. And not try to do something else just because of what others are doing or to feel like you have accomplished something.

In the same way, another woman may be given a calling outside or in addition to being a wife and mother, and she too can be personally fulfilled in her calling. Just don't let anyone devalue you if you are "only" a wife and mother. That calling is incredibly challenging—and one God values immensely!

So both men and women are called by God. Everyone isn't created to do the extraordinary, but we are all created to do whatever we do in an extraordinary way. Esther and Daniel are examples of this.

VIII. YOUR RELATIONSHIP

Another clue to your calling is who you are connected to and which people you get along with best. Those with whom you connect easily may not be the people from your own culture. *You will get along well with the people of your calling.* God will give you supernatural favor with the people to whom you are assigned.

Paul was called to the Gentiles, but his passion was for the people from His culture, so he kept going back to them. However, each time he went back to them he was rejected, beaten on many occasions, and eventually kicked out. Conversely, when he went to the Gentiles, they welcomed him or had a supernatural breakthrough in most places. Moses and Aaron, Peter and Andrew, and James and John are examples to this.

IX. PROVISION

Another clue is found in where your provision comes from. Who is God using to provide for you? Your provision is in the place of your calling. Your calling is in the place of your provision. God is committed to provide for you. He will always send someone to help you, no matter where you are. If there is no human available, He will send a bird or other creature.

X. DREAMS

Sometimes God will communicate your calling to you through your dreams. There are multiple examples of this in the Bible. Joseph in the Old Testament is the best example. We need to be open to God in whatever way He chooses to communicate His Word and calling. We cannot dictate to God what He must to do and how He should do it. He is God.

RECOGNIZING YOUR CALLING
IS IMPORTANT FOR THE FOLLOWING REASONS:

YOUR PROVISION IS CONNECTED TO YOUR CALLING

Your financial blessing is attached to your calling. The reason for poverty on earth is because people don't know their purpose and calling.

Many nations think population is the reason for poverty. Population is not the problem; productivity is the problem. People not knowing their purpose is the real problem. Many developed nations do not have enough people to do the work, so they allow people from other nations to immigrate to their countries.

YOUR PROVISION IS IN THE PLACE OF YOUR CALLING

Your calling is also connected to a place. Once you discover your calling, you need to know where you are supposed to fulfill it. Depending on the season of your life and your calling, you might be required to move to a new location. This is the geographic will of God. Many miss God because they are hesitant to move when they should. Each person has a specific place and nation in which they are supposed to live to fulfill their purpose.

CALLING GIVES YOU FREEDOM

We all like having the freedom to do what is really important to us. We like to see places and help other people. We have been duped by our culture, which says that money grants us freedom. Because they believe this lie, people try to make money through all sorts of evil ways and end up destroying their lives.

When you are doing what you were created to do, it frees you from being a slave to a system and being tied to a mundane schedule. Once you recognize your calling, you will be able to make your own schedule.

CALLING GIVES YOU FULFILLMENT

Nothing else gives you more satisfaction and fulfillment than doing what you were created to do. Many people are not satisfied and feel unfulfilled, so they try to find fulfillment in the wrong places. Some feel they need a hobby to make them happy.

CALLING GIVES YOU SIGNIFICANCE

One of the fundamental needs of every human is to feel significant. The solution to feeling insignificant is to recognize your calling and gifts and function in them. When you have a calling that is different from everyone else's, it naturally makes you feel significant. People in the world do all kinds of crazy things to be appreciated and noticed by others. They are trying to fill that need for significance.

CALLING GIVES YOU DIRECTION AND FOCUS

Many people do many things, but they don't do anything well because they don't have any focus. Every journey has a destination. Your life has a destiny, which is your destination. When you know what you are supposed to do, you can really focus on it. It also gives you direction about where to go with your life.

CALLING GIVES YOU BOUNDARIES

Everything God created has a boundary. Jesus said the path to life is narrow and difficult (Matthew 7:14). This means that living dedicated to your purpose is not easy. Your calling keeps you on target and on a narrow path.

GIFTS DO NOT DEFINE YOUR CALLING

This is very important to understand. People in the body of Christ often decide what they are called to do based on their gifts. That should never be the case. It's not the fault of the believers that this is happening; it is something their leaders have taught them.

There are many programs, techniques, and trainings to help identify a person's gifts. Then they tell them they are called into some office of ministry based on those gifts. But this is not how it works. Jesus first called the disciples and then gave them gifts to fulfill that calling. That is the way God operates, and that is His order for doing things.

For example, if a believer possesses a gift of healing, they automatically think they must be an evangelist. If a person casts out demons, they think they must take up the mantle of the apostle. They put a title in front of their name and print a business card that says "Apostle So-and-so." Some too quickly start a church or a ministry. This is part of the reason we have so many divisions in the body of Christ.

The truth is that anyone in the body of Christ can operate in the gift of healing or cast out a demon. Jesus said so:

> And these signs will follow those who believe: In My name they will cast out demons; they will speak with new tongues; they will take up serpents; and if they drink anything deadly, it will by no means hurt them; they will lay hands on the sick, and they will recover. *(Mark 16:17–18)*

The only qualification to operate in the gifts of the Holy Spirit is faith to believe that Jesus heals. That does not qualify a person to call themselves into the office of an evangelist or an apostle or any other ministry office. We must follow God's order. He first defines the purpose (that is most important to Him), and then he tells the person what he or she is called to fulfill that purpose. Then He gives them gifts to fulfill that calling.

We have been taught the opposite. We go looking for a gift to decide what we are called to do. People will travel the seas and pay any money to obtain a gift. Then we try to decide our purpose. This has created chaos in the body of Christ, and because the body of Christ is in chaos, the rest of the world is a mess, too.

The gifts of the Holy Spirit are given to each and every believer in Christ (1 Corinthians 12:7). That doesn't mean each believer is called into the five-fold ministry. The Bible clearly tells us in Ephesians 4 that only "some" are called into the five-fold ministry.

Just because a person operates in the gift of prophecy doesn't guarantee that he or she is called into the office of prophet. This confusion has been going on in the body of Christ for a long time, causing disorder and dysfunction. This happened because of poor teaching and a misunderstanding of the Scriptures.

There is a world of difference between the gift of prophecy and the office of a prophet. Similarly, someone who sells medicine is not necessarily a doctor. If they try to open an office without the proper education, they would end up in prison.

THE KEY TO LIVING OUT YOUR CALLING

As Jesus said, many are called, but few are chosen. The moment you see in your spirit what you are called to do, it is your responsibility to follow the leading of the Holy Spirit into next step.

The key to fulfilling your calling is to *do whatever He tells you to do*. If the Holy Spirit tells you to go and study something, then go. If the Holy Spirit tells you to move to another country or state, then move. If He tells you to start a business, then study everything about that business and start one.

We all take detours every now and then, but that doesn't mean you blew it and God cancelled His calling. He will wait for you to get back on track and keep going. Even if you fall or make mistakes seven times a day, He will not cancel your calling.

That is why the Bible says the righteous may fall seven times, but he will get back up (Proverbs 24:16). The gifts and calling of God are irrevocable (Romans 11:29).

Recognizing your calling does not guarantee its success. It just means you are called. God is giving you an opportunity to prove to Him that He can choose and trust you. Now the process begins in which you will qualify to be chosen by Him to fulfill the assignment.

That is why the Bible says many are called, but few are chosen (Matthew 22:14). The calling goes to every single human being ever born. Not everybody fulfills it.

Helping discover people's purpose and calling was a mystery to me. Many people struggle through with this in their lives. However, God made it very simple and easy from the beginning, but we didn't know it. Nobody taught us how it worked. Finally, God has revealed these principles again, so we may teach the next generation the right ways of God.

Many are stumbling in the dark or trying to copy someone who has become famous or prosperous. Don't try to copy others in their calling. Your calling is unique and special; nobody else can do what you were created to do.

If you are in ministry, don't try to copy someone else. Even if you have been raised up by someone, you will never be the same as that person. Discover your unique path. It took me a long time to come to peace with what I was called to do. I dreamed of becoming like others or tried to imitate others, but nothing worked for me.

There were no other samples. I couldn't find anyone to compare and copy in my life. My calling was so unique that I didn't fit in anywhere. I tried. Believe me, I wanted to fit in. Many times I felt rejected by others, and this made me feel nervous.

You need to be cautious with each step you take. One wrong step can deviate from the path God has ordained for you.

The moment you take the first step to fulfilling your calling, God steps in and starts to move on your behalf. He will make sure you have what you need. That doesn't mean everything will come to you with ease. There will be many battles and trials you need to overcome along the way.

As I said earlier, you must do what the Holy Spirit tells you to do. Either He will appoint someone to give you what you need, or He will tell you what to do to get it. Obedience is the key.

Don't tell God what to do or try to get Him to approve your decisions. That is humanism. Make Him the King of your life and His kingdom the number one priority in your life. Follow each step where He leads.

PART III:
MANIFESTING THE KINGDOM

CHAPTER 13

MANIFESTING THE KINGDOM

The kingdom of God is within you. (Luke 17:21)

What are you supposed to do after you see the kingdom and recognize your calling? There are specific steps we need to take to fulfill the calling we received. Just because you saw it, nothing is guaranteed. We are going to learn about those steps in this chapter.

STEPS IN MANIFESTING THE KINGDOM

BECOME BORN AGAIN

We have learned extensively about being born again, so I will not repeat it again. Read and study those subjects until that teaching becomes part of you. It will take time to change our old paradigm into kingdom understanding.

Suffice it to say that *seeing* the kingdom means you will *see* in the spirit, with the eyes of your imagination, the reason God sent you to this earth. You will understand your specific role in manifesting God's kingdom. That's what you will see in your spirit. We call it a vision or a dream. What you see is your calling.

The reason the kingdom is not manifesting yet is because there are not very many people who see it. You were sent here to manifest an aspect of God's kingdom. That is what you should have seen when you were born again.

Each of us was sent to demonstrate an aspect of God's kingdom to the rest of creation. We are uniquely made, so none of us can be duplicated. When we do not fulfill what we are sent to do, that part remains undone or missing on the earth. Unfortunately, the majority of the people are not fulfilling what they were sent to do. Therefore, we see much that is not functioning properly.

There are inventions and solutions from God's kingdom that have yet to be tapped into that would solve a problem we have. That part remains broken or missing. Do you want to know what's wrong with the world? Those sent to fix something didn't do their jobs, so that area remains empty or out of order. Instead, they are all waiting to escape this planet and go to heaven. By the time we leave this planet, it should be a better place than when we arrived.

When we are naturally born, we are born as citizens of various countries. We were not originally the citizens of this earth; we were sent here by a King from another country. When we arrived, we were taken captive by the enemy and kept under the bondage of sin. When we believe in Jesus, we are reborn a second time and receive our original heavenly citizenship. That's why we see the country of our origin when we are born again. From that time on, the devil and his kingdom has no legal right over our lives.

When we receive our heavenly citizenship, we get access to everything that is in heaven. Our birthright and assignment is to see what is happening in heaven and manifest it on the earth—to see God's will done on earth as it is in heaven.

However, not everyone sees what's happening in heaven or what their heavenly Father is doing. Their minds and souls still remain under the bondage of the enemy or attached to their past wounds and mistakes. Most of us need to go through a cleansing or healing process from our past.

Additionally, our minds have been programmed by our culture and language, so they need to be renewed on a daily basis with the Word of God. Most of us think our minds are renewed and that we think according to the Word of God because we know some Bible verses and stories by heart, or because we have been attending a church for the last thirty years.

If you check your words and actions, I can guarantee you that ninety percent of what you say and do will be according to the culture you grew up in and has nothing to do with the kingdom of God. That means the strongholds that have been formed in you as you grew are still controlling your life. That means the Babylonian system still has a hold on you.

Once we are born again and see our calling, we move to the next step.

CATCHING THE VISION

Once you see the kingdom and catch the vision, you need to receive it into your heart by faith. This will be beyond your natural capabilities and resources, but you need to take hold of it by faith and not let it go. When I was in Bible school, I remember putting a poster up in our living quarters that said, "Pray for a nation and catch the vision." This was to encourage fellow students to pray for nations, asking God to put His vision in their hearts when they prayed.

That's what happened to me when I was a teenager. I received the vision for my life through prayer meetings. I saw the kingdom. We had a small youth group prayer meeting that met once a week and prayed from 8:30 at night until 4:30 in the morning. Those prayer meetings were the foundation of the life I live today.

God birthed His vision in my spirit during those prayer times. He drew my destiny into my spirit. It was not a little "bless-me" prayer meeting in which we told God what we wanted Him to do. In our prayer time, we were becoming one with the blueprint (our scroll) in heaven. We were becoming one with the heart of God and praying to manifest His will on earth.

I was becoming the vessel or the body through which my Father could manifest His kingdom. I had no other agenda. I didn't ask Him for anything personal. Every request was focused toward fulfilling His desire in and through me.

We were young and we did not have mentors who taught us these things. Holy Spirit was our Mentor and Teacher. I never read a Christian book about faith, miracles, the kingdom, or any other subject until I was in my late twenties. The only book I had was my Bible. I read it morning, noon, and evening. That was my spiritual food.

I didn't receive much from the church that I attended, either. I didn't know what I was reading at that time. It all sounded like a foreign language to me. But I ate His Word like a hungry child who had found his mother's milk.

Today, everything I read in God's Word is coming to life. All these books He gave me to write are coming from the Word I sowed into my spirit when I was young. Every verse I quote in these books comes from my heart. What I saw at that time seemed quite impossible to me in the natural, but it is now becoming possible day by day. There was no chance of it coming to pass based on my education, financial background, or nationality.

However, I believed it in my heart, and even in those times I tried to get rid of it because of frustration or disappointment, God, in His mercy, didn't take it away from me. My cry to God was, "Lord, don't let me go! Even if I try to run away, don't let me go!" He hasn't. I didn't tell God that I wouldn't let Him go. I have no confidence in my ability. My trust is in His ability. If He doesn't show up, I am done.

If you are not sure about the vision He gave when you were born again, spend time in prayer. Prayer is the incubator through which kingdom destinies and purposes are conceived and birthed on earth. If you don't pray, don't even try to live for God or call yourself a child of God. When God is looking for someone to use, *He is looking for someone who prays.*

Many things are not birthed on earth because there is no one praying. Our churches teach our kids to pray as if they were ordering God to take care of their lists. They tell God what to do, treating Him like their slave. I got so irritated by this kind of prayer that one day I stopped my kids from praying and explained to them that telling God what to do wasn't prayer. Instead, we must ask Him what He has in store for us to do.

I once saw a vision of a storeroom in heaven with piles of inventions. God told me those are inventions were supposed to have manifested on earth, but there was no one to receive them and birth them on earth. There they are in heaven, now outdated, and thrown into a heap. Heaven won't wait for us. Either we will catch up with His timing, or we will miss the train. God is always moving and doing something new.

We have no idea what we are missing because we aren't in line with God's heart and vision for our nations. We are stuck in a religious rut and think we are waiting for God to do something. Actually, *He is waiting for us.*

When God released you to this planet, He wanted to manifest something of His kingdom through you. Something of His nature and character is supposed to come through you to the rest of creation.

When we see what God wants us to see, we are supposed to be led by what we saw and not by our circumstances or natural sight after that. That is why the Bible says we walk by faith and not by sight. There are huge differences between natural eyesight and vision from God.

Below are the ten differences between sight and vision.

SIGHT	VISION
Sight is of the body	Vision is of the Spirit
Sight is limited	Vision is unlimited
Sight is natural	Vision is spiritual
Sight is temporary	Vision is eternal
Sight is deceiving	Vision is real
Sight is earthly	Vision is heavenly
Sight is of material things	Vision is of spiritual things
Sight keeps changing	Vision is permanent
Sight is personal	Vision is from God
Sight is of the natural man	Vision is of the spiritual man

Once we receive a vision from God, we are supposed to be led by it for the rest of our lives. Every decision we make has to be based on that vision. If we don't do this, we will delay our progress or deviate from the path God has ordained for us. The enemy's tactic is to keep us focused on our natural sight and the things around us instead.

Materialism corrupts our vision. The enemy constantly throws things in front of our eyes to keep us distracted and busy. This prevents us from focusing on the vision God placed in our hearts. Most people are stuck in the material world and can't take their eyes off of it. Once we catch the vision, we move on to the next step.

BELIEVE

You need to believe what you see, even though it may not make any sense to your natural mind. Do you think it was easy for Mary to believe when the angel told her she was going to have a baby? That was beyond her natural comprehension, but she believed it—and the rest is history.

It's not our job to try to figure out all the details. That's God's business, and we are His vessels through which He can do whatever He chooses. It is interesting to note that Jesus told people to "only believe." That's our responsibility. Instead, we try to come up with all kinds of excuses as to why we are not able to believe. We cannot believe because we are looking for all the details first.

We try to help God out by coming up with ideas for how to fulfill the vision He gave us. Remember Abraham and Sarah? God promised them a son. Sarah came up with an idea to have a son by her handmaiden because she was old and barren. It wasn't God's plan, so they gave birth to Ishmael. Ishmael should have never been born.

Whatever is born of the flesh is flesh. It will fight against the spirit. When we try to help God with ideas about how to fulfill His vision, we give birth to things in the flesh.

People came to Jesus and complained about their problems and impossibilities. He had only one answer for them all: "Only believe!" Does your destiny seem impossible? Only believe! Let's move to the next step.

WRITE THE VISION DOWN

Once you believe what you see, take out a journal and write it down. After I saw the vision when I was seventeen, I wrote it down. Not only did we write, but we also drew pictures of the things we saw and began to declare them to manifest in the natural. It was a baby step, but everything we saw, wrote, drew, and declared manifested, it still continues to do so.

> Then the Lord answered me and said: "Write the vision and make it plain on tablets, that he may run who reads it." *(Habakkuk 2:2)*

I am still running to finish the race that I saw when I was born again. When we write something down, it becomes the evidence of what we believe.

Faith is the substance (words) of things not seen and the evidence (what we write down) of things hoped for (Hebrews 11:1).

When God visits us to fulfill His destiny or promise, He is looking for evidence of our faith. The evidence shows that you believe what you saw or what He showed you. What you speak and what you wrote are two evidences of the faith you have in your heart. God is looking for both evidences. One is what you have written down. The Bible says out of the mouth of two or three witnesses everything is established. The next step is the second evidence.

SPEAK THE VISION

The whole kingdom of God functions on two fundamental principles. They are seeing and speaking. What you see in your heart and imagination, you will eventually speak. What you speak will eventually manifest in your life. Our destinies and the destiny of this world are governed by words.

One of the primary responsibilities we have in activating and manifesting our vision is beginning to speak it. That is our responsibility in the partnership with God. It's not our job to worry about money or how everything is going to take place. We must simply speak forth the vision we have as often as we can. Then we must declare that things manifest in accordance to the vision we received from God.

When we study the lives of the people in the Bible, we see this same pattern. Joseph had a dream and he shared it with his brothers and his family. When you speak your vision, two things will happen. There will be polarization of people; one group will agree and support it, and the other will oppose it. One group is for you, and the other group is not.

The group that is for you will help you fulfill the vision. The group that opposes is there to help develop your character. Both groups are equally important to the plan of God has for your life, so never hate your enemies or those who oppose you. That is why Jesus said to love your enemies and bless those who curse you (Matthew 5:44). We never fight against people.

One of the main purposes of speaking is to find those people who are going to stand with you. You need them. They are the ones whom God has appointed to help you carry out the task. The other group will teach you patience and perseverance.

When Jesus began His ministry, He went to a synagogue in the town He grew up in to announce the assignment His Father had for Him. He opened the book of Isaiah and read a few verses.

> "The Spirit of the Lord is upon Me, because He has anointed Me to preach the gospel to the poor; He has sent Me to heal the brokenhearted, to proclaim liberty to the captives and recovery of sight to the blind,

> to set at liberty those who are oppressed; to proclaim the acceptable year of the Lord." Then He closed the book, and gave it back to the attendant and sat down. And the eyes of all who were in the synagogue were fixed on Him. And He began to say to them, "Today this Scripture is fulfilled in your hearing."
> *(Luke 4:18–21)*

When He finished reading and preaching His first sermon, people were so angry they tried to kill Him (Luke 4:28–30). They couldn't kill Him because no one can destroy your life before the time as long as you are walking in obedience to the call of God. God has His protection around you all the time, and He will deliver you from every trouble as He did Jesus.

When you speak the vision God gave you, don't expect everyone to be happy and accept you. In the beginning, you will face more rejection than acceptance. You will need to learn to walk a lonely walk. At first, there may not be anyone to help you or believe in you. You need to be prepared to face that.

People and demonic spirits will ask you: "Who are you to do what you are doing?" "Who gave you the authority to do this?" They did that to Jesus, and I had to face that in my personal life as well. This won't be coming from people in the world, but from those who think they are spiritual and from leaders in the church.

.When we first begin to operate in the law of faith by speaking the promises God has given us, our hearts and minds will have difficulty accepting it. Our internal communication is as important as what we speak with our mouths.

Because we are born with an unbelieving nature, it will take time for our internal communication to come into alignment with our mouths. We should not quit speaking what God promised us. We should declare it as often as we can until our hearts and the thoughts in our minds come into total agreement with what our mouths say. In time, they will all say the same thing.

When the twelve spies went to spy out the Promised Land, ten came back with a negative report, but the other two saw things differently. The ten saw the giants and considered themselves as grasshoppers. Their vision was overwhelmed by the circumstances around them. What we see will eventually manifest. In other words, we will keep manifesting what we see with our spiritual eyes.

The ten spies spoke about what they saw with their natural eyes and lost the opportunity to enter the Promised Land. Make sure your words are in line with the heavenly vision God placed in your heart. Don't speak about the challenges or the limitations around you. Speak in alignment with the vision; speak what God has spoken and shown you.

You will attract that which you imagine and proclaim. Many people underestimate the power of their words. Then they wonder why they have not made any progress or why things are going from bad to worse. If you are in such a situation, check the words you speak.

DISCERN OPPORTUNITIES

Once you receive your calling, every decision you make after that needs to be in line with what God showed you. This is so important. Everything you do after you receive your vision has the power to make or break you. What you choose to study, who your friends are, the one you choose to marry, and where you live are all connected to your calling.

In other words, once you receive your calling, everything you choose has to be in support of it. Otherwise, you will make it harder to walk in what you are called to do, or maybe you will not fulfill your calling at all, depending on the situation.

The last step in manifesting the kingdom is to discern the doors and opportunities that will come your way. Once you begin to speak, God will start opening doors for you. He will use what you proclaim to begin to create circumstances that line up with your vision so you can fulfill your calling.

God will open some doors or bring some opportunities to you. You need to jump onto these opportunities like your very life depends on them! If not, that opportunity will keep moving and go to someone else. You will end up waiting for your next season. Opportunities are doors God opens for you. Step into them and keep moving with God. Of course, you must make sure the opportunity is from God first; but once you do, don't let your puny little brain talk you out of it.

How do you know if an opportunity is from God? If it is appropriate for the next step in fulfilling what God already showed you, then it's from Him. If the opportunity will take you away from the vision, then you need to say no and stay away from it.

Many people make mistakes in this by jumping into an opportunity that looked beneficial to them personally. Or perhaps it looked attractive to fulfill a personal ambition or feed their ego. Don't do it. Avoid those. Don't accept any opportunity without consulting with God and without discerning whether it will propel you toward the vision or derail you from it. If the opportunity deviates from the vision God gave you, then don't even look in that direction. Turn and walk away.

You also need to remember that we have an enemy. He doesn't want you to fulfill your calling. His purpose is to derail you from that calling and destroy your life before you even start. He will bring distracting opportunities and pull on you with evil impulses through your flesh.

Many abort their calling by making poor or unwise choices. God is not to be blamed. This is all too common. Remember Adam and Eve and the choice they made. Remember Abraham and Sarah and the unwise choice they made to produce Ishmael.

Unless you stay in tune to your spirit and the Holy Spirit, there is no way you will make it. A countless number of people began and never finished what they started out to do. The enemy came with "opportunities," and they did not consult God before they jumped in and said yes. Just like Eve; when the serpent came to her, she did not consult God or her husband. The result was tragic, and we are still paying the price for that one act of disobedience.

I'm not saying it was an easy road for me, either. I have been through hell a few times. I had to fight many life-and-death battles. I still stand because of the grace and mercy of God and the prayers of many saints around the world.

Remember the story of Gehazi? He was the servant of Elisha. He was supposed to succeed Elisha and carry his anointing, but he saw (and took) an opportunity to receive some gifts instead. Through new clothes and blankets from Syria, he lost his destiny. If he had not made that choice, we would probably be reading the stories about all the amazing miracles Gehazi did alongside Elisha. If only he had resisted that temptation and rejected that opportunity!

Elisha did double the miracles Elijah did, and Gehazi would have done double of what Elisha did. Instead, he lost everything and became a leper. When Naaman from Syria came to Elisha for the healing of his leprosy, he brought gifts to give to Elisha. Elisha did not accept them. However, his servant thought it foolish to pass up this once-in-a-lifetime opportunity to wear some expensive clothing. He ran after Naaman and lied to him to receive the gifts.

Elisha knew this in the spirit and pronounced a curse upon his servant. The leprosy that was upon Naaman came upon Gehazi and his children forever. That is the result of accepting wrong opportunities and making wrong choices.

Rest assured that every one of us will make at least one major mistake in the process of unfolding our calling. Everyone in the Bible did, so we are not an exception. Don't dwell on your mistakes. God will help you circumvent any event and turn it around for good. It will be hard and painful, but it's possible. We may have to live with an Ishmael for the rest of our lives, but that doesn't need to end God's calling on your life. It didn't end the calling for Abraham and Sarah. They had their Isaac, too.

GOD NEVER STARTS WITH MONEY FIRST

One of the major hurdles we all need to overcome is the issue of money. Once you receive the vision, the next question your natural mind brings is, "Where is the money to fulfill this vision going to come from?"

Many people who have great vision run around looking for money and support. Others are waiting for a major financial breakthrough to start their ministry or fulfill whatever God called them to do. They wait and wait for many years, and nothing seems to happen. This happens because they don't understand this kingdom principle: God never starts anything with money first.

We don't see a single incident in the Bible in which God started anything He wanted to accomplish with an amount of money or a budget first. That's not the way He operates. We should never think money is a limit or the decision maker in what God called us to do.

God never called anyone and then asked how much they had in their bank account. God will never do that. The money never comes first.

There is something that you will never tell Jesus. This is very serious—and I want you to capture this in your heart.

You should never tell Jesus this: "Lord, let me go and start a business or work and make enough money to support myself and my family and secure some in the savings, and then I will come and serve You." That is the most insulting thing you could tell any king or our Lord Jesus.

Why? That's not the way His kingdom operates. A king would never expect you to come up with the resources to accomplish a mission for him. That's not the way kings operate—especially our King Jesus who created the whole universe with His word.

There was a man who Jesus told to follow Him, but the man replied to Him, "Lord, let me first go and bury my father" (Luke 9:59). This man wasn't talking about his father because he cared for him. He was concerned about his estate. According to his culture, only after the father dies would he receive his inheritance.

This man was saying, "Once my father is dead, I will receive my inheritance, and then I will come and serve You." Note the word "first" in the above verse? Jesus told us to seek *His kingdom* first—not our savings or estates. Jesus was not impressed. He told him to let the dead bury their own dead, meaning to let those who are spiritually dead and had no vision bury any others who were spiritually dead. Jesus exhorted the man to go and preach the kingdom of God instead (Luke 9:60).

To accomplish the vision God gave us (and because the vision is from God), we need to learn to operate and function like Him. How does God function? When God wants to accomplish something, what does He do? This is the most important key to everything you do in the kingdom.

We are created in the image and likeness of God, so He expects us to operate in the same way He does. You might say, "Oh my goodness, how can a mere human being like me operate like God?" It is as simple as counting 1-2-3. I will show you from the Word.

To show us how to operate in the image and likeness of God, He gave us the best example in Genesis 1. He started with the most hopeless situation on the entire planet.

What do I mean by that? The earth that we see in Genesis 1:2 is the most hopeless piece of matter we could ever see. The Bible says the earth was void, without form, and darkness was on the face of the deep. There was no light and no chance of any life. It was out of shape, and it looked hopeless and useless in the natural.

How did God start remodeling the planet? He didn't hire the largest construction company to come and help him. He didn't sit down and come up with a budget about how much it was going to cost Him to make the changes He had in mind. He didn't call for a board meeting in heaven to see how much money He needed to start the project and get everyone's feedback on whether it was a worthy endeavor. No, never.

God *spoke* what He wanted to see happen. What He spoke He saw it materialized in the natural. Everything in the kingdom begins by speaking—not with money. That's why the Bible says, "In the beginning was the Word" (John 1;1a). I want you to capture this revelation with your whole being. If you miss this, you will miss everything else—you will miss your calling and your assignment on the earth.

God wants us to follow His footsteps in fulfilling the kingdom assignment He has for us. I understand there is a place for budget and other technical things, but if you wait for a budget to start what God has called you to do, you may never start. If the vision you have can fit into your budget, then it's not from God.

After you see what God wants you to see, you need to speak what you see by faith. You call for everything you need by faith as if it already existed. That's what happened to me. When I was sixteen, I called those things out that I saw in my spirit. I declared them to manifest.

I had no budget—not even a dime. I had never even heard of the word *budget* at that time. (Today we do have a budget for our ministry for the sake of accountability, but it doesn't decide what we should or shouldn't do.)

To be honest, I am still walking in the fulfillment today of what I proclaimed when I was sixteen. God is faithful to His Word. That is why He said that when He sends His Word, it never comes back void. It will always accomplish the purpose for which it was sent.

I started the kingdom life with words, not money. There was nothing in my hands. All I could do was speak, so I spoke and declared everything God showed me like a crazy fellow. That is why the Bible says, "In the beginning was the Word" (John 1:1). The beginning of everything is the Word.

Anyone can do what God has called them to do. Instead of waiting to have all the money you need to start, start with words. Your education level, language, or economic situation does not matter. To be honest, the more educated you are, the more difficult walking in faith and trusting God can be.

People who are more educated have a tendency to depend on knowledge instead of what God says. Education can become a crutch and can sabotage our kingdom assignment if we depend on it too much. That's what this world's education does to a person. Kingdom education does the very opposite. It will train a person to walk in faith and live by faith.

Paul says we have the spirit of faith, and therefore we speak (2 Corinthians 4:13). If you have faith, it will show up in the words you speak. Unbelief and doubt will show up in your words as well. You will reap the harvest of the words you speak (Proverbs 13:2; Isaiah 57:19a).

God cannot make kingdom living simpler than this. How could we miss this? Our logic and the reasoning of our peanut brains cancel out the very plan and calling God has on our lives. We made life complicated by trying to figure things out and became stupid as a result.

CHAPTER 14

WHY THE KINGDOM OF GOD IS NOT MANIFESTING

That I may make it manifest, as I ought to speak.
(Colossians 4:4)

I couldn't find a single doctrine in the church that I grew up in that would prepare a believer for anything that is good on this earth. That is very sad. Not a single doctrine prepared a believer to become productive and fruitful in any area of life. Every doctrine was geared toward making a person more religious and useless for anything here.

Many churches' motto is preparing people for heaven. How about your church? Can you find one doctrine or training that prepares you to become effective for God's kingdom on earth? If not, I would encourage you to run from that kind of church.

The church I knew believed they were the most spiritual and holy people in the whole world. The deception of the religious spirit is that strong and powerful. The religious spirit will render you absolutely useless for God's mission here on earth. How? By telling you that you were created to go and live in heaven, and that there is a mansion waiting for you there. All you have to do on earth is sing to

Jesus once a week and make Him feel happy. This is how the devil uses the religious spirit to steal everything that belongs to us.

Do you know how many Bible colleges and seminaries are out there that take an individual and castrate them, making them into a religious nutcase? When they come out of these institutions, they will be zealous for their religion and think they are fighting for and serving God, just like Paul was before his conversion. Most of these religious institutions will not teach you anything about kingdom or your purpose.

We are supposed to be the most productive people on earth because we are God's children. Our God is the most productive and creative person in the whole universe. We are created to represent and manifest Him on earth.

When Jesus started His ministry and called His disciples, He didn't promise them any monthly support. Today someone will start an organization and beg for money from other people and send out some ministers, promising them monthly support. The kingdom of God doesn't work like that. That is this world's religious system.

Jesus wants each of His followers to discover His kingdom and live dependent on it, and not on an organization or human leader. That is why the kingdom of God isn't manifesting through us. We have been programmed and are following a Babylonian system.

Paul didn't do this, either. He didn't promise anyone any monthly support and send them out to start a church. If he had done that, he wouldn't have been as effective as he was. He taught and preached the kingdom as Jesus did, and the people who worked with him tapped into the same resources he did. He taught them how to do that. This is the way every ministry should be done. Ministry means whatever you are called to do in the kingdom.

The Bible says Paul made many rich by teaching and imparting to them kingdom business principles (2 Corinthians 6:10). Today most ministers work for a salary. No one did that in the Bible. They lived dependent on the kingdom economy.

Sometimes people have come to work with me, and their first question was how much I would pay them monthly. None of those who did that were effective in fulfilling their calling. They didn't last long. Why? Their motive was the salary and not the vision. They were looking for an opportunity to survive.

Can you imagine what it was like when the disciples left their businesses to follow Jesus? They did that because they had a revelation of who Jesus was and their destiny. They understood that if they truly followed Him, they would not lack for anything. They didn't take days to discuss and pray about it, either; it was an immediate decision.

Today people ask for a month so that they can pray and consult with others on whether to obey the call or not. There's nothing wrong with praying. People need to hear from God for themselves. The disciples didn't follow Jesus based on someone else's experience or revelation. They each had a personal encounter with Jesus.

If you look at the people God used, you will see that they all followed this same principle. They made God and His kingdom their source. Whenever they needed anything, they learned to tap into kingdom resources by faith and waited for its manifestation. When you learn to do this in your life, you are ready to fulfill your kingdom assignment.

This is how each child of God should function today. When we err from God's way, we get into trouble. We begin to worry about our livelihood and then depend on other humans instead of God.

The first revelation every believer and every minister should receive in their lives is about the kingdom of God. I was surprised and shocked to read that when a person is born again, they do not see Jesus, but the kingdom of God. From God's point of view, the revelation of the kingdom of God is that important to a human being.

Each minister should learn to see and manifest the kingdom of God to fulfill their life's mission. Their provision and everything they need in the natural is connected to that vision.

Any time we define the purpose of our lives and the earth, and interpret major doctrines of the Bible, we need to look at them in the light of God's eternal plan, the original design He revealed in the first two chapters of Genesis. Genesis 3 explains why life on earth is the way it is now, as well as when and how all the problems we see and experience on earth today began. Sickness, sin, poverty, religion, death, division, racism, and everything else began because of what happened in Genesis 3.

When I refer to "manifesting the kingdom of God," I am not describing some mystic, eerie world where everything floats in a smoke-filled airy place, as we see in some computer-generated cartoons or movies. When the kingdom of God manifests, the earth will still be the earth and heaven will still be heaven. The difference is we will see God's will being done on earth as it is in heaven.

What will the kingdom of God manifesting physically look like?

- We will have free and easy access to heaven and the things of the Spirit.
- There won't be any sickness and curses, lying, or cheating.
- Everyone's needs will be met.
- Everyone will be free to fulfill their destiny.
- Nations will be serving Jesus as their King and Lord.

The body of Christ has been preaching doom, gloom, and despair for too many years. We haven't provided the world with any hope. People in the world are already going through hell; they don't need to come to church to hear more about hell. What they need to hear is the gospel of the kingdom. The only hope we provide is life after death found in heaven. We are supposed to be giving hope to people for this life. That's why Jesus came.

The reason the whole body of Christ has wandered into darkness is because our vision is not right. What we see about our future has been distorted by the religious spirit. We do not see anything good about the future of our nations. We were taught to see gloom and despair. Everything is going to go from bad to worse. Do you believe that?

Though Jesus took away the sin of the whole world and died on the cross to pay to redeem us from everything sin brought upon us, not even one nation or city can say they have appropriated what Christ died and paid for.

Is there one location on this planet in which the church has appropriated and fixed what was broken in the community, nature, government, or any other arena of life? It should shame us to participate in our religious rituals every Sunday morning and think we are doing God some kind of favor. He is ready to vomit us out when He hears and sees what we are doing in our churches.

It's a bad thing that the people of the world exhibit greater sense about life on earth and the responsibility toward it than most churchgoers. They are more productive and useful, while most holy rollers are waiting to go to heaven and give Jesus a religious sloppy wet kiss.

The whole Bible is divided into two groups of people. The first group saw what God wanted them to see, and the second group saw only what their flesh saw. The first thing that needs to be corrected when we are born again is our vision. If our vision is not right, our whole lives will malfunction. That's why our nations are out of order.

If you haven't received a vision for your future and your place in God's kingdom when you were born again, then I would question your salvation experience. You might have had a religious experience by hearing a religious gospel. When the people in the Bible had an encounter with God, their vision was corrected, and a new vision was instilled into them to make something that was broken on the earth better than it was before.

As generations go by, I personally believe that the more we manifest the kingdom and God's will, the more life will progress and transform to become more and more like heaven. In time, everything on earth will be one with heaven. The earth will be restored to the original order we see in Genesis 2.

According to the Bible, the earth has gone through three renewals already. First was the one we saw in Genesis 1:1. That was the first state, which did not have the sun and moon as we see them today. The Luciferian earth was not lit by any solar lights. He was the light and the light bearer. Then that earth was destroyed by a flood. We read about that flooded earth in Genesis 1:2. God restored it again and created the sun and moon to give light. We marred the earth with Adam's fall. The third time it was renewed was when the flood happened during Noah's time.

This earth will be restored once again. We read about it in Revelation 21–22. In that earth, there won't be any sun or moon. Jesus will be the Light of that earth (Revelation 22:5).

THE GREAT EXODUS

Another reason the kingdom of God is not manifesting is because the people whom God sent here to manifest His kingdom are stuck in the Babylonian system for survival, as we saw in the first chapter. They need to be set free from this so they can fulfill their God-given destiny. That is the whole purpose of this book.

It will take some time for God's people to capture the vision and prepare themselves to leave the bondage of Babylon and then move into the kingdom and start flowing in their calling and gifts. We need to equip the body of Christ to discover their kingdom assignment. That is why we are starting Kingdom Schools in different parts of the world.

KINGDOM SCHOOLS

If you are interested in studying the kingdom of God in-depth and want to discover your kingdom assignment, we have several courses available for you online. Visit our website at www.TheKingdomNetwork.org and sign up for a course today. We have different options to choose from for students from different parts of the world. Close to a hundred people have signed up to be in the first classes, and that number keeps growing every day.

FLESH AND BLOOD CANNOT INHERIT GOD'S KINGDOM

> Now this I say, brethren, that flesh and blood cannot inherit the kingdom of God; nor does corruption inherit incorruption. *(1 Corinthians 15:50)*

In a royal family, the next in the bloodline will inherit the throne or the kingdom after the death of the king or prince. In the kingdom of God, it doesn't work that way. Just because I'm in the kingdom of God doesn't guarantee that my children or wife will inherit the kingdom.

Many children of believers grow up in a Christian home and they are active in ministry or church stuff from their childhoods. They assume they are born again and a child of God. Many turn away from their Christian backgrounds in time because they have no root to sustain them. They do not own their faith—all along, they were running on someone else's revelation or calling. After a while, they burn out.

At some point, salvation and the kingdom of God has to become personal in each one of our lives. We can't inherit the kingdom because we are born into a certain family or church. We all have to go through the process individually.

In the Old Testament when the Israelites came out of Egypt, everyone was taken into the wilderness. They all had to complete the wilderness process to inherit the Promised Land—all of them, not just the leaders. They all had to overcome their flesh and pass all the tests before they could step into the Jordan River.

HOLY SPIRIT AND LIFE IN THE KINGDOM

There is only One person who knows the callings and gifts God deposited into your spirit when He created you, and that person is the Holy Spirit. Holy Spirit is the only person who knows what is in the heart of God. He searches out the heart and mind of God and finds out things concerning your life.

Holy Spirit's responsibility is to communicate with you what He finds out from the Father. I was surprised when I discovered the depth of the involvement of the Holy Spirit in Jesus's life. He was conceived by the Holy Spirit, but that wasn't enough for Him to fulfill His calling.

At His baptism, the Holy Spirit came upon Jesus a second time, and His public ministry began that day. Throughout His life, Jesus was led by the Holy Spirit. When He was buried, He was raised up by the Holy Spirit. Before He left, He gave His followers assurance about the coming of the Holy Spirit.

If the Holy Spirit was that active in the life of Jesus, how much more do we need Him today! Jesus couldn't do anything without the Holy Spirit. We are introduced to the Holy Spirit in the very first chapter of the Bible. In Genesis 1:2, we read that the Spirit of God was brooding over the waters.

Holy Spirit is very active in relation to our planet. His work is to help us manifest the kingdom of God on earth and execute the will of God on earth as it is in heaven. Throughout the Bible, nobody did anything for God without the Holy Spirit.

The Holy Spirit is the Spirit of Wisdom and Understanding. He is the most precious gift the Father has ever given us. He is the Spirit of truth, and always speaks truth. He doesn't get into anyone's business. God didn't send Him to tell you to comb your hair and brush your teeth. He gave us our brains to help us to do those things. The Holy Spirit's job is to help us manifest the kingdom in and through our lives.

We need to have the Word in us if the Spirit is going to start working in us. The proportion of how much you are led by the Spirit is directly related to how much of the Word you have in you. The Word and Spirit work together; they are inseparable.

They worked together at creation. The Spirit of God was hovering over the water. Nothing happened until God spoke His Word. You need to receive the Word before the Spirit comes upon you. The Spirit comes to fulfill the Word you have received. The Spirit comes to quicken the Word. The Word receives life and manifests the purpose for which it was sent.

Before His ascension, Jesus told His disciples to wait in Jerusalem for the promise of the Father. They received the Word and waited ten days. Then the Holy Spirit came upon them on the day of Pentecost. Do you see a pattern here? In each instance, the order is same.

There are different spirits other than Jesus's on the earth. Not everybody who calls on Jesus is talking about the Jesus in the Bible. Not everybody who prophesies and heals is doing this through the Holy Spirit. All spirits are not from God. Most are demonic in origin. There are different gospels, as well. Many receive the gospel that takes them to heaven and renders them good for nothing on earth.

> For if he who comes preaches another Jesus whom we have not preached, or if you receive a different spirit which you have not received, or a different gospel which you have not accepted—you may well put up with it! *(2 Corinthians 11:4)*

Any spirit or "Jesus" that doesn't promote or manifest the kingdom of God is not from God. They are religious spirits pretending to be from God. They are demonic spirits pretending to be angels of light. Don't be deceived. Many believe they received the Holy Spirit, but have no clue what God gave them, nor do they know what they are supposed to do with their lives. Often it is not the Holy Spirit they have received; most of the time, it's a religious spirit. I had the religious spirit for a long time because I grew up in church.

I had no clue about the things God had given to me. I thought I had the Holy Spirit, and I was acting like everybody else in the church. I clapped my hands and sang songs and acted holy, saying, "Praise the Lord." When a church is full of people who are possessed by the religious sprit, you won't know any difference. It will seem normal because everybody is doing the same thing. They think it is the Holy Spirit, but it is not.

When I was delivered from the religious spirit, then I knew the difference. I ran out of the religious circle I had attended and never looked back. Thank God for His mercy and grace to deliver! When I encounter that religious circle today, it feels uncomfortable. It is the most difficult place in which to minister God's Word.

Jesus came to set the captives free. We limit that process only to demons, bad habits, or addictions and sin, but there is so much more. Jesus came to set our destinies free as well. Our destinies and the destinies of our nations have been held captive by the enemy kingdom for too long. Jesus wants to set us free and release us into our destinies. Only when individuals are free to fulfill their destinies will the destiny of a city or a nation also be set free.

ESTABLISHING GOD'S KINGDOM AND WILL TODAY

When we are born again and see the kingdom of God, He will show us an aspect of the kingdom that He wants to manifest through us on earth. What each of us sees will differ. What you see is your calling. This is how you discover your calling.

What you see will be how life should have been on earth if Adam had not fallen. God will show you His original idea for that area of life on earth. He will put that blueprint in your spirit man and He wants you to manifest it. When God shows you something, the picture will always look perfect because it is His will in heaven about that area.

God will show you how life should have been on earth. The current situation in that area will be dark, chaotic, broken, and out of order. It will be under the influence of the evil one, wicked people, and the kingdom of darkness.

God wants you to manifest His will on earth as it is in heaven there. That's why you were born again. Right now, the will of the devil is accomplished in almost every nook and cranny of our planet. However, you will take the vision God gave you and forbid the operation of the gates of hell over that area, and establish the will of God.

How do we do this in everyday life? Let's take the example of education in our countries. Whose will is being accomplished right now through the world of education? Who is making the syllabi that are taught in our schools? I have heard that in some countries they teach about same-sex marriage in elementary schools.

That is wickedness. They also teach that mankind came from monkeys and that the earth was formed from an explosion. Those ideas are not based on God's Word. Instead, the enemy's will and agenda are being accomplished through our educational system.

To establish God's will, He will put a picture of how the educational system should be in a person's spirit when they are born again. They will see that aspect of the kingdom (kingdom education).

Those who are called to the world of education when they are born again will see how they can do something to make a difference for God. They need to follow that exact vision from that day forward. Step by step, God will supply His strategies to bring change.

Kingdom education refers to raising up the sons and daughters of God to manifest His image and likeness here on earth. It deals with people's identities first. It helps people discover their purpose, recognize their calling, identify their gifts, and then develop them and release them to the world. That is kingdom education.

This objective of the world's system of education is to raise up a new labor force to serve its system. It produces more slaves to serve the Babylonian system.

You may be a teacher working in a public school, and you may not have the freedom, influence, or authority to decide what to teach your students. The problem with most Christians is that they are looking for a miracle or a quick fix. Most of the time, God and the devil doesn't work that way. They have long-term plans.

The people who come into positions of power in any field do not get there overnight. They have been thinking, planning, and working for many years. Those who accomplish the devil's evil agenda in any area of life reached there because of their meticulous planning and the excellent execution of their plans for many years, sometimes even generations.

While Christians sit in their churches and talk about their football teams and drink free coffee while they wait for the rapture, the devil's children have been busily planning and executing their father's agenda, so that when the children of these believers go to school on Monday morning they get "educated" in that.

If the devil's children can plan something generationally, how much more should we be planning and executing the will of our Father, too? It is time for us to wake up from our sleep.

If we can't change the situation, at least we can pray, mobilize, and raise up someone to occupy that gate ten to fifteen years from now. Believe me, we have ten to fifteen years of time and more left. Don't let the spirit of rapture steal your destiny. God has an assignment for you right now on the earth.

DIFFERENT PEOPLE NEED A DIFFERENT FOCUS

I believe every local *ekklesia* should have a team that they are raising up to address each sphere of society. They should have a group of educators with a focus to see a kingdom agenda accomplished in the field of education in their city or town.

There should be a group for kingdom government, in which everyone called to be in government and politics is trained to influence the government and politics in their cities and towns. We need to see God's will done through government here as it is in heaven.

We need to have groups for each and every area of society, including kingdom farming, kingdom innovation, and manufacturing. Eventually the goal of all these groups would be raise up the right people to occupy those gates in their cities and eventually the whole nation. We need to sing less and train more so our people can do kingdom work and fulfill their calling.

When we come to meet as an *ekklesia* on Sunday, or whichever day is convenient for people, we should not put everybody in the same fold and preach a common sermon. We should separate each group and train them according to their calling, so they can be released to fulfill their destiny. This is the true job of a minister called by God.

Nobody eats the same food every day everywhere. God has created a variety of foods. Different seasons in our lives require different diets. Even restaurants have menus from which we can choose what we want to eat. We should not be serving the "same meal" to someone who just became born again and someone who has been in church for thirty years. Their needs are not the same.

There have to be specific classes for different groups of people based on their calling and assignment in the kingdom. The church needs to be a training ground where we equip the saints to fulfill their destiny. There should be training happening seven days a week in every church building. It should not be left closed six days a week. Because these courses are so effective and life-changing, people from the town should throng outside to get in to sign up for a course. Each church needs to be a center for community education and transformation.

The Israelites did not possess the Promised Land overnight or in a week. It took years of planning and preparation. It took them forty years to finish the wilderness journey. It was a new generation that actually went in and possessed the Promised Land. It is with faith and patience that we inherit the promises of God and possess the land.

WAITING FOR "REVIVAL"

Don't go after revival or talk about it after each major event. What do I mean by that? In the US, whenever something major happens—especially disasters—all of these so-called prophets come up with a prophecy about revival. I am writing this in March of 2020. We are in the midst of the COVID-19 crisis. Everybody is talking about a "Corona revival" in the church.

For God's sake! Every church building is shut down and people are not even allowed to gather. God did that purposefully. Before COVID-19, we had a Super Bowl game in February. When a particular team won, everybody began to jump and shout, saying the revival was here because that team had won after so many years. That was our Super Bowl revival.

Before that, everybody was talking about the 2020 revival. Apparently, the year 2020 is something special. Preachers started milking their believers, promising all kinds of blessing in 2020. Now every business is struggling, people are being laid off, and the whole world is going through a huge crisis instead.

When will we talk about the kingdom of God? When will we focus on the dream and the plan Father God has for us and for this planet? It's sad that people have not caught the right vision after all these years.

I have seen many precious believers who don't do anything because they think the rapture is going to happen tomorrow. They don't go to school and they don't send their children to school. They don't do any work and don't marry; they're just waiting. These are the foolish virgins mentioned in the parable by Jesus in Matthew (Matthew 25:7–9).

They are waiting without preparation. They will miss everything God has for them on earth and in heaven. In heaven, we will receive the reward for what we did while on earth.

WE MUST RECLAIM THE GATES

Every gate of our society might be occupied and operated by the enemy and his kingdom. As kingdom citizens, it is our job is to reclaim those gates for the kingdom of God and our King Jesus.

Another example is government. How do we establish God's will in the government of our country? God never intended for the wicked to be in places of authority. If Adam had not fallen and died, he and his children would still be ruling the earth. He was a son of God (Luke 3:38). The earth should be ruled by God's sons and daughters. That was His plan from the beginning.

That is why the Bible says that when the righteous are in authority, people rejoice, but when the wicked rule, people groan (Proverbs 29:2). When God's will is accomplished in any area of life, personal or social, the kingdom of God will manifest in that area.

What is the kingdom of God? The kingdom of God is where His rule and will are accomplished. God's will was accomplished in the garden of Eden, in the Promised Land, and in the early church for a time period. It is absolutely possible for God's will to be established on earth as it is in heaven in our day and time.

The government was on Adam's shoulder. That means the right to rule this planet was given to him and his children after him. When Adam failed, God sent another Adam called Jesus, about whom the Bible says the government shall be upon His shoulders (Isaiah 9:6). How do we know the will of God concerning an area? That is why we were born again. When we were born again, we saw the kingdom of God, and then He gave us the Holy Spirit. He showed us how things on this earth should be. Holy Spirit searches the heart and mind of God and finds out His will. Then He shows us the blueprint when we are born again.

God will send each of His sons and daughters to an area on earth that needs to be brought back into order and beauty. We need to exercise the image, likeness, and creativity of our heavenly Father and restore that area to His original plan and design. That is our assignment. That is the plan God has for us while we are on the earth.

May the Lord help each one of us do this successfully. To partner with God in accomplishing His will on earth as it is in heaven is a high calling.

When we, the church, administer the kingdom of God in the nations of the world, the change we have been looking for will come. Souls will be brought to the kingdom like no time before. Nations will be discipled and restored to Him. May you hear the invitation of the Lord in your spirit and respond to be part of this kingdom movement.

Most people on earth are doing what they are paid to do instead of what they were created to do. Only when people see the kingdom and discover their calling and gifts and are released into their destiny can they fulfill the assignment God has for them.

When every single believer in Christ discovers their purpose, fulfills their calling by functioning in their gifts, and manifests the kingdom of God, this world will be a whole different place in no time.

Our nations will explode with development and restoration. Everything the enemy has stolen from us will be restored to us and to their original Owner. The glory of God will manifest as it was in Eden, the Promised Land, and in the early church. There won't be any sick among us, or anyone in need.

That is God's dream, and my dream as well. I gave my life away to see that dream fulfilled. The good news is that it is beginning to happen in different parts of the world.

> Truly, as I live, all the earth shall be filled with the glory of the Lord. *(Numbers 14:21)*

> The glory of the Lord shall be revealed, and all flesh shall see it together; for the mouth of the Lord has spoken. *(Isaiah 40:5)*

Now let's find out how each one of us will need to transition into the kingdom of God so that we can live out our calling or our assignment in the kingdom. That is what the next chapter is all about.

CHAPTER 15

TRANSITIONING INTO THE KINGDOM

The law and the prophets were until John. Since that time the kingdom of God has been preached, and everyone is pressing into it. (Luke 16:16)

The kingdom of God is not a philosophy, concept, good teaching, religion, church, principle or even just a good idea. When people hear the message of the kingdom, many get excited about it and try to add the message to whatever else they were believing and have been doing before. But that's not the way the kingdom of God works.

So far, people who have been preaching the kingdom were either preaching the philosophy of the kingdom or they were preaching religion, thinking it was about the kingdom. People who heard it received the message, but remained in the same old religious system that they were part of. Because of that, the kingdom is not being manifested anywhere.

The preachers did not tell the people the whole story. Instead leading them out of Egypt and Babylon they left them where they were. So many believers and ministers around the world live in hunger or are struggling to survive. In the Western world, believers went back to their jobs and continued to do what they always did.

THREE SHIFTS MUST COME

Once we hear the message of the kingdom of God, there has to be shift in three major areas of our lives.

First we need to shift from religion into the kingdom of God. Christianity is a religion and it has nothing to do with the kingdom of God. The kingdom of God is a country. A simple definition of religion is doing the same thing again and again and expecting a different result. Religion is made of rituals and practices. It is trying to please God through certain behaviors, habits, and outward appearances. There needs to be a shift from religious thinking to kingdom thinking.

Secondly, we need to shift from a church to an *ekklesia*. Churches belongs to the Christian religion, the same way synagogues belongs to Judaism. Jesus did not come to start church or a synagogue as we know it today, but He said that He will build His *ekklesia*, which is the governing body of His kingdom.

The third transition has to do with each person's individual life focus. Once a person hears the gospel of the kingdom, they need to shift from doing a job or employment and be released to start doing the kingdom assignment that God sent them to this earth for. Too many people are just working day in and day out—*and they are doing practically nothing for the kingdom*. They are trying to survive.

If these three shifts do not happen in a person's life, they have not understood the message of the kingdom. These are not the only areas that a shift needs to take place, but they are the most important ones.

There is so much talk and teaching on the kingdom nowadays. Very few are willing to make the transition, leaving what they were believing and doing until then, and enter into the kingdom way of living and start doing their kingdom assignment.

Just because we add the word *kingdom* to our existing "Christianese" vocabulary, it doesn't make us people of the kingdom. The people of Israel had to leave Egypt to receive the Promised Land as their inheritance. Unfortunately, the majority of the people who have heard the message of the kingdom today are not willing to leave their Egypt, so they remain slaves to their culture, employment, religious system, and task masters.

THE KINGDOM COUNTRY

The kingdom of God is a country, not an idea or a doctrine. When you hear the gospel of the kingdom, there has to be a radical shift in your life. There has to be a drastic change in what you were doing before and what you started to do as the result of hearing the gospel of the kingdom.

When you receive the message of the kingdom you are required to shift from the country of your birth into the kingdom of God. Until then, you lived according to the system and culture of your country, but when you receive and enter the kingdom you will begin to live based on the culture and system of the kingdom of God.

Today, many people migrate from the country of their origin to a developed country for employment and other opportunities. What I have noticed is that even though these people have moved from the country of their birth and are living in a foreign country with different language, culture, food and way of living, they will create or form an alternative or subculture that is based on the country of their origin—and will not change or adopt to the new culture of the country they are currently living in.

We have a Chinatown in New York City. If you visit the Chinatown, you will feel as though you just stepped into China. People from China took the same culture, food, and lifestyle from their country and copied it in New York City. That is what happened to us; God delivered us from the power of darkness and brought us into the kingdom of His dear Son, Jesus.

If you go to Chicago, there is a street called Devon Avenue. There you will see hundreds of Indian stores and you will feel like suddenly you were transported to India. Even though you stand in the soil of the United States, the atmosphere and culture you will feel like it does in India.

Many Christians are like these citizens, who are so accustomed to their way of living that they are not willing to forsake it and adopt to the new culture of the kingdom. When you come into the kingdom, whatever culture we lived in until that day needs to give way to the kingdom culture.

WE NEED TO TRANSITION

Until you start living by the gospel of the kingdom, you functioned by the economy of the country you were brought up, but then you need to live based on kingdom economy. We see this transition in the lives of the people in the Bible. They were brought up in various cultures and were doing a job or business to make a living, but when they heard the gospel of the kingdom they made a transition.

How did this transition happen? They recognized that if whatever job they had to supply their income was not in line with the gospel of the kingdom and God's plan and mission for their life, then they stepped into their kingdom assignment—and the kingdom of God began to supply what they need. From that day onward, they were carrying out their kingdom assignment. God and His kingdom became their source and provider.

The gospel of the kingdom is the word that the Lord gave you or spoke over you regarding your destiny—that is the gospel of the kingdom for you. For Abraham, the gospel of the kingdom was about a land God wanted him to possess. It was kingdom territory. For David, the gospel of the kingdom was about becoming a king of Israel. The gospel of the kingdom will vary from person to person. *Gospel* simply means "good news."

When Jesus met Peter, James, and John, they were fishermen. The fish they caught were the source of their income and provided whatever they needed. If they did not catch any fish, then they did not make any money. Fishing was how they made their living.

But when these men met Jesus, we see that Peter left his boat, his net, and the fish he caught, and began to follow Jesus. How did Peter survive from that day? How did he support himself and his family? Peter didn't just make a decision to follow Jesus that day; he transitioned from one world to the next, from one economy to a different economy—from his business to his kingdom assignment.

Peter transitioned from the Jewish culture to kingdom culture; from one king to another King; from one form of government to the kingdom government; from one religious system to the kingdom way of living and relating with God; from this world's economy into kingdom economy; from doing job or business into his kingdom assignment. That type of transition needs to happen in every single believers' life if they are going to fulfill their kingdom assignment. That's the only way the kingdom of God will manifest on the earth.

WILLING TO SHIFT

This is where the challenge comes in. Because of fear or unbelief, many people may not be willing to make the shift. Others won't make the transition because they are not sure of what their specific kingdom assignment is. They just hear the kingdom message and continue to do what they always did—and they won't see any change in their lives. This is where people failed to make that switch from the old to the new. This transition is not easy.

Peter made that switch in one day, but the time period and the way the shift happens will vary from person to person. God will wait patiently until we are completely transitioned into His kingdom, but the sooner we make that transition, the better it is for us.

One day a rich ruler came to Jesus and asked what he could do to inherit eternal life. Jesus answered and told him to keep the commandments, to which the man said he was keeping all them from his youth. Then Jesus told him he still lacked one thing before he could follow Him, which was to go and sell all that he had and distribute to the poor, and then he would have treasure in heaven (see Luke 18:18-24).

Jesus was not against having riches; He was against the riches having us. Not fulfilling our destiny and losing our kingdom assignment for the sake of making some money is not worth it. Jesus was giving this man an opportunity to make the transition from trusting in his riches to the kingdom economy, but he was not willing to do it because he was very rich.

I understand his concern. I'm sure he wondered how he would survive if he were to give up his riches, how he would feed himself and his family the next day? Jesus didn't tell the man to save some for his family—He said to give it all away. That's scary in the natural! But Jesus knew something this man didn't know or see in that moment. That's why Jesus told him to come and follow Him. Once he would have started to following Jesus and do his kingdom assignment, then the King and His kingdom would become responsible for providing for him.

Jesus wasn't intending to make him poor or turn him into a beggar—His desire was for this man to become a kingdom citizen, depending on the resources of the kingdom in order to fulfill his kingdom assignment.

Right away, Jesus began to talk about how difficult it is for people with riches to enter His kingdom. He said it is like a camel going through the eye of a needle. Jesus didn't say that it's impossible for rich people to enter the kingdom, but difficult. People with riches know they can get things done with their wealth. They don't feel the need to do God's will and depend on God or the kingdom economy for their provision. Most people are not brought up learning to trust God for these things; they were brought up trusting in their own ability or a job to provide for themselves—and if nothing works, they were taught that they can just borrow some money to get by.

A DIVINE PANDEMIC

This pandemic is a supernaturally orchestrated, worldwide, that supposed to help the body of Christ make this transition into the kingdom of God. It will help us all move from religion into the kingdom of God; from church to kingdom ekklesia; from this world's economy into kingdom economy; from people doing a job or looking for an employment to discovering and walking in their kingdom assignment.

People all over the world are worried about their lives and their future. They do not fully understand what is happening and what is going to unfold in the near future. Believers have become entrenched in the world and they feel stuck and are afraid for their future.

As the Bible says that all things working together for the good of those who are called according to God's purpose (Romans 8:28). There's no better time than now to make this transition. When we live in God's economy, we will not be affected by what is happening in the world. There is no recession in God's economy.

Remember the life of Isaac? When the famine came, it did not affect him. When everyone was worried and complaining about their future, Isaac went out into his field and began to prepare the ground to sow the seed. It's quite likely that the people around him might have made fun of him, but what they didn't realize that Isaac was living in a different economy. He was living in God's kingdom. What happened outside didn't affect the way he lived or what he did with his life. He sowed and received a hundred-fold harvest. That's how God's people should be living.

Isaac was prospering when everybody else was talking about lack and hunger. He was living in a different system than the people around him. They couldn't perceive the spiritual kingdom he was living in; they only saw what their natural eyes could see. If you are prospering while everyone else is struggling to survive, that's how you know if you are living in God's kingdom or not.

When the people of Israel came into the wilderness, God began to provide for them with bread from heaven, water from the rock, air conditioning with clouds by day, and fire by night. That's kingdom living! The wilderness is a place of scarcity and lack. But if you live in God's kingdom it doesn't matter which place or part of the world you are living in. Kingdom provision doesn't depend on our outward circumstances.

Once you start your journey to fulfill your kingdom assignment, God will become your provider and protector. Remember, after the crucifixion Peter decided to go back to fishing. He was worried about his livelihood. In his perception, Jesus was dead and all hope was lost—his future was now in his own hands.

Then Jesus showed up on the shore and asked them if they caught anything. The disciples recognized that it was Jesus but might have felt embarrassed because they didn't believe that He would rise again on the third again.

It is interesting thing to notice is that Jesus brought them breakfast. Even after the resurrection Jesus was faithful to feed them and take care of them. Why? Once you give your life to fulfilling your assignment, God will go any length to take care of you and your family.

It takes tremendous faith to make that transition. We need to hear a clear and absolute word from God about what He wants us to do. It's not about taking a blind step—but taking the exact step in obedience to what He tells us to do.

LIVING FOR BROKEN DREAMS

So how do we live out our kingdom assignment in a practical way? Many Christians I know are waiting for a miracle or for someone to give them something for free. But that's not the way kingdom life happens.

When we were born in the natural, our parents took care of us every moment of every day until we were old enough to go to school. Then we spent at least twelve years e learning how to survive on the earth and learning how to make a living when we grow up. We spent five days a week in that school for nine months of the year, for twelve long years.

Then many of us went to college after that and spent three or more years learning things to earn a degree. We made that investment hoping that one day someone would hire us and give us a job so that we can generate enough money to support ourselves and our family.

People go through enormous pain and struggle to finish their schooling. Many borrow money, take out loans, and travel to other countries to finish their college education. They spend hours and hours studying and doing homework and experiments. They read books and go to libraries to borrow books. Burning midnight oil to complete assignments and research papers is normal.

This is the way we learned how to survive in this world. Then when we became "educated," this world system and a company became our source of income and our provider. We began to be dependent on this world and worried what we will do if we lost that job.

Many of us had parents who put dreams into our hearts when we were little; they dreamed that their child would become a doctor, engineer, a sport's star, or someone famous. We believed those dreams, but looking back, ninety-nine percent of the time the dreams did not materialize. We also have our own personal dreams and ambitions, most of which never came to fruition. So many people carry the weight and scars of a broken or unfulfilled dream.

In reality, we spent all those precious years of our life in school or college, learning how the Babylonian world system works. How sad!

LIVING THE KINGDOM LIFE

When you come into the kingdom of God, the same principle applies, but in a different system altogether.

When we are spiritually born again, our heavenly Father put His dream in our heart or in our spirit man. He enrolls us into His kingdom school. The dream or calling He put in our heart is the system by which He provides for His children in His kingdom. As long as people fulfill what they are called to do they won't lack anything in their life. As long as we won't deviate from what God has called us to do, we will not lack anything.

When we discover God's kingdom and our assignment in it, He and His kingdom become our source, our provider. We won't need to worry about anything. What many people don't realize is that just like we spent years studying how to survive in this world, now we will need to invest time to study and learn how His kingdom operates and to fulfill what we are called to do in it. And this won't happen overnight or by a miracle. We didn't jump to college from primary school in an instant or by miracle—it was a long journey. It's the same with the kingdom.

This world system will only hire people who are educated or trained in a particular field to do a particular job. If you never went to medical school, nobody will hire you as a doctor. If you never went to a flight school and obtained a license to fly, no airline will hire you as their pilot.

This is the same way it works in the kingdom. Before God releases us to do what He called us to do, He will take us through a in-depth training. His training takes longer than when we were trained in the world and it requires more from us than preparing for an employment in a company.

REQUIREMENTS FOR KINGDOM LIVING

What is required from us to live and fulfill God's kingdom assignment? Every atom and every fiber of our being is necessary to fulfill what God has called us to do. We were designed and created by God for one reason—to fulfill His kingdom agenda on earth. People think that just because they go to church for two hours on a Sunday, they are doing some kind-of favor for God or for themselves. Lord have mercy! They have no clue about God's kingdom or what He has called them to do.

People brag about paying tithe and their employment without knowing that their very life was given to them and that they exist because of His kingdom. The more time you to put into learning to walk in what you are called to do in His kingdom, the more you will get out of it. The more you learn to yield to the Holy Spirit in what He wants you to do, the more progress you will make in your journey of fulfilling His assignment.

If you invest at least five years of your life toward what you are called to do, you will see great result in your life. Remember Jesus, spent more than three years with His disciples to train them in the kingdom and their calling. He didn't just lay hands on them and said, Be the apostles I want you to be—He walked and lived day to day with them for three long years.

We don't have the luxury of physically walking with Jesus like the disciples did, but we have the Holy Spirit living inside of us, leading and guiding us. We have to follow the leading of the Holy Spirit moment by moment.

We won't become what God called us to be by someone laying hands on us. There is a place for miracles, prayer, and laying on of hands, but we can't use any of those things as a shortcut. They cannot replace the time we need to invest to go through God's training. There are no shortcuts in God's kingdom. If we try to take a shortcut we will short circuit our destiny and calling.

Miracles or laying on of hands will often propel us into the training God wants us to go through. The same amount of time you invested in your schooling while growing up is what you will need to invest into kingdom schooling or training, so you can learn how the kingdom of God works and where you fit in the kingdom with your calling.

People tell me, "Abraham, I read one of your books about the kingdom, but there's no kingdom manifesting in my life." Others will express how they took one of the courses from our Kingdom School but they have no calling manifesting and no money is coming in. Instead, they will feel as though they are going through enormous pressure and battle as they have never experienced before.

That is absolutely normal! Imagine if you were training for a game for a sport team? How many hours and days did you go to practice?

Were those practices and training easy? Did you cry sometimes because it was so tough? Kingdom training is more intense than that—and it requires every single part of our being.

Our whole spirit, soul, and body need to go through the transformation. In sports it was mainly physical training, and it was still tough. Imagine your spirit, soul, and body going through the process of change all at the same time. We will cry for help or will feel like quitting or running away.

If you are being educated to be doctor, you won't complain the second year of your schooling because no income is coming in, right? You will patiently go through the education until it is finished. If you quit in the middle, then all that investment goes to waste. But I can guarantee that God will be faithful to provide what you need from day one of your training.

Remember the testimony I shared in the beginning of this book? It all started with me in a whole night prayer meeting from 8:30 at night to 4:30 in the morning. That was an investment I was making into my future and to my calling. It was not a waste of time. It was laying the foundation for the rest of my life. Things are still being fulfilled in my life now that I prayed in those prayer meetings so many years ago.

I encourage you to pursue your calling with everything you've got; don't do it as a side business. When things get tough, the tough get going. Don't quit or give into the temptation of looking for an easy road. As long as you stay in the course, God will continue to strengthen, provide, and protect you. God bless you.

I would encourage you to read this book more than once and really study it. You will not receive everything God has for you by only reading it once. Keep this book as a manual for your kingdom living. There is much "treasure" in these concepts, and you need to keep digging to get everything out. Pray as you study it. Enroll in our Kingdom School and take the course Seeing, Entering, and Manifesting the Kingdom. This book and the course are pivotal for fulfilling your purpose and calling in this life. May the Lord help you do that. Amen.

List of Other Books and Resources

Discipling Nations series

Kingdom Mandate (for any donation)
Discovering the Lost Kingdom (Volume 1) $14.00
Purpose, Calling, and Gifts (Volume 2) $15.00
God's Original Design (Volume 3) $20.00
Seeing, Entering, and Manifesting the Kingdom of God (Volume 4)$20.00
The Ekklesia (Volume 5) $30.00
The Gospel of the Kingdom (Volume 6) $20.00
Power and Authority of the Church (Volume 7) $15.00
Kingdom Family (Volume 8) $15.00
The Birthing of a kingdom nation (Volume 9) $20.00
What Happened to God? (Volume10) $20.00
7 Dimensions and Operations of the Kingdom of God (Volume 11)$15.00
Kingdom Economy (Volume 12) $15.00
Kingdom Government (Volume 13) $15.00
Releasing Kings and Queens to their Original Intent (Volume 14) $10.00
Kingdom Secrets to Restoring Nations Back to God (Volume 15) $20.00
Keys to Fulfilling Your Kingdom Assignment (Volume 16) $15.00

Kingdom Living series

The Three Most Important Decisions of Your Life $15.000
Recognizing God's Timing for Your Life $12.00
Overcoming the Spirit of Poverty $10.00
Seven Kinds of Believers $10.00
7 Dimensions of God's Glory $5.00
7 Dimensions of God's Grace $10.00
7 Kinds of Faith $7.00

Kingdom Books for Kids

Genesis 1:26 Three Volume set for boys $25.00

To place an order, contact us at:

www.TheKingdomNetwork.org
Phone: 1-800-558-5020
Email: info@TheKingdomNetwork.org

Are you struggling to discover your **PURPOSE ?**
You are not supposed to fit in but stand out !

Sign up today for the upcoming
FREE Online Kingdom Course

DISCOVERING

THE LOST KINGDOM

In this course you'll DISCOVER:

>> Your true identity and purpose
>> What God is doing on the earth and how you can partner with Him in it
>> Why God created the earth and put us on this planet

And much more ...

Why are people becoming more and more disinterested in **church and religion** globally?
Join the course, and discover
what your soul has been searching for all along.

FREE BOOK AND STUDY GUIDE

other courses available
>> DISCOVERING PURPOSE, CALLING AND GIFTS
>> SEEING, ENTERING AND MANIFESTING THE KINGDOM
>> GOD'S ORIGINAL DESIGN | FEBRUARY 2024
>> The Ekklesia
>> The Next move of GOD

And more ...

Register Now @ www.TheKingdomUniversity.org

Welcome to

KINGDOM DELIVERANCE
— WORKSHOP —

Are you tired of waiting and looking for breakthroughs? Kingdom of God has the answer.

This kingdom deconstruct workshop is divided into EIGHT major categories which deal with the seven major areas of our life. Each one is connected to the next, and so if one of these areas dysfunctions, it will affect all other areas of your life.

1. Relationship with the Father
2. Spiritual Healing
3. Emotional Healing
4. Recognizing Purpose and Calling
5. Identifying and Mastering Natural and Spiritual Gifts
6. Finances—Learning to Live in Kingdom Economy
7. Healing Relationships
8. Physical Health

Take action now. Order all 8 workshop manuals today !

Thank you so much for taking the courses from The Kingdom University. Taking a course is only the first step. We are pleased to present you with the next step—that of going through the process to get rid of all the extra weights that have been slowing and hindering you from fully living out your kingdom assignment.

Call 1 800 558 5020   www.TheKingdomNetwork.org

www.ingramcontent.com/pod-product-compliance
Lightning Source LLC
Chambersburg PA
CBHW070050080526
44586CB00013B/986